Laurence Braddon

Innocency and Truth Vindicated

an account of what hath been, or is ready to be deposed, to prove the most treacherous and cruel murder of the Right Honourable Arthur, late Earl of Essex

Laurence Braddon

Innocency and Truth Vindicated

an account of what hath been, or is ready to be deposed, to prove the most treacherous and cruel murder of the Right Honourable Arthur, late Earl of Essex

ISBN/EAN: 9783337196394

Printed in Europe, USA, Canada, Australia, Japan

Cover: Foto ©Andreas Hilbeck / pixelio.de

More available books at **www.hansebooks.com**

Laurence Braddon

Innocency and Truth Vindicated
an account of what hath been, or is ready to be deposed, to prove the most treacherous and cruel murder of the Right Honourable Arthur, late Earl of Essex

ISBN/EAN: 9783337196394

Printed in Europe, USA, Canada, Australia, Japan

Cover: Foto ©Andreas Hilbeck / pixelio.de

More available books at **www.hansebooks.com**

Innocency and Truth Vindicated.

AN ACCOUNT

Of what hath been, or is ready to be depoſed, to prove the

Moſt Treacherous and Cruel Murder

Of the Right Honourable

ARTHUR, late Earl of ESSEX.

With Reflections upon the Evidence, and the moſt material Objections againſt this Murder, diſcuſs'd and anſwered.

In a Conference between three Gentlemen concerning the preſent Inquiry into the Death of that

Noble Lord and true Patriot.

Whoſo ſheddeth Man's Blood, by Man ſhall his Blood be ſhed, Gen. 9.6.
——*For Blood it defileth the Land, and the Land cannot be cleanſed of the Blood that is ſhed therein, but by the Blood of him that ſhed it.* Numb. 35. 33.

Magna eſt Veritas & prævalebit.

Printed in the Year MDCLXXXIX.

To t' e Right Honourable the LORDS of the (late) COMMITTEE, appointed to examine into the Death of that Noble LORD and True PATRIOT, ARTHUR late EARL of ESSEX.

MY LORDS,

COuld I have manag'd the Evidence in Proof, of the Murder of this Honourable Lord, with that ſtrength and efficacy they are capable of, nothing would more plainly have appeared to the impartial Reader, than this (to me) great Truth, (viz.) That the Right Honourable Arthur, late Earl of Eſſex, was moſt Treacherouſly and Barbarouſly Murdered. But ſuch as it is, I do, with all Humility, caſt it at your Lordſhips Feet, to whoſe great Judgments I ſhall, with intire reſignation, ſubmit.

My Lords, Having long known, and been lately much converſant with Mr. Braddon, I have had often Opportunities of diſcourſing almoſt every Witneſs in this Caſe examined; and ſuch as I my ſelf have not ſpoke with, I have from him been informed what ſuch have declared: And though the Account I have here given of what theſe have related, which have been examined before your Lordſhips, be more large and particular than their Depoſitions, (becauſe I have had repeated Opportunities of hearing their Relations) yet, if themſelves ſay true, nothing in theſe Papers is contradictory to or inconſiſtent with what they have depoſed before your Lordſhips.

My Lords, In the Account at large I have firſt ſtated, the Caſe, as to the pretended Self-Murder, as it was and is endeavoured to be proved by thoſe immediately attending on my Lord; and then I have divided the Proofs for this Murder into three General Heads, as they have relation to Time: Whether,

Firſt, Before the Day of my Lord's Death.
Secondly, The Day of his Death.
Thirdly, Subſequent to the Day of his Death.

And after every Proof, I have raiſed all ſuch Objections I could in Converſation ever meet with, or my ſelf could object, which carried the leaſt colour of Argument againſt ſuch Evidence; and the Solutions, with all humility, are ſubmitted to your Lordſhips Cenſures.

In the Abſtract, I have obſerved this Order: Firſt, I have ſtated the Caſe, as repreſented and ſworn by thoſe that would prove the Self-Murder; and then detected the Falſity of every Part of thoſe Relations. After which I have briefly conſidered the other Proofs in the ſame Order of Time as the Diſcourſe at large.

My Lords, Several things here mentioned have not as yet been before your Lordſhips, ſome of theſe Relations having not been known to Mr. Braddon before your Lordſhips Committee was diſſolved : But theſe after-Teſtimonies, and ſome other things not here taken notice of, will be brought before your Lordſhips, as ſoon as your Lordſhips ſhall think fit to move, that thoſe Depoſitions and Examinations. now ſealed up, may be taken out of the Houſe by your Lordſhips, and to thoſe added ſuch other Teſtimonies as have been taken before ſeveral Juſtices, (ſince the Report made) or are ready to be taken; and then, that, as well ſuch as are now ſealed up, as thoſe others which have been, or ſhall be depoſed, may be reported by your Lordſhips, in ſuch Method,

A 2 *as*

as to your Lordships great Wisdom shall seem most meet. After which I doubt not but all your Lordships, and the whole World, will be convinced of that Truth which the Interest of so many have industriously endeavoured to stifle: But there is no Power of Earth, and Hell, when conjoined, can make that Thing never to have been, which was. And therefore if my Lord was treacherously and barbarously murdered, no Interest or Strength what-ever can make him a Self-murderer. Truth may be destroyed in its Credit, but never in its Being; and the Measures that have been taken to discredit the Proof of this Murder, have been sufficiently detected as false, which hath not a little increased the Credibility of that which those Counter-Evidences would have rendered incredible and false.

My Lords, No two Truths in Nature are inconsistent; for then a Thing would be, and not be, at the same time: wherefore when Men would subvert the belief of a Truth, they do raise some Falshood which stands in opposition to such Truth; but if once this Falshood appears in its true Colour, then doth it give stronger credit to that Truth, which before it was designed to prejudice.

My Lords, every Man's Defence virtually concludes. If my Defence be false, my Charge is true. This Conclusion the Law makes in all Civil Actions, and it's according to the Reason of the Thing: For all Men presume that every Man accused, will make use of the best Arguments (especially in Matters of Fact) he can for his Defence; and if those appear false, he falls under a Self-Condemnation. My Lords, tho this Discourse is printed, it's not published, nor above 200 printed, as is ready to be proved; neither will one of these be communicated to any, if your Lordships shall so order it; for all are kept till Mr. Braddon receives your Lordships Commands as to their disposal. My Lords, I could wish I had not been so large in this Discourse, seeing your Lordships whole time is so ingrossed by the Publick, that I fear the State can scarce allow your Lordships any hours of perusal. My Lords, tho I can't but humbly beseech your Lordships Pardon for this Presumption, yet I could not, without being guilty of the greatest Injustice, any otherwise dedicate this Discourse, seeing what hath been already discovered, is chiefly owing to your Lordships unwearied Diligence in those many Committees, in which your Lordships have so often sat in search of a Truth, which the Impenitency of some, and the industrious Interest of others have strongly opposed. But maugre all Oponents, the matter is (as I do humbly conceive) so far detected, as Circumstantial Evidence is (almost) capable of; and those that will not be convinced of the Truth of a Murder, unless positive ly attested, demand such Proof for their Conviction as no Law requires. Now that the God of Wisdom, Righteousness and Truth, may direct and prosper your Lordships in this, and all other Undertakings, is the Humble Prayer of,

My Lords,

Your Lordships most Humble

and Obedient Servant,

P. V.

The CONTENTS.

p. *for* Page, c. *for* Colume.

THE *Introduction,* Pag. 1. Col. 1.
False Reports to prejudice the Discovery, p. 2.
Two Orders of the Lords, p. 3. C. 1.
How this Case first came before the Lords, p. 3. C. 2.
My Lord of Essex's *Commitment to the* Tower, p. 4. C. 2.
Bomeny's *Information (before the Coroner) printed,* p. 5. C. 2.
Russel *and the two Chirurgeons Informations before the Coroner,* p. 6. C. 1, 2.
The Substance of what was sworn before the Coroner, to prove the Self-murder, p. 6. C. 2.
What Monday *declareth,* p. 6. C. 2.
What Major Hawley *declareth,* p. 7. C. 1.
Bomeny, Monday, Russel, *and* Lloyd, *denied the letting in any Men to my Lord, that morning my Lord died,* p. 7. C. 1.
The Order into which the Evidence is divided, p. 7. C. 2.
Do. Smith's *Evidence to prove the Papists Resolution, nine days before my Lord's Death, to cut my Lord's Throat,* p. 8, 9.
An Objection against this Evidence, p. 9. C. 2.
An Answer to this Objection, p. 9. C. 2.
D. Smith's *Evidence no new made Story, but long since revealed,* p. 10, 11, 12.
Farther Objections against D. Smith's *Evidence, and these Objections answered,* p. 12. C. 2. p. 13, to 22.
Many Reports in several Parts of England *before my Lord's Death, that the Earl of* Essex *had cut his Throat in the* Tower, p. 22, 23.
All Reports agree in the Manner how, and Place where, p. 23. C. 2.

An Objection against the Reports, p. 24. c. 1, 2.
An Answer thereunto, p. 24. C. 1, 2.
F―― *Evidence proves, that the Report before my Lord's Death, sets forth not only the Manner how, and the Place where, my Lord died, but likewise the pretended Reason wherefore my Lord cut his Throat,* p. 22, 24.
An Objection against F―― *Evidence,* p. 24. C. 2. p. 25. C. 1.
An Answer to this Objection, p. 25. C. 1, 2.
How the Earl's Death became so generally reported in so many Places; and particularly as to Manner, Place, and pretended Reason, before he was dead, p. 26. C. 1, 2.
A short Inference from these Reports, p. 27. C. 1.
What passed the day my Lord died, p. 27. C. 1.
The letting in the Ruffians to my Lord just before his Death, p. 27. C. 2. p. 28, 29.
An Objection against this Evidence, p. 30. C. 1.
An Answer to this Objection, p. 30. C. 2.
M. B. *proves a great bustling between three or four Men in my Lord's Room, just before my Lord's Death; and one in this bustle crying out, very loud, and very dolefully, Murder, Murder, Murder,* p. 31. C. 1.
This Evidence of B. *not now made, but revealed by* B. *just after my Lord's Death,* p. 31. C. 1, 2.
The Reason that M. B. *refused to depose what she knew in this Case,* p. 31, C. 2. p. 32.
B's *Testimony confirms* Loyd's *Confession,* p. 33. C. 1.
An Objection against B's *Evidence,* p. 33. C. 1.
An Answer thereunto, Eodem.

a T*he*

The Contents.

The Sentinel a Confederate, p. 33. c. 1, 2.
The D. of Y. sends the Ruffians to murder my Lord, p. 33. c. 2. p. 34. c. 1.
An Objection against this, p. 33. c. 2.
An Answer to this Objection, p. 33. c. 1, 2.
Further Evidence of the Duke's sending the Men to my Lord's Chamber to murder my Lord, p. 35. c. 1.
An Objection against such Evidence, p. 35. c. 1.
An Answer to this Objection, p. 35. c. 1.
Further Evidence of these Ruffians being sent by the Duke to the Earl's Lodgings, p. 35. c. 2.
A further Answer to an Objection against what R. and M. declared the day my Lord died, p. 36. c. 1.
Major Hawley suspected to let in the Ruffians into my Lord's Lodgings, p. 36. c. 2.
An Objection against this, p. 36. c. 2.
An Answer to this Objection, p. 36. c. 2. p. 37. c. 1.
Sir C— —t to the Old-Baily, to give notice of my Lord's Death, but forgets who brought Orders from his then Majesty for his going, p. 37. c. 2. p. 38. c. 1, 2.
Bomeny and Russel suffered to hear each others Examination before the Coroner, p. 38. c. 2.
Bomeny's first Information taken by the Coroner, p. 38. c. 2. p. 39. c. 1.
Bomeny suffered to go from the Jury into the next Room, and there to write his second Information, p. 39. c. 1.
Bomeny's Information which he so wrote, p. 39. c. 2. p. 40. c. 1.
Bomeny's Information, which was printed by Authority, is different from that which he swore to, p. 40. c. 1.
The Reason Bomeny's Information was printed, contradictory to what he had deposed before the Coroner, p. 40. c. 2.
Monday declared, the day before my Lord died, and confirmed it afterwards, that he saw my Lord of Essex, with the Razor in his Hand, as soon as the Gentleman-Goaler had opened my Lord's Chamber-Door, and this above two hours before my Lord's Death, and long before Russel stood Warder at my Lord's Chamber Door, p. 41. c. 1, 2.
No Razor delivered to my Lord, appears by the Contradictions between Bomeny, Monday, and Russel, p. 42, 43. c. 1.
An Answer to those Contradictions, p. 43. c. 1.
This Answer insufficient, Eodem.
Bomeny, Monday, and Russel swore, or declared, that my Lord pared his Nails with the Razor, that morning my Lord died, p. 43. c. 2.
This appears false, p. 43. c. 2.
The Closet-Door not-locked upon my Lord, as Bomeny, Monday, and Russel, have sworn or declared, p. 43. c. 2. p. 44. c. 1.
For what Reason Bomeny, Monday, and Russel, have sworn, and declared, that my Lord's Closet Door was locked upon the Body, p. 44. c. 2. p. 45. c. 1.
Further Evidence against the Closet Door being locked, p. 45. c. 1.
No Razor lying by my Lord in the Closet, when my Lord was first discovered, p. 45. c. 1, 2.
W— —E— — proves a bloody Razor thrown out of my Lord's Chamber-Window, before my Lord's Death was known, p. 45. c. 2.
An Objection against W— —E— — Testimony, p. 45. c. 2.
An Answer to this Objection, p. 46, 47.
J. L. proves this bloody Razor being thrown out as before, p. 48. c. 1.
An Objection against J. L's Evidence, p. 48. c. 2.
An Answer to this Objection, Eodem.
Further Evidence of the bloody Razor's being, as before, thrown out of my Lord's Chamber-Window, p. 49, 50, 51.
What might occasion the throwing out of the Razor, before my Lord's Death was known, p. 51. c. 1.
Alice Carter supposed to take up this Razor, and first to discover my Lord's Death: Her Defence false in every part, p. 51. c. 2. p. 52. c. 1, 2.
The Razor broke at the top, and several Notches in the Razor, argue its fall some distance, p. 52. c. 2.
Farther Arguments against my Lord's cutting his Throat in the Closet, p. 52. c. 2. p. 53. c. 1.
The bloody Room and Closet washed before the Jury saw the Body, p. 53. c. 2.

The

The Contents.

The unfair Management of the Coroner's Jury, p. 54. c. 1.
Why the Body was stripp'd, and the Clothes carried away and denied to the Jury, p. 54. c. 2. p. 55. c. 1.
A large Knife, the supposed Instrument of my Lord's Death; and Holland suspected as concerned therein, p. 55, 56.
An Answer to Holland's Letter to the Earl of Feversham, p. 57, 58. c. 1.
Major Hawley suggested to the Coroner's Jury, that Self-murder was my Lord's Principle, p. 58. c. 2. p. 59. c. 1.
Major Hawley denies his being with the Jury where they sat, or that he did ever suggest this, or ever heard it said to be my Lord's Principle, p. 59. c. 1.
The Reason of Major Hawley's now denial, p. 59. c. 2.
Some short Inferences from such denial, p. 59. c. 2.
Major Hawley prevented the Coroner's Jury from adjourning their Inquisition, by suggesting that his then Majesty had sent for the same, p. 60. c. 1.
Major Hawley ever disaffected to the present Interest, p. 60. c. 2.
The Coroner's Jury went not according to Evidence, p. 61. c. 2. p. 62. c. 1.
Some of the Jury unwilling to discover what they knew, p. 62. c. 2.
The Averseness of the then Government from any Inquiry into this Murder, p. 64.
The Reason of such Averseness, p. 64. c. 1.
The late crowned Heads endeavoured to subvert the Crown, p. 65. c. 1, 2.
Very unreasonable Bail demanded of Mr. Braddon, p. 68. c. 2. p. 69. c. 1.
The Habeas-Corpus Act defective, p. 70. c. 1, 2.
Mr. Braddon informed, (a little after he had first moved herein) that his Highness had thretned his Ruin, p. 71. c. 2.
An Inference from that, p. 71. c. 2.
Mr. Braddon a sole Conspirator, p. 72. c. 1.
Mr. Braddon thretned by Sir R. S. just before he was tred, p. 72. c. 1.
Innocence a support under Trouble, p. 72. c. 2. p. 73. c. 1.

Mr. Braddon's Jury well paid, p. 73. c. 2.
Sir Hugh Middleton, Foreman of Mr. Braddon's Jury, since turned Papist, p. 74. c. 1.
His late Majesty crossed only Mr. Braddon's Name in that List of his King's-Bench Prisoners, which was delivered him, p. 74. c. 1.
An Inference from his late Majesty's Irreconcilable Hatred of Mr. Braddon, p. 74. c. 2.
The Coroner's Inquest used as a Means to prevent the Discovery of my Lord's Murder, p. 75. c. 1.
The detecting Sir Thomas Overbury's Murder, the same Offence Mr. Braddon was guilty of, but met not with such Discouragement, p. 75. c. 2.
King James the First his Speech, upon the discovery of Sir Thomas Overbury's Murder, p. 75. c. 2.
A Comparison between the Murder of the late Earl of Essex, and that of Sir Thomas Overbury, p. 75. c. 2. p. 76. c. 1, 2.
The Lord-Keeper North insinuates to Mr. Braddon the Danger of this Prosecution, p. 76. c. 2.
The Reasons that moved Mr. Braddon to ingage in this Prosecution, p. 76. c. 2. p. 77. c. 1.
Bomeny (shortly after my Lord's Death) is supposed to have writ a Letter, wherein he declared he would fully discover this Murder upon a Pardon, p. 77. c. 2.
An Objection against this, p. 77. c. 2.
An Answer to this Objection, p. 78. c. 2.
Bomeny supposed to be a disguised Papist, p. 79. c. 1.
A certain Divine's Argument for the Self-Murder, p. 79. c. 2.
An Answer thereunto, p. 80. c. 1, 2.
The Contradictions between Bomeny, Monday, and Russel, as to the (pretended) Self-Murder, of themselves are sufficient to clear my Lord of this infamous Imputation, p. 81. c. 1, 2.
Mr. Billingsley's Objection against this Murder, deserves no Credit, p. 82. c. 1, 2. p. 83. c. 1.
The Earl of Essex feared neither Danger, nor Death, but was ready chearfully to lay down his Life for his Country, p. 83. c. 2.
The most popular Objections against this Murder, answered, p. 84, to 90.

Injunctions

The Contents.

Injunctions of Secrecy laid upon the Souldiers, the next day after the Earl's Death, p. 90. c. 2.

M. presumed to be murdered, to prevent his testifying what he knew as to my Lord's Murder, p. 91.

R. sent to the Indies, and there shot to Death, p. 91. c. 1.

A third Souldier fear'd he should be murdered for what he had discovered, with relation to my Lord's Murder, Eodem.

Hawley the Warder supposed to be murdered, to hinder the Discovery of what he knew, p. 91. c. 2. p. 92.

A Souldier barbarously whip'd, only for saying, He would not say he did believe the Earl of Essex cut his own Throat, p. 92. c. 2. p. 93. c. 1.

Old Edwards turned out of his Place in the Custom-House, only (as presumed) for his Son's Relation, p. 93. c. 2.

Major Webster brings home my Lord's bloody Handkerchief, and forty nine Guinies, and a Pistol, &c. p. 94.

His Wife tells him, she could hang him, and one in the Tower, p. 94. c. 2.

Webster then in no danger of a Prosecution, or Punishment, from what his Wife could discover, p. 94. c. 2.

The Relation of a Wife will not excuse her concealing a Murder committed by her Husband, p. 95, 96.

Major Webster, before the Lords, disown'd his having produced a Purse of Gold to O. but since pretended he had won the Mony at Gaming, p. 96. c. 2.

Holms's Wife tells her Husband, he was a Murderer, and she could hang him, &c. p. 97. c. 1.

Murderers falling out, Murder is detected, p. 97. c. 1.

An Abstract of the Whole, p. 97. c. 2. to 104.

A Lincolns-Inn Gent. SIR, I rejoyce I hav thus fortunately met you here; for ever since I came to Town, I have longed to see you, because I have been defired by many of our Countrymen to give them what Information I can, how the Cafe of the late Earl of *Effex* now ftands; whether there have been any Informations, or Examinations herein, taken before the Honourable Houfe of Lords (for we have heard their Lordfhips, upon their firft fitting, took the matter into Examination) and what you have heard to be the Subftance of thofe Depofitions and Examinations, whether fufficient to prove that unfortunate Lord treacheroufly murdered, as he was generally believed to be.

A Templer. Sir, you could never have met me more opportunely for your Satisfaction in this, feeing I have now about me the Subftance of all thofe Depofitions and Examinations that have been taken before the Secret Committee of Lords appointed by the Houfe for this purpofe, and fome time fince reported to the Houfe; and likewife Copies of many Informations herein taken before fome Juftices of the Peace; befides all which, I have Copies of fuch Depofitions as have been fworn to, deftroy the Credit of what hath been materially depofed to prove that unfortunate Lord villianoufly murdered; and further, I have feveral Informations taken to ftrengthen my Lord's Evidence, in Anfwer to thofe Depofitions, on the behalf of the Prifoner. Of all which I have had an Opportunity to take Copies, by being daily converfant with that Gentleman, whofe Misfortunes have made him of all Men the beft acquainted with this Cafe. Sir, there is hardly a Witnefs herein fworn but what I have difcourfed; neither do I believe there is any Objection can be raifed againft the Proof of my Lord's being murdered, but what I can fufficiently Anfwer. All which your Authority fhall command from me, who rejoyce in this Occafion of ferving you. But I queftion whether it may not be thought a divulging of what a Secret Committee hath had under Examination, and ought ftill to be kept private.

L. You can't but know that this Secret Committee is diffolved, by the Reports being made to the Houfe, where the Depofitions having been read, it can no longer be thought a Secret: And it being for the Intereft of the Kingdom it fhould be publifhed (if there be any Evidence to prove this Murder) I can't imagine how your communicating this matter can in the leaft prejudice this Caufe, the juft Succefs whereof no Man living can defire with greater impatience than my felf, who fhall (its probable) by your now-Affiftance, be able to ftop the Mouths of thofe Gainfayers, which not fo much out of Malice, as Mifinformation, feem totally to disbelieve this matter; of which number Mr. *O.* of *Grays-Inn* (our Friend, and old Acquaintance) is one; he did appoint to be here precifely at this time. He is now come.

A Grays-In Gent. Gentlemen, your moft humble Servant.

T. Sir, We are both cordially yours, and rejoyce you are thus opportunely come.

G. I hope my Company doth not hinder private Bufinefs; if fo, I will leave
B ycu

(2)

you till such your Discourse is ended, and then shall esteem my self happy in the Injoyment of both your good Companies.

T. Sir, the Business we are upon you are free to hear, and I do very much rejoyce in this Opportunity of making you a Convert.

G. In what (pray Sir?) for if I am in any Error, I hope I am not thereto so wedded, but upon good Cause shewn, shall readily sue a Divorce, and thank you heartily for my Conviction.

L. This Gentleman is about giving such Reasons as will convince (not me, for I do already believe it, but) you, That the late Earl of *Essex* was treacherously and villanously murdered.

G. Pish! there is not the least ground for such a Belief, neither hath there been any colour of Evidence for it produced to the Lords. Moreover, all my Lord's Relations are so firmly possessed with the Belief, that the late Earl of *Essex* did indeed cut his own Throat, that neither of them hath thought fit in the least to move in this matter, but all of them wish that this Cause had never been revived, because it renews the Remembrance of that sad and deplorable Accident which hath been so great a Misfortune to that Honourable Family.

T. Sir; I perceive you have been abused in every part of your Information, for your Author scarce told you one Word of Truth. As for the Families not appearing in (but being very averse to) this Prosecution, I do assure you (Sir) this is far from being true; for no Gentleman could shew more Honour, and greater Zeal in a Cause, than the Right Honourable Sir *Henry Capel* (the late Earl's only Brother) hath done in this, and caused some to be taken up for endeavouring to abuse the World with the Belief, that he had not engaged in this matter. The now Earl of *Essex* was not returned from his Travels when this Prosecution was renewed; but as soon as he came, his Lordship approved of what was done, and hath been at the Charge of this Prosecution, in which you may believe there hath been no small Expence, there having been in this Cause such a number of Witnesses examined, and so many several Committees. And whereas you say there was not the least Colour of Evidence produced to the Lords: Did you ever hear what Persons were sworn before their Lordships, and after examined by this Honourable Committee.

G. Not in every particular, but in part I have, and in general have been informed, That the Witnesses produced by that Gentleman, who pretended to prove it, were looked upon as altogether insufficient for that end; and therefore the House of Lords, upon reading the Informations in this Case taken by the Committee, immediately rejected them as frivolous, thereupon ordering, that all such as had been taken up, as suspected concerned in this pretended Murder, should be discharged.

T. I perceive in this also you have been misinformed, as to both particulars; for the House of Lords upon reading what was taken by the Honourable Lords of this Committee, neither rejected the Evidence as insufficient, nor ordered the discharge of such as in this case were taken up, but the Depositions being read before the House, when three of the four Honourable Lords of this Committee were out of Town (*viz.*) the Earl of *Devon*, the Earl of *Monmouth*, and Lord *Delamere* (the Earl of *Bedford* being the first in this Committee) the House ordered all those Depositions and Examinations to be sealed up, and kept by the Clerk of the Parliament, till these three Lords returned, and in the mean time the farther Debate hereupon to be suspended: To prove all which, pray Sir, read this Order made *Die Jovis* 23°. *Maii,* 1689.

Die.

(3)

Die Jovii 23º. *Maii.* 1689.

After reading several Papers and Depositions relating to the death of the late Earl of Essex, It is Ordered by the Lords Spiritual and Temporal in Parliament Assembled, that the Consideration of this business shall be suspended until the return of the Lord Steward, the Earl of Monmouth, and the Lord Delamere, who were of the Committee, before whom they were made, and who are now in the Country in His Majesties Service. And its further Ordered, that the said Depositions and Papers shall be Sealed up, and kept by the Clerk of the Parliament in the mean time.

G. Then I find my Information in this Particular false.

T. As to the Second, That the Lords have not ordered the discharge of such as were in this Case apprehended, but contrarywise, that all these should be bound over by the Court of *Kings Bench*, to appear the first day of the next Term, appears by an Order of the House of Lords, made the 15º. *June* 1689. which you may read if you please.

Die Sabati 15º. *Junii* 1689.

Ordered by the Lords Spiritual and Temporal, in Parliament Assembled, that such Persons as are now under Bayl by Recognizance, concerning the death of the late Earl of Essex, shall be by the Court of *Kings Bench* bound over to appear the first day of Michaelmas Term next.

G. I thank you, Sir, for your Information herein, and its very probable those who gave me such false Information as to the Lords Proceedings in this Matter, may have likewise forged what Arguments they thought might sway with me to believe my Lords self Murder; what those are I shall give you an Account. But I first desire to hear what Evidence in particular hath been produced to prove my Lords being murdered by others.

T. Before I give you an Account of the Informations that have been in this Case taken, I think it proper first to inform you how the Case came before their Lordships, and what by them therein hath been done, and how the Case now stands before the House.

G. Pray, Sir, use your own method.

T. The 21st of *January* last, (being the day before the Convention sat) several Persons were taken up, as suspected to be privy to my Lords Murder; amongst whom was Major *Hawley*, (Major of the *Tower*) in whose House my Lord was murdered, and *Thomas Russell*, one of the two Warders that stood upon my Lord at the time of his death: these two belonging to the Tower, and consequently under the Command of the Right Honourable the Lord *Lucas* Governour of the Tower, were not taken up by any Constable; but his Lordship having seen the Warrant out against them, ordered both to be secured. The next day, being the 22d, several Informations were taken before *John Robins* Esquire, one of the *Middlesex* Justices, who carried Coppies of these Informations to my Lord *Lucas*. His Lordship the 24th moved the House of Lords for their Lordships Order, as to the keeping, discharging, or removing *Hawley* and *Russell*, as before secured by his Lordships Command; and then produced to the House those Informations brought his Lordship, as before by Mr. *Robins*; upon reading which, after some Debate, the House of Lords ordered Mr. *Braddon* to be called in before their Lordships, and after

B 2   his

his Examination, their Lordships constituted a Committee of Lords, of which the Right Honourable the Earl of *Devonshire* (now Lord Steward of His Majesties Houshold) was Chairman. After this Committee had several times met, there was a secret Committee ordered to examine into the Matter; which Committee consisted of these Four Honourable Lords, (*viz.*) the Earl of *Bedford*, the Earl of *Devon*, the Earl of *Monmouth*, (then Lord *Mordant*) and the Lord *Delamere*; after this Committee had many times sat, and taken about Fourty Depositions and Examinations, the Earl of *Monmouth*, and the Lord *Delamere* were sent by His Majesty into the Country, as two of the Lords Commissioners to regulate the Army. After these two Lords were thus out of Town, the Earl of *Devon* (being Chairman of the Committee) brought these Depositions and Examinations into the House; but it being then late in the day, none were read, but an Order made that they should be read the next Morning; but His Majesties Affairs Commanded likewise the Earl of *Devon* the next Morning to go into the Country; so that when these Informations were read in the House, not one of the four Lords of this Committee were there besides the Earl of *Bedford*: Wherefore the House Ordered the Debate of the matter to be suspended, as you have before heard. And thus the Case came at first before their Lordships, and so it now stands.

G. Sir I thank you for undeceiving me, and desire you to proceed in such a Method, as you think may give us the most Regular Notion of the Matter.

T. Before I give you any Information to prove my Lord by others barbarously Murdered, I think it proper to state the Case as it was represented by those who would have the World believe my Lord a Self-Murderer; for without this you cannot understand what use can be made of many Informations that have been in this Case taken, because you will not be able to see wherein they contradict what was sworn before the Coroner, to prove my Lords self-destruction, and whatsoever proves their representation of the matter to the Coroner false by a very natural Consequence, proves my Lords being murdred by others.

L. Without doubt, for what end (I pray) should any swear to a Lye but to conceal a Truth, there being no other reason to be given for it?

T. I shall begin with my Lords Commitment to the Tower. The Right Honourable *Arthur*, late Earl of *Essex*, was committed to the Tower the Tenth of *July* 1683. and the first night lay at Captain *Cheekes*, the then Lieutenant of the Tower, but the next day was removed to Major *Hawleys*, (then Gentleman Porter of the Tower) and the two Warders placed upon his Lordship were *Nathaniel Munday* and *Thomas Russel*, one to stand at my Lords Chamber-door, or in his Chamber, and the other at the Stairs-foot, and thus by turns. *Paul Bomeny*, my Lords Servant, was permitted to be with his Lordship. At Mr. *Hawleys* my Lord lay *Wednesday* night and *Thursday* night, but *Friday* Morning about Nine of the Clock his Lordship was found with his Throat cut through both Jugulars and Arteries, even to the Neck-bone on both sides the Neck. The next day—

L. Sir, Pardon this Interruption, I find that my Lord first lay at Captain *Cheeks* one night, and then was removed to *Hawleys*, where after two nights his Lordship was found dead; how came it to pass that my Lord had not continued to lye at Captain *Cheeks*, it being very usual for Prisoners of his Lordships Quality to lye at the Lieutenants House, as now my Lord *Salisbury* doth at the Lord *Lucas*'s.

T. The true Cause of this Removal I cannot give you, but the Colour I can; It is pretended that Captain *Cheek* would not be troubled with any Prisoners in his own House; for which reason (as pretended) his Lordship was removed; but this I believe not to be the Cause, but (as I said) the

the Colour only ; as for the true reason hereof, I refer you to the *Men of Secrecy* in this Cafe. But to proceed, The next day being *Saturday*, the Jury fate, and before them were fworn the aforefaid *Paul Bomeny, Thomas Ruffel*, and the two Chyrurgeons.

Which Informations are as followeth according to the Print ; but that (as I fhall obferve in its own proper place) varies from the Original in *Bomeny*'s Information.

The Information of Paul Bomeny *Servant to the late Earl of* Effex *for about Three or Four Years now laft paft taken upon Oath the* 14*th day of* July, Anno Regni Caroli Secondi Dei gratia Angliæ, Scotiæ, Franciæ, & Hiberniæ Regis, Fidei Defenfor, &c. Tricefimo Quinto, Annoque Domini 1683.

SAith, that when my Lord came to Captain *Hawley*'s, which was the 11*th* inftant, my Lord of *Effex* asked him for a Penknife to pare his Nails, as he was wont to do, to which this Informant anfwered, being come in hafte, he had not brought it, but he would fend for one, and accordingly fent the Footman with a Note for feveral things for my Lord, amongft which the Penknife was inferted ; and the Footman went and gave the Bill to my Lords Steward, who fent the Provifions, but not the Penknife, and he told the Footman he would get one the next day : When the Footman was come, my Lord asked if the Penknife was come, this Informant anfwered No, but he fhould have it the next day, and accordingly he on the 12*th* inftant in the morning before my Lord of *Effex* was up, this Informant fent the Footman home with a Note to the Steward, in which amongft other things, he asked for a Penknife for my Lord ; and when the Footman was gone about or a little after eight of the Clock,

my Lord fent one Mr. *Ruffel* his Warder to this Informant, who came, and then he asked him if the Penknife was come, this Informant faid, No my Lord, but I fhall have it by and by, to which my Lord faid that he fhould bring him one of his Rafors, it would do as well ; and then this Informant went and fetched one, and gave it my Lord, who then went to pare his Nails ; and then the Informant went out of the Room into the paffage by the Door, on *Fryday the 13th inftant*, and began to talk with the Warder ; and a little while after he went down Stairs. And foon after came the Footman with the Provifions, and brought alfo a Penknife, which this Informant put upon his Bed, and thought my Lord had no more need of it, becaufe he thought he had pared his Nails. And then this Informant came up to my Lords Chamber about Eight or Nine in the Forenoon on *Fryday the 13th*. inftant wich a little Note from the Steward ; but not finding his Lord in the Chamber, went to the Clofe ftool Clofet Door, and found it fhut, and thinking his Lord was bufie there, went down and ftaid a little, and came up again, thinking his Lord had been come out of the Clofet, and finding him not in the Chamber, he knocked at the Door with his Finger thrice, and faid, My Lord ? But no body anfwering, he took up the Hanging, and looking through the Chink, he faw Blood and parts of the Rafor, whereupon he called the Warder *Ruffel*, and went down to call for help, and the faid *Ruffel* pufhed the Door open, and there they faw my Lord of *Effex* all along the Floor without a Perriwig, and all full of Blood and the Rafor by him. And this Deponent further depofeth, that the Rafor now fhewed to him at the time of his Examination is the fame Rafor which he did bring to my Lord, and which did lye on the Ground in the Cloffet by my Lord.

The

The Information of Thomas Russel *one of the Warders of the Tower, who had the Custody of the Earl of* Essex, *taken the Fourteenth day of* July, Anno Regni Caroli Secundi Dei gratia Angliæ, Scotiæ, Franciæ & Hiberniæ Regis, Fidei Defensoris, *&c.* Tricesimo quinto. Annoque Domini, 1683.

Saith, That on *Fryday* the 13*th* instant, about Eight or Nine of the Clock in the Forenoon, he was present when he did hear the Lord of *Essex* call to his Man Mr. *Bomeny* for a Penknife to pare his Nails, and then for a Razor, which Mr. *Bomeny* brought him ; and then my Lord walked up and down the Room ⸱ scraping his Nails with the Razor, and shut the outWard door ; Mr. *Bomeny half a quarter of an hour afterwards* not finding my Lord in his Bed chamber, went down Stairs again, believing that my Lord was then private in his Closet, *Bomeny* came up about *a quarter of an hour* afterwards and knocked at the Door, then called My Lord, My Lord, but he not answering, peeped through a Chink of the Door, and did see the Earl of *Essex* lying on the Ground in the Closet ; whereupon he did cry out, that my Lord was fallen down sick, and then the Informant went to the Closet Door, and opened it, the Key being on the out-side, and then did see my Lord lye on the Ground in his Blood, and his Throat cut.

The Information of Robert Sherwood *of* Fanchurch-street, *Chyrurgeon, taken the* 14*th day of* July, Anno Regni Caroli Secundi Dei gratia Angliæ, Scotiæ, Franciæ & Hiberniæ Regis, Fidei Defensor, *&c.* Tricesimo quinto, Annoque Domini 1683.

Saith that he hath viewed the Throat of the Earl of *Essex*, and does find that there is a large Wound, and that the *Aspera Arteria* or Wind-pipe, and the Gullet with the Jugular Arteries are all divided, of which wound he certainly dyed.

The Information of Robert Andrews *of* Crutchet-Fryars *Chyrurgeon, taken upon Oath the* 14*th day of* July, Anno Regni Caroli Secundi nunc Regis Angliæ, *&c.* Tricesimo Quinto, Anneque Domini 1683.

Saith, That he hath viewed the Throat of the Lord of *Essex*, and does find that it was cut from the one Jugular to the other, and through the Wind pipe and Gullet into the Vertebres of the Neck, both Jugular Veins being also quite divided.

Upon these Informations the Coroners Jury found my Lord *Felo de se*.

The substance of these Informations in short is, That my Lord of *Essex* called for a Penknife to pare his Nails, but the Penknife not being ready, his Lordship required a Razor, which was delivered him, with which Razor his Lordship retired into his Closet and Lock'd himself in ; but soon after the Closet door being opened, my Lord was found with his Throat cut through both Jugulars and Arteries to the Neck-bone, and the Razor (as before delivered) lying by him.

Nathaniel Monday (the other Warder on my Lord at the time of his Death) now declares, that assoon as my Lord of *Essex*'s Chamber Door was opened by the Gentleman Jaylor about Seven of the Clock, (that morning my Lord died,) he stood Warder upon my Lord till about a quarter of an hour before my Lord was found dead, and then he called up *Russel* and left him at the Door, and then went down Stairs, where he had not been a quarter of an hour before *Bomeny* cryed out, My Lord is fallen down sick ; whereupon he ran up Stairs, and found *Bomeny* and *Russel* endeavouring to open the Closet Door, but neither could stir it, because my Lords body lay

(7)

lay so very close and strong against the Door; wherefore he being stronger than either *Bomeny* or *Russel*, put his Shoulder against the Door, and thrusting with all his might broke it open.

Major *Hawley* (at whose house my Lord was Murdered,) saith, That about Five of the Clock that Morning my Lord died, he went out to open the Tower Gates (according to the duty of his place,) and came not home nor nigh his own house till Note about *Nine* of the Clock, when *Monday* the Warder came to him and told him my Lord of *Essex* had cut his Throat; whereupon *Hawley* going home found it true, and immediately thereupon went to his Majesty *Charles* the Second (then in the Tower) and did inform his Majesty of the same.

Bomeny, *Russel* and *Munday*, (and likewise *Lloyd* the Sentinel at my Lords Lodgings that Note Morning my Lord dyed,) did *ever deny* (till *January* last) that any men were let into my Lords Lodgings before his Death any time that Morning my Lord dyed. The two first upon their Oaths denied it before the Coroner and *Bomeny*. *Russel* and *Lloyd* did at Mr. *Bradon*'s Tryal *pag.* 55, 56, 57, upon their Oaths declare, that no men were let into my Lords Lodgings, (that Morning my Lord dyed) before my Lords Death was known. *Monday* and *Russel* still persist in their denial of any mens being let into my Lord before his Death that Morning my Lord dyed.

This is the state of the Case, as it was represented by those that were immediately attending upon my Lord at the time of his death. I shall not in this place make any Observations upon the several Contradictions and Incoherences of these Relations, nor yet say what is prov'd to falsify all that hath (as before) by these been declared and sworn, but shall leave this to a more proper place, and shall in my method begin with such things as were first in order of time.

The Informations and Examinations in this Case taken are nigh Sixty, I shall range them in this order I shall place those.

First, That have relation to what passed before the day of the death of the late Earl of *Essex*. Secondly, those that relate to what passed the day of his death. And in the third and last place, such as have relation to what was subsequent to the day of his death; upon hearing all which, I doubt not but fully to convince every unprejudiced person.

L. Such I am I do assure you, for its neither my interest nor desire that this Murder (if such indeed it were) should not be detected; but I do heartily wish all such of whatsoever quality sex or condition as stood concerned in contriving, privy to, or acting in this Murder, may be brought to condign punishment.

G. If this be proved to be a Murder, I shall always think it the most villanous that was ever acted on our Stage; and as soon as I shall be throughly convinced hereof, shall as heartily desire (with you) that all Actors and Abetters herein, may receive according to their demerit. And indeed I shall hardly think any punishment too severe for such an Act, or any thing too ill to be thought of any who were in the least concerned in this treacherous complicated Murder (in Person and Reputation) if it be proved to be any. But pardon me if I think it not true, but invented by heretofore Disloyal and Disaffected Men, to raise an aversion against the most Unfortunate among Princes, who was treacherously, (I had almost said Treasonably) deserted by his Souldiers as well as others in the midst of the greatest dangers. We have had much noise of this (pretended) Murder, and (as some falsly call it) of the Murder of *Charles* the Second of the suppositiousness of the Birth of the Prince of *Wales*, and of the Private *French* League; but all this hitherto hath been but *talk*, and I now think (as I ever did) there is not any good grounds for the belief of either, for if there had, we should long since (for the Vindication of what is past, which I shall

forbear

orbear to call by its proper Name) have had it made more publick.

T. *Bona verba, quæso,* not this great heat.

G. But Paſſion is very natural to every honeſt Man that had any ſparks of true Loyalty upon ſuch Reflections as theſe.

T. Paſſion ſerves not, but prejudices an Argument, and generally ſpeaking where there is the moſt Paſſion there is leaſt Reaſon.

G. I will endeavour for the future to be more calm.

L. I ſhall tell you at our next meeting what I have heard concerning the Death of *Charles* the Second, and the Birth of the *pretended* Prince of *Wales*, and its probable may inform you in both of what you may have never heard, nor as yet made publick by any; but I deſire not any longer to detain this Gentleman from proceeding in his intended Method.

G. I beg both your Pardons for this Heat and Interruption, and I do impatiently wait to hear what can be ſaid.

T. I ſhall proceed; and,

Firſt, as for ſuch Informations as have relation to what paſſed before my Lord's Death, theſe are of two ſorts; the firſt proves a Reſolution (by Papiſts) ſeveral Days before my Lord's Death, to cut my Lord's Throat. The

Second, Many Reports in ſeveral parts of *England* (before my Lord's Death) that the Earl of *Eſſex* had cut his Throat in the Tower. For proof of their previous Reſolution to cut my Lord's Throat; pray read this Paper which I have taken for my own ſatisfaction, and the Information of ſome Friends, from the Perſon's own Mouth.

G. D. S. ſaith, 'That a little before
' the Death of the late Earl of *Eſſex*, as
' ſhe was Servant in the Houſe of one Mr.
' *Holmes*, a Papiſt, then living in *Baldwins*
' *Gardens* about Nine Days before my
' Lord's Death, ſome Papiſts (among which
' one Mr. *Lovet*, whom this Informant
' knew) met in her ſaid Maſters Houſe,
' ſhe being then in the Kitchin with one
' *W. A.* then Apprentice with the ſaid Mr.
' *Holmes*; the ſaid *W. A.* went a little up
' ſtairs, and ſtopping, beckoned to this Informant to come to him, which this Informant accordingly did; but the ſaid *W.*
' *A.* ſoon went up ſtairs into the Garret
' (as this Informant ſuppoſes) to work,
' and left this Informant on the Stairs;
' and this Informant heard the aforeſaid
' Papiſts diſcourſing in the Room juſt over
' the Kitchin, concerning the ſaid Earl of
' *Eſſex*; and the ſubſtance of what ſhe then
' heard, was to the Effect following (*viz.*)
' one of them curſing the ſaid Earl, called him Villain and Dog (or ſuch, with
' ſeveral ſuch approbrious Terms) ſaying,
' *He knew ſo much of their Deſigns, and*
' *was ſo very averſe to their Intereſt, that*
' *unleſs he was taken off, they ſhould never*
' *carry them on*. Upon which it was then
' anſwered by another, That they had
' been with his 𝕳𝖎𝖌𝖍𝖓𝖊𝖘𝖘, and his 𝕳𝖎𝖌𝖍=
' 𝖓𝖊𝖘𝖘 was for *Poyſoning* the ſaid Earl;
' but his 𝕳𝖎𝖌𝖍𝖓𝖊𝖘𝖘 was told, that manner
' of Death would not look well to the
' World; it was then alſo declared, that
' one had propoſed to his 𝕳𝖎𝖌𝖍𝖓𝖊𝖘𝖘,
' *Stabbing* the Earl, but that was likewiſe
' not agreed on; 𝖆𝖙 𝖑𝖊𝖓𝖌𝖙𝖍 𝖍𝖎𝖘 𝕳𝖎𝖌𝖍𝖓𝖊𝖘𝖘
' 𝖈𝖔𝖓𝖈𝖑𝖚𝖉𝖊𝖉, 𝖆𝖓𝖉 𝖔𝖗𝖉𝖊𝖗𝖊𝖉 𝖍𝖎𝖘 𝕿𝖍𝖗𝖔𝖆𝖙 𝖙𝖔
' 𝖇𝖊 𝖈𝖚𝖙; 𝖆𝖓𝖉 𝖍𝖎𝖘 𝕳𝖎𝖌𝖍𝖓𝖊𝖘𝖘 𝖍𝖆𝖉 𝖕𝖗𝖔𝖒𝖎=
' 𝖘𝖊𝖉 𝖙𝖔 𝖇𝖊 𝖙𝖍𝖊𝖗𝖊 𝖜𝖍𝖊𝖓 𝖎𝖙 𝖜𝖆𝖘 𝖉𝖔𝖓𝖊;
' (but this Informant remembers not any
' Place mentioned where the Earl's Throat
' was to be cut.) This was the Subſtance
' of what this Informant heard the firſt
' meeting: But about three Days after
' ſome of the aforeſaid Perſons met again
' at the ſaid Mr. *Holmes*'s Houſe, and this
' Informant liſtned (as before) to their
' Diſcourſe, and heard one of them ſay,
' *That the cutting the Earl's Throat was a-*
' *greed on*, *but they would give it out*, *That*
' *he had done it himſelf*; *and if any ſhould*
' *deny it, they would take them up, and pu-*
' *niſh them for it*. This Informant further
' ſaith, That being much troubled in mind
                                              ' for

Note.

'for what she had heard, as above re-
'lated, she was willing to have disco-
'vered to some Justice of Peace what
'she knew, as aforesaid, being willing
'the Mischief, as above-designed, might
'be prevented. Whereupon she went to
'a Friend of hers to advise with (*viz.*)
'one Mr. *B.* since dead (who bfore that
'time had been her Master) who liv'd
'not far from Mr. *Holmes*'s House, and
'informed him as before set forth.
'Whereupon the said Mr. *B.* did *advise*
'*her to be silent*; *for the Papists carrying*
'*all before them*, *she was ruined*, *if she*
'*spoke of it.* Upon which she did not to
'her remembrance then reveal it to any
'other. This Informant further saith,
'That the very day of my Lord's death
'she was (not long before Dinner) at
'a Chandlers (not far from the said
'*Holme*'s House) *viz.* one Mrs. *Hinton*'s, in
'*Leather-lane*, where there then came some
'who declared, That the Earl of *Essex*
'had cut his Throat in the Tower:
'upon which she went home to Mr.
'*Holmes*'s, and was extreamly troubled,
'and immediately taken with Fits, ha-
'ving, as before, heard their Resolution
'to cut the Earl's Throat. This Infor-
'mant further declareth, That about two
'or three of the Clock the same day the
'Earl died, some of the aforesaid Con-
'sult met again at her Master *Holmes*'s
'House, and she heard them leap about
'the Room; and one of them struck him
'upon the Back, and cry'd, *The Feat*
'*was done (or we have done the Feat.)*
'Whereupon the said Mr. *Holmes* re-
'plied, Is the Earl's Throat cut? To which
'the other answered, Yes; 𝔞𝔫𝔡 𝔣𝔲𝔯𝔱𝔥𝔢𝔯
'𝔰𝔞𝔦𝔡, 𝔥𝔢 𝔠𝔬𝔲𝔩𝔡 𝔫𝔬𝔱 𝔟𝔲𝔱 𝔩𝔞𝔲𝔤𝔥 𝔱𝔬
'𝔱𝔥𝔦𝔫𝔨 𝔥𝔬𝔴 𝔩𝔦𝔨𝔢 𝔞 𝔉𝔬𝔬𝔩 𝔱𝔥𝔢 𝔈𝔞𝔯𝔩 𝔬𝔣
'*Essex* 𝔩𝔬𝔬𝔨𝔢𝔡 𝔴𝔥𝔢𝔫 𝔱𝔥𝔢𝔶 𝔠𝔞𝔪𝔢 𝔱𝔬 𝔠𝔲𝔱
'𝔥𝔦𝔰 𝔗𝔥𝔯𝔬𝔞𝔱? The said Mr. *Holmes*
'did then say, Was his Highness there?
'To which the other Papist replied, Yes.
'This Informant further saith, That she
'did, about four Years since, discover to
'one Mr. *R.* (with whom she then lived

'as a Servant) his Wife and Daughter,
'That she had heard at Mr. *Holmes*'s
'House aforesaid, some Papists (several
'days before my Lord's Death) declare,
'That the Earl's Throat was to be
'cut: but her said Master *R.* command-
'ed her to hold her peace, and not to
'tell him such dangerous things, lest, as
'he said, being over-heard, she should
'ruine him, and all his Family, or Words
'to that effect.

G. It's improbable that any should discourse a matter of this Consequence and
Secrecy, thus to be over-heard by the Servant.

T. I do hardly know any House more
convenient for a secret Meeting, provided
all the Family be true to the Design; and,
it's probable, these Men did not know
that this Maid was a Protestant, or that
upon the Stairs in the Kitchin their
Discourse could be over-heard; but indeed it could be there heard almost as
plain as in the very Room it self, unless
you whisper.

L. Besides, consider the Circumstances of Time when this Consult was held.
This was when our Government in its
Corruption was grown to such a pitch,
that some People were *Loyally mad*, and
(through blind prejudiced Obedience, I
hope, more than Malice) were offering
up as Sacrifices to the Court Popish and
Arbitrary Interest the Blood of those
brave Men, who did zealously oppose those
cursed Designs, the Popish and Arbitrary
end whereof we then saw through a
Glass, but since (to our Cost) face to
face. Should therefore this poor Maid
have revealed what she heard, it's ten
thousand to one but this Truth would
have met with such a Disbelief in some,
and such Hatred in others, that through
both, it would have been severely punished; for be sure these bloody Men would
have deposed, and, in probability, by
others of their Party, proved, that they
at that time were somewhere else; and
C with-

without all doubt our then Juries would sooner have credited the many oaths which would, though falsely, have contradicted her Testimony, than her own single Evidence: And therefore I think Mr. *Billinger*'s Caution (as before) given this Maid, was grounded upon great Reason, and what would have proved too true should it have been put to the Tryal.

G. Hath this Woman been sworn?

T. Yes; and as I have been told, deposed the same in Substance before the Lords.

G. She here speaks of several that she long since informed of this matter; is there any that have, or will depose the same? for otherwise I shall look upon it as a new contrived Story maliciously to traduce the most unhappy crowned Head in Christendom (King *James* the Second I mean) and therein to serve a present Interest.

L. I should agree with you in the same Opinion, if it were not, nor could be proved by those to whom she revealed it; but to satisfie you that it both can, and hath been proved long since to be discovered by this *D. S.* pray read what Mr. *R.* his Wife and Daughter (before-mentioned, in *Smith*'s Information) do declare, and are ready to depose.

'*G.* 'Mr. *R.* his Wife and Daughter do 'declare, and are ready to depose, That 'about four years since the aforesaid *D. 'S.* did declare, that she had heard a 'Consult by Papists several days before 'the Earl of *Essex*'s Death, wherein it 'was declared the Earl's Throat was to be 'cut. And the said Mr. *R.* further saith, 'that he did check the said *D. S.* for 'speaking of it, and would not hear her 'freely declare what she would have said 'in that matter, because it would have 'been of dangerous Consequence to him-'self and Family, should such her Dis-'course be over-heard, as it easily might

'by any that might have listned at the 'Window. And the said Mrs *R.* further 'saith, That the said *D. S.* about four 'Years since did declare, That she could 'say much more than she had to them 'revealed, and that she did hope she should 'live to see that day wherein she might 'with safety speak the Truth in this mat-'ter.

L. Have either of those there been sworn before the Lords?

T. Yes, Mr. *R.* and his Daughter, and they have declared to me they have deposed the same in substance before the Lords.

L. How long hath Mr. *Braddon* known of this Evidence?

T. No longer than about *February* last.

G. How doth that appear?

T. By those two Informations following; by the first of which you will perceive, that what this *D. S.* knew in this matter, she was much afraid to reveal to every one.

L. She had great reason so to be; for had it been long since known to some that she knew so much, in all probability she would not now have been in the Land of the Living to have given this Information.

T. The Information you may read.

G. R. M. of *London*, Goldsmith, deposeth, That some time after the Death of the late Earl of *Essex*, observing *D. S.* to be very melancholy, and much concerned and troubled in mind, the said *R. M.* desired the said *D. S.* to tell the reason of such her Dejection; but the said *D. S.* at first was very unwilling, saying, She was afraid to reveal her mind to any. Whereupon the said *R. M.* advised her to discover it to some particular Friend whom she could safely confide in: Upon which the said *D.* replied, *That somewhat which she knew, with relation to the Death of the late Earl of Essex, was the*

cause

(11)

cause of her trouble, and it was not safe for her to reveal it (or words to that effect;) whereupon the said *R. M.* advised her not to reveal it to any one, till she might with safety. The said *R. M.* farther saith, that about *February* last, the said *R. M.* finding it safe to ask, and no danger to the said *D. S.* to reveal what she knew with relation to the said Earls Death, he then desired her to inform him what she knew with relation thereunto. Whereupon the said *D. S.* told him she had heard a Consult before my Lords Death to cut his Throat, and that some great Person was named at that meeting as concerned in contriving the said Earls death, (or words to that effect;) upon which this Deponent (without being very inquisitive into particulars,) spoke to one Mr. *T.* to acquaint Mr. *Braddon*, whom the said *R. M.* knew not, nor to his knowledge ever saw; and sometime after the said Mr. *T.* told the said *R. M.* that he had spoken to the said Mr. *Braddon* about it, and that the said Mr. *Braddon* did desire him the said *R. M.* to bring the said *D. S.* to the *Cross-Keys* in *Watling-street*, where this Deponent and the said *D. S.* with one Friend of hers more, met the said Mr. *Braddon* and Mr. *T.* and then the said *D. S.* gave the said Mr. *Braddon* a particular account of what she knew with relation to the Earls death. And this Deponent doth verily believe, that before that time the said *D. S.* never saw the said Mr. *Braddon* or Mr. *T.*

W. *T.* Gent. deposeth, that about *January* last, discoursing with one *R. M.* concerning the death of the late Earl of *Essex*, the said *R. M.* told this Deponent, that he knew one *D. S.* which could say what was material, with relation to the death of the late Earl of *Essex*; whereupon this Deponent declared, that he would inform Mr. *Braddon* of the same, of which the said *R. M.* seemed very willing and desirous: This Deponent did so accordingly, but the said Mr. *Braddon* spoke to this effect, (*viz.*) That he did believe the Papists did endeavour to put sham-Evidence upon him, which they being able to detect, would from thence argue against the truth of all that should be said. And therefore the said Mr. *Braddon* declared, that unless the said *D.* appeared to be of good reputation, and that she had some years since discovered what she knew in this Case to some Friends; so that it did appear, that it was not a new contrived Story, either to serve the present Interest, or to baffle what else should be sworn, he would not believe whatsoever she should say, neither would he have her Sworn, whatsoever she declared, unless it appeared as above, confirmed by those to whom she revealed it. This Deponent told the said Mr. *Braddon*, that he knew not the said *D. S.* neither (to his remembrance) had ever seen her; But if the said Mr. *Braddon* would appoint some time and place, he might discourse the said *D. S.* and hear what she could say; which the said Mr. *Braddon* declared he would do, if he knew where to speak with her; upon which, this Deponent went to the said *R. M.* and desired the said *R. M.* to bring the said *D. S.* to the Cross Keys in *Watling Street* such a day and hour, for there the said Mr. *Braddon* and this Deponent should then be. This Deponent further deposeth, that the said *R. M. D. S.* and another, met this Deponent, and the said Mr. *Braddon* accordingly; and this Deponent saith, that he this Deponent, the said *R. M.* and another Person, were present when the said Mr. *Braddon* discoursed the said *D. S.* who then gave the said Mr. *Braddon* a particular account of two meetings of Papists several days before the Earl of *Essex's* Death; wherein it was declared how the Earl of *Essex's* Throat was to be cut, and by whom ordered, and likewise of what passed the day the Earl dyed, at the same house where they met before his Death. This Deponent further deposeth, that the said Mr. *Braddon* then spoke to the said *D. S.* to this effect, That unless she could produce Persons of very good Reputation, to

C 2   whom

whom she had some years before revealed it, he would look upon it as a new contrived Story, either to serve the interest of the Government, or invented to baffle what else should be sworn; for though it was of very dangerous consequence to reveal it, yet he could not believe she had been so secret in it as not to reveal it to any; and thereupon this Deponent heard the said *D.S.* declare she had revealed it to several which she named, but she was by all cautioned to Secresy, as she valued her safety. The said *D.S.* did then further declare to the effect following, *viz.* That for some time after my Lord's Death it did extreamly trouble her, and she went to a Divine for his Advice in the matter, for she was extreamly concern'd to think that the Papists should lay the Earls death to his own charge, when she had (as before) heard how they themselves had resolved to cut his Throat; but the said Divine told her, (as she then said) she must be quiet and silent in the matter, till such times should come, wherein she might with safety reveal it. This Deponent farther deposeth, that he (to his best remembrance) never saw the said *D. S.* before this Meeting. And this Deponent doth verily believe, that the said Mr. *Braddon* never saw the said *D. S.* till (as before) at the *Cross-Keys* in *Watling Street*. And this Deponent farther believeth, that the said Mr. *Braddon* never did hear of the said *D. S.* or *R. M.* before this Deponent had (as above deposed) given him Information of them.

T. I have often heard Mr. *Braddon* declare, that he never heard of the said *D. S.* before Mr. *T.* (as before) Informed him of her, and this he would Depose if thereto called.

L. I think that matter is as plainly proved as the thing is capable of; for no man can Swear possitively (besides Mr. *Braddon*) that Mr. *Braddon* never heard of, or saw the said *D.* but through the Information of Mr. *T.* but by all circumstances, as before deposed by Mr. *M.* and *T.* he never did.

G. Mr. *M.* deposeth, that about *February*, he did inform Mr. *T.* and Mr. *T.* deposeth it was about *January*: here seems some variation.

T. None I think; for when a man is to be examined to a Fact about six Months after the Fact done, the certain time whereof he did not set down, he may be well uncertain as to a week or much more. Now neither of these Informants being positive as to the time, but Mr. *T.* being more inclin'd to believe it to be in *January*, and Mr. *M.* thinking it was the beginning of *February*, each being to Swear as himself believeth (as to the time) thus came the seeming difference. Besides, when a man speaks of an action to be done about such a Year, Month, or Week, certainly (in common acceptation) about a Year, includes either the very Year, or the Year before or after; and about such a Month, either the very Month, or the Month before or after, *&c.*

G. I am herein satisfied; now this Information of *D. S.* thus strengthened, would alone convince me of the truth of my Lords being Murdered, were it not that I had heard some Informations read in the Court of King's Bench (upon a Motion made for the Bailing of Mr. *Holmes*,) which with me, and indeed with all men, must totally destroy the Credit of this pretended Consult.

If I mistake not, those Informations proved this *D. S.* for suspition of Theft to have been turned out of Mr. *Holmes*'s Service in *April* before my Lords Death; whereas she Swears her self a Servant with *Holmes* at the time of my Lords Death, which was *July* the 13*th*. I remember not the Names of these Deponents, but I am almost possitive this was what was sworn; and if I mistake not, there was somewhat else deposed by a Countrey Parson, which in some other particulars contradicted *D.S*'s Information.

T. I

(13)

T. I will herein arm you against my self, and produce you Copies of these Informations you speak of.

The first is of one *Dorothy Hewit*, Sister in Law to Mr. *Holmes*, a very violent Papist, and otherwise not of the best Reputation. The second is of one *Elizabeth Christopher*, once reputed of a very loose Character. And the third of, *Nathaniel Swan*, Clerk, to whose Character I shall speak in a more proper time and place.

These are the names of the Informants, and here are the Informations, which you may read if you please.

G. ' *Dorothy Hewit* of *Hatton-Garden*,
' in the County of *Middlesex*, Widdow,
' maketh Oath, That one *Dorothy* (now
' called by the name of *Dorothy Smith*,)
' was Servant to *William Holmes* of
' *Baldwins* Gardens, in the County of
' *Middlesex*, Varnisher, and Brother-in-
' Law to this Deponent, and lived with
' the said *William Holmes* as his Maid Ser-
' vant about the space of a Month, and
' went away from the said Service in the
' Month of *April*, in the Year of our
' Lord 1683, and was turn'd away upon
' suspicion of Stealing a Silver Spoon, for
' which the said *William Holmes*'s Wife
' refused to pay her any Wages, and af-
' ter a long dispute, the said Mr. *Holmes*
' did detain 4 *s.* and 6 *d.* or 5 *s.* for satis-
' faction of the said Spoon ; upon which
' the said *D.* in the presence and hearing
' of this Deponent, did give the said Mrs.
' *Holmes* very opprobrious Language, and
' declared that she would be reveng'd of
' her, or words to that effect. And about
' Two or Three days after the said *Do-*
' *rothy* was turned away as aforesaid, one
' *Elizabeth Cadman* came into her place,
' and lived with the said *William Holmes*
' for the space of Nine Months and up-
' wards. And this Deponant further ma-
' keth Oath, that the 6*th* day of *July*, in
' the said Year of our Lord, 1683, this
' Deponent went with the said *William*
' *Holmes* from the said *William Holmes*'s
' House into the Country, and went that
' day to *Wickam*, in the County of *Bucks*,
' and the next day went to the City of
' *Oxford*, where this Deponent and the
' said *William Holmes* continued till the
' 9th day of the said *July*; and the said
' 9th day, this Deponent and the said
' *William Holmes* went from thence to *Al-*
' *derminster* in the County of *Worcester*,
' to the house of one Mr. *Nathaniel*
' *Swan*, Minister of the said Town, and
' continued there till the 23*d* day of the
' said Month of *July*, and then returned
' towards *London*, and came to *London* the
' Six or Seven and Twentieth of the said
' Month of *July* 1683.

' *Elizabeth Christopher*, late *Elizabeth*
' *Cadman*, now Wife of *John Christopher*
' of *Winford* Street near *White-Chappel*,
' Clothworker, maketh Oath, That she this
' Deponent was Servant to, and lived with
' *William Holmes*, Varnisher, from the
' Month of April, in the Year of our Lord
' 1683, which said Mr. *Holmes* then lived
' in *Baldwins* Gardens, in the County of
' *Middlesex*, and is now a Prisoner in the
' Gaol of *Newgate*, and that this Depo-
' nent continued his Servant as aforesaid,
' and lived in his House from the said
' Month of *April* for the space of Nine
' Months and upwards then next follow-
' ing; and that there was not in that time
' any other Female Servant living with the
' said Mr. *Holmes*. And this Deponent
' farther maketh Oath, That the said Mr.
' *Holmes* in or about the beginning of
' the Month of *July* then next following,
' did go into the Country with Mrs. *Do-*
' *rothy Hewit*, Widdow, his Wives Sister,
' and continued absent for about Three
' Weeks; and she this Deponent hath
' heard the said Mr. *Holmes* his Wife and
' Sister declare, that they went into
' *Worcestershire*, and in their absence, this
' Deponent did hear of the Death of the
' late Earl of *Essex* in the Tower of
' *London*.

Nathaniel

(14)

'Nathaniel Swan of Alderminster in the County of Worcester, Clerk, maketh Oath, That about the 5th day of July, in the Year of our Lord 1683, William Holmes of Baldwin's Gardens, in the County of Middlesex, Varnisher, now a Prisoner in Newgate, London, with and in the Company of Dorothy Hewit of Hatton Garden, in the said County of Middlesex, Widdow, Sister-in-Law to the said William Holmes, and Grand-daughter to this Deponent, came to this Deponents House in the said Town of Alderminster, and continued there with this Deponent till about the Three and Twentieth day of the said Month of July, 1683, and then departed thence towards London.

G. What can you say in Contradiction to these Depositions, either of which being true, your pretended Consult falls down to the ground, and your first Evidence proved false? Of the same nature are (I believe) all the rest, though they may not be so happily detected, as this Smiths Evidence is by these Depositions.

L. I believe these Depositions will be of but little service to you, because your Adversary did so readily furnish you with them; I am therefore apt to think he may be able to destroy the credit of these, as these seem to do the credit of Smiths. And if it shall appear, that these Informations are false, such a detection will add great force to the credibility of Dorothy Smiths Deposition; for whosoever flies to Lyes for a Defence, hath nothing of truth and innocence for protection.

G. I must confess there cannot be a greater Argument of Guilt, than a false defence, seeing every man in his defence doth virtually conclude, If my Defence be false, my Charge is true.

L. The Law concludes the same in all Civil Actions; for instance, he that is sued upon a Bond, and Pleads non est factum, or solvit ad diem, or a Release, or a former Recovery, &c. Whatsoever such general Issuable Plea is pleaded, and the Plaintiff denies this Plea to be true, and thereupon the truth hereof being tryed, if what is pleaded appears false, the Law immediately gives Judgment against the Defendant; for its to be supposed, that every man will first plead the best, (and consequently the truest) Plea he can in bar of the Action; and if his first Plea proves false, its presumed he can give no true and just Cause to exclude the Plaintiff his Action; for if he could, he would first have pleaded it.

T. The same holds good upon Criminal Prosecutions, for if a man shall be accused (though but upon suspicion) of having committed a Robbery within two miles of Salisbury, such a day, upon such a Coloured Gelding, and to avoid this Charge, the Prisoner pretends he was never within Thirty miles of Salisbury in his life; and he likewise produces some, (not of the best Reputation) who declare, that for Ten days before that Robbery, and as long after, the Prisoner being very sick, kept his Chamber, and stirred not out of it; if in Contradiction to this, it be positively sworn by Persons of undoubted Credit, who well knew the Prisoner, that the very day of the Robbery committed, within a very short time before the Robbery appears to have been committed, they met the Prisoner nigh the place where, &c. the Prisoners Gelding, and all other circumstances, in his Cloaths, &c. agreeing with the description the Prosecutor gave, I say, if this be credibly proved in contradiction to the Prisoners Defence, it cannot but satisfy any Judge and Jury, that the Prisoner is really Guilty; neither are they to answer at the last day for his Blood, should he prove innocent, but his Blood shall be required at his own hands, seeing by his false Defence he became a Self-destroyer, according to the common Judgement of all Mankind.

The

(15)

The like may be said in a thousand other Cases.

L. Innocence is naturally suspected as Guilt, when the falsity of its Defence is detected; for if a Person of a very ill Reputation charged a Man with a Crime, if I knew the Disreputation of the Accuser, the bare denyal of the Accused might more influence my Belief, than the Oath of the Prosecutors; but if once I found the Prisoner false in his Defence, that Charge which before I disbelieved as false, I should then immediately as firmly credit for Truth; but I desire to know what can be said in answer to these Counter-evidences.

T. Dorothy *Hewits* Deposition declares, That *D. S.* was turned away in *April* before my Lord's Death, upon suspicion of stealing a Silver Spoon; and upon her being so turned away, she threatned Mr. *Holmes* with Revenge. This Deponent further deposeth, That she went with Mr. *Holmes* into the Country the 6th. of *July*, and tarried with him till about the 27th. so that Mr. *Holmes* was not at home the 13th. of *July*, as *Smith* deposeth.

Elizabeth *Christopher* deposeth, That she came to Mr. *Holmes's* Service in *April* 1683. and tarried there for Nine Months, and no other Maid Servant was with Mr. *Holmes* all that time.

Mr. *Swan* deposeth, That Mr. *Holmes* was with him from *about* the 9th. of *July* 1683. till about the 23d. or 24th. of the same Month.

Hewit and *Christopher* have sworn further back from my Lord's Death than the Case required; for, if they had deposed, that *D. S.* went away the first or second of *July* 1683. it had been more difficult to have disproved them; but having allowed almost three Months to prove them forsworn, it hath been done with the greater ease; whereas these two swear, That *D. S.* went away in *April* before my Lord's Death; by these two Depositions following it appears that she came not a Servant to Mr. *Holmes* till after *May*, 1683.

Pray read these Depositions:

G. 'S. D. of *Little Brittain, London*, 'Widow, deposeth, That in *June* and '*July*, 1683. she lodged next Door to 'Mr. *Holmes's* in *Leopards Alley* in *Baldwin's* Gardens, and in *June* or *July*, 1683. 'she knew *D. S.* to be then a Servant 'to the said Mr. *Holmes*, and whilst the 'said *D.* was there a Servant, she did several times borrow a Bible of this Deponent, and eat *green Pease* with this 'Deponent, *Pease being then three pence* '*or a Groat a Peck*. This Deponent further deposeth, That the said *D. S.* 'whilst she was a Servant, as aforesaid, 'to the said Mr. *Holmes*, came crying to 'this Deponent, and told this Deponent, 'that whilst she was out of her Masters 'House there was a Silver Spoon lost, and 'her Mistress told her she should pay 'for it, which the said *D. S.* crying, 'did much complain of. This Deponent 'further saith, That she saw the said *D.* 'several times after this Spoon was said 'to be lost, and whilst the said *D.* was 'Servant to the said Mr. *Holmes*: But 'how long the said *D. S.* tarried Servant 'with the said Mr. *Holmes* after the Spoon 'was lost, or when she left the said Mr. '*Holmes's* Service, this Deponent knoweth not. But this Deponent saith, That 'the said *D. S.* came not to the Service 'of the said Mr. *Holmes* till some time 'after the 27th. of *May* in the Year aforesaid.

The Information of R. B.

'R. B. of *Oldstreet*, Blacksmith, deposeth, That he knew *D. S.* in *May* or '*June*, 1683. and about Twelve Weeks 'next before, to be Servant to one Mistress '*Ward* in *Oldstreet*, where this Deponent 'then lodged; and the said *D.* did not 'go from the said Mistress *Ward's* Service to be Servant to Mr. *Holmes* in Note Baldwins

'Baldwins-Gardens, till after Green Beans
'were fit to eat. This Deponent further
'deposeth, That about the end of *June*,
'or beginning of *July* in the year afore-
'said, this Deponent went into *Baldwins
'Gardens* and sent to the said Mistress
'*Holms*'s to speak with the said *D. S.*
'who did thereupon come and speak
'with this Deponent at one Mr. *Billin-
'gers* (with whom the said *D.* had been
'before a Servant) but when the said *D.*
'left the said Mistress *Holmes*'s Service,
'this Deponent knoweth not.

L. I perceive *Hewit* and *Christopher*
have sworn *D. S.* to have gone away
from *Holmes*'s above a Month before she
came there to Service; but what farther
Evidence have you of this matter?

T. I desire these Depositions may likewise be read.

The Information of A. D.

'*A. D.* of *Oldstreet*, Spinster, deposeth,
'That some time after *Midsummer* in the
'year 1683. either the end of *June*, or
'beginning of *July* of the same year, this
'Deponent saw *D. S.* then a Servant in
'the House of Mr. *Holmes* in *Leopards
'Alley* in *Baldwins Gardens*; but when the
'said *D.* went from the said Mr. *Holmes*'s
'Service, this Deponent knoweth not.

The Information of K. C.

'*K. C.* of *Baldwinds Gardens*' maketh
'Oath, That in, or about the Month of
'*July*, 1683. she met *D. S.* by *Leopards
'Alley* in *Balwins Gardens* with Green
'Pease, and the said *D. S.* crying, this
'Deponent asked the reason; to which
'the said *D.* answered, that her Mistress
'(Mrs. *Holmes* of *Leopards Alley* in *Bald-
'wins Gardens*, with whom she said she
'then lived) whilst she was at Market,
'that Morning had lost a Silver Spoon,
'and told her she should pay for it, or
'words to that effect. This Deponent
'further maketh Oath, That several Days
'after this she saw the said *D.* in *Bald-
'wins Gardens*, whilst the said *D.* was (as
'she then declared) a Servant to the said
'Mrs. *Holmes*.

The Information of E. M.

'*E. M.* Wife of *R. M.* of *Vine-street* in
'*Hatton Garden*, Pavier, deposeth, That
'in *July* 1683. she lived next Door to
'Mr. *Holmes*'s in *Leopards Alley* in *Bald-
'wins Gardens*, and she knew *D. S.* to be
'a Servant in the House of the said Mr.
'*Holmes* in the same Month of *July*, 1683. Note
'after the Death of the late Earl of *Es-
'sex*; but this Deponent knoweth not
'how long the said *D. S.* tarried with
'the said Mr. *Holmes* a Servant. This
'Deponent further deposeth, That the
'said *D. S.* in the same Month of *July*
'1683. told this Deponent, that her Mi-
'stress had lost a Silver Spoon, and told
'her she should pay for it: Whereupon
'this Deponent said, it was well if the
'right Owner had not mislaid it to make
'her pay for it, or Words to that effect.
'This Deponent farther deposeth, That
'the said *D. S.* remained a Servant with
'the said Mr. *Holmes* several days after
'the said Spoon was lost.

L. Here are five Depositions against
your two, and unless these five appear
to be of very infamous Characters, Mrs.
Hewit and *Christopher* deserve a Pillory
for swearing falsely in Protection of Murder. What is sworn by these five seems very
natural, because most agree in this, That
D. S. was a Servant with *Holmes* in that
time of the year when Green Pease were
very plenty, and cheap: Now this is a natural Evidence, that it was long after *April*; for all men know Pease are not
then a Groat a Peck, nor indeed to be
had for any Price.

G. These Depositions contradict *Hewit*
and *Christopher* as to that part which
proves

proves D. S. to go from Mr. *Holmes* in *April*, but how do you prove Mr. *Holmes* was in Town the 13th of *July*, 1683, seeing Mr. *Swan* as well as *Hewit* prove him in the Countrey.

T. As for Mrs. *Hewits* Deposition in that point, it is of no credit at all, for if it be once disproved in any particular, (as I think it sufficiently is,) the credit of the whole is destroyed; *for perjured or foresworn in one thing, believed in nothing.* But seeing Mr. *Swan* (which by the way is fallen into ill Company in this his Evidence) deposeth, That *Holmes* came to his House *about* the 9th of *July*, 1683, and tarried till the 23d. Mr. *Swan* hath sworn very indefinitely, as to the first part, for what allowance he will have made for *about*, I can't imagine, if he thinks reasonable that *about* shall include the 16th, (seeing the time is so long past, to which he swears, this objection falls of it self; but if the Parson will be more certain, and depose, that Mr. *Holmes* was at his House before the 13th of *July* 1683, and tarried there till the 23d, then will his Oath be some Objection, which otherwise is none. Nevertheless it appears by the Informations following, that Mr. *Holmes* did not go into the Countrey with Mrs. *Hewit*, till D. S. left *Holmes*'s Service, and it is Sworn by E. M. that D. S. did not leave Mr. *Holmes*'s Service till after my Lord's Death; therefore according to these Informations, *Holmes* did not go into the Countrey till after the Death of the late Earl of *Essex* : Pray read this Information.

6. 'W. A. Declareth, and is ready to 'Depose, that whilst D. S. was Servant 'to Mr. *Holmes*, in the Year of our Lord '1683, this Informant being then Ap- 'prentice to the said Mr. *Holmes*, remem- 'bers that Mrs. *Holmes* pretended she lost 'a Silver Spoon; but this Informant saith, 'that the said D. S. was not imme- 'diately hereupon turned away, for she

'tarried sometime after, to the best of 'this Informants remembrance about a 'Fortnight. This Informant further saith, 'That Mr. *Holmes* did not go his Journey 'into the Countrey with Mrs. *Dorothy* '*Hewit*, until after the said D. S. left his 'Service. But this Informant at present 'can't be positive what Month the said 'D. S. went from Mr. *Holmes*'s Service.

T. This Information doth further prove that the said D. did remain a Servant with *Holmes* some time after this Spoon was lost, and was not immediately turned away, as was pretended by *Hewit*. But a stronger Evidence to prove *Hewit* in Town, whilst she swears she was with Mr. *Holmes* in the Countrey, then any you yet heard, is a Taylors Book ready to be produced, by which it appears, that Mrs. *Hewit* had a Dust-Gown, (a peculiar Riding upper Garment,) made for her the Week next after she swore she went out of Town, (this Gown was made the Week my Lord Died,) the Gown appears to be made about the *Wednesday*, which was the 11th of *July*, the second day next before my Lord's Death; but the Taylor can't be positive what day of this Week he did deliver this Gown to Mrs. *Hewit*. The Taylor's Information is as followeth.

'*J. W.* of St. *Dunstans* declareth and is 'ready to depose, that in *July*, 1683, he 'lived in *Poppins Alley*, nigh *Fleetstreet*, 'very near Mrs. *Dorothy Hewit*, and often 'wrought for the said Mrs. *Hewit*, and 'between *Monday* the 9th of *July* 1683, 'and *Monday* the 16th of the same Month 'and Year, this Informant made or cau- 'sed to be made, a Dust-Gown for the 'said Mrs. *Hewit*, as appears by this In- 'formants Book, ready to be produced; 'and the very same Week, (*viz.*) be- 'tween *Monday* the 9th of *July* 1683, and '*Monday* the 16th of the same Month and 'Year (but in the very Day, this Infor- 'mant is not certain,) this Informant 'carried the said Dust-Gown to the 'said

'said Mrs. *Hewit*, who did then pretend
'she was about going into the Countrey,
'but how long after the Duft-Gown so
'delivered, the said Mrs. *Hewit* did go
'into the Countrey, this Informant know-
'eth not.

T. This entry before my Lord's Death
is so clear an Argument of the falcity of
Holmes's Defence——

L. And consequently of the truth of
his charge.

T. That there can't be a more satisfactory Evidence in this part produced.

G. How came this entry to be found
out.

T. When Mr. *Braddon* found that *Holmes*
endeavoured to prove (as before sworn
by *Hewit*) himself out of Town from the
6th of *July* 1683, to the 26th or 27th of
the same Month Mr. *B.* did endeavour to
enquire out all such as either Mr. *Holmes*
or Mrs. *Hewit* were well known to or
traded with, and therefore he made inquiry after all those with whom (in that
Month and Year) they bought of or sold to
all Shopkeepers, Taylors, Butchers, Fish-
mongers, Shoemakers, Hatters, &c. and
such as upon inquiry he received such
Characters of, as he might expect fair
satisfaction from, he did desire to see
their Books in that Month of *July*, to see
whether any Goods were bought in Town
by the said Mr. *Holmes* or Mrs. *Hewit*,
(for proving *Hewit* in Town, proves
Holmes likewise in Town, because its
sworn and can be prov'd, they both went
out of Town together,) or any Money
paid between the 6th and 26th of *July*, by
either of these. After a very long and
tedious Inquiry, (all those Tradesmen
being altogether Strangers to Mr. *Braddon*.)
he providentially met with this Mr. *W.*
who very readily shewed his Book,
wherein is entred as before ⟨ ⟩. This
Book hath not been of any use to Mr. *W.*
for almost five Years, and it was a very
great Providence this had not been torn
out, seeing the Book for some Years had
been used as waste Paper, and the very
next Leaf to this torn out and lost.

L. Upon the smallest matters things of
the greatest moment many times do
depend ; who could have thought this
entry so preserved, would have been
serviceable in so weighty and just a cause.

T. No one Providence is independent,
but the most considerable occurrences
are often brought about by things of the
least consideration. *Joseph*'s Dream preserved his Aged Father, and all his Bre-
thren, and in them all that sprang from
them, from that pale Famine that otherwise might have devoured not these only, but *Egypt* it self. And *Ahasuerus* not
being able either to Dream or Sleep, not
only saves the *Jews* from their Enemies,
but destroys their very Enemies themselves.

L. What can *Holmes* and *Hewit* say in
Vindication of this notorious false Defence.

T. As soon as Mrs. *Hewit* understood
such a Taylors entry was against her Oath,
she with *Holmes*'s Wife went to this Taylor, and desired to see his Book, which
being shewed, *Hewit* first pretended that
this Entry was forged and new ; but when
Mr. *W.* declared he could safely, and
would depose that the Entry was real, it
was then pretended that the Gown was
sent into the Country after Mrs. *Hewit* ;
but when in answer to that, Mr. *W.* declared he could depose, that Mrs. *Hewit*
was in Town when that Dust-Gown was
made and delivered, and that she then
pretended she was about going into the
Countrey, (but how many days after she
did go, he could not tell.) Mrs. *Hewit* told
him if he did Swear that, he would take
off her Brothers life, and *Holmes*'s Blood
would be upon his head.

L. This is a Villanous and False Suggestion, to prevent the detection of Blood,
and evade the punishment for the vilest
Murder. I am sure of this ; if Mr. *W.*
should upon Oath deny what he can with
safety assert, he would draw the guilt of
Perjury on his Head. And not only so,
but

(19)

but this Perjury being in protection of a Murder, to that Perjury, he would add the guilt of my Lord's Blood, seeing by that Perjury he doth endeavour to stifle the Discovery, and prevent the Prosecution of the most Treacherous, Barbarous and Cruel Murder (in all circumstances consider'd) our Nation ever knew. If he that protects a Murderer (being well assured that he is such) in his House, to avoid the common methods of Justice, deserves in our Law to answer this Evasion, (which makes him accessary after the fact) with nothing less than his Life. How much more criminal (before God) is he that by Perjury endeavours to frustrate the Execution of Justice upon the the like offender ; the first doth an action in it self abstracted from the end hospitable, nay, it may be charitable, and his intentions (which argues his after assent to the Murder,) renders him a Criminal. But the second commits one of the greatest Transgressions (which in it self deserves almost Death,) with the same ill design as the first ; wherefore most certainly he is the greatest Criminal of the two, by that addition of Perjury to the same offence. And though our Law in this case punish not the second Offender with Death, yet I am sure (and I think all men will own) that the second most deserves it.

'That D. S. was a Servant at Holmes's 'the day of my Lord Russel's Tryal, and 'my Lord of Essex's Death, and that Mr. 'Holmes and Mrs. Dorothy Hewit were then 'in Town, farther appears from the words 'of a Dying man, who upon his Death-'bed did several times declare he knew 'D. S. then there a Servant, and Holmes 'and Hewit then in Town, and both 'Holmes and Hewit that morning, pre-'tended they would go to my Lord 'Russel's Tryal : This Person did often for 'several days before his Death, declare 'this, as what he could answer as a great 'truth before that God, before whom he 'was shortly to appear; and all this he

This is ready to be prov'd by several.

'did confirm with almost his very last 'breath. This Person did farther declare, 'that when D.S. was a Servant to the said 'Mr. Holmes, and a little before she left 'Holmes's Service; she told this Informant 'she was much troubled with somewhat 'which lay upon her mind ; upon which 'this Informant was desirous to know what 'it was, but the said D. would not tell, 'being unwilling and afraid ; upon which 'this Informant advised her to go to some 'Divine and disclose it.

L. If the positive Depositions of the Living, and the last Breath of a Dying man then dropping into Eternity, where this Relation (had it been false,) would ▬▬ eternally torment him) may be credited, Hewit and Christopher are most notoriously perjured, (and the Parson himself *about* being forsworn, for *about* hath sav'd him from a flat Perjury,) and consequently Mr. Holmes's Defence thus sworn to, is false throughout.

T. Who then can otherwise conclude, but that his charge is true.

L. It's very probable, that some or other that knew Mr. Holmes or Mrs. Hewit, might see one or both of them at my Lord Russel's Tryal, (if they were there,) or might that night hear them confess their having been there ; for this was a very notorious thing, and a sight which People of their Religion and Characters would rejoyce to see and delight much in the Repetition of.

G. It's not unlikely but that others may remember they saw them that day, and heard them give an account of both my Lord Russel's Tryal, and the Earls Death ; for both these things are so remarkable, as may fix the remembrance of Holmes's and Hewits being in Town in some of their acquaintance.

T. I think the Taylors Book before observed, and the words of a Dying-man will be sufficient to convince all mankind. Nevertheless I can't but say this, that it's the duty of every Person that can be positive in Hewits or Holmes's being in Town

D 2   that

(20)

that day the Earl of *Essex* was murdered, which was the same day my Lord *Russel* was try'd, or their being in Town the day just before or next after, (for that Week proves *Hewit* Perjured, who Swears she and *Holmes* went out of Town the Week next before, and returned not till the 26th of the same month;) I say whosoever can be positive in this, and reveals it not, consents to the Death of my Lord; and though Humane Law reach him not, the Divine Law-giver will one day lay it to his charge, as consenting to this Blood.

G. This Doctrine I do not well understand.

L. The Doctrine (I think) is both true and plain, and I will give you an Instance somewhat like this. A Gentleman such a day very early in the morning was found Murdered between *London* and *Highgate*, with one Glove lying by the Body, and not any Person at the first by his Relations particularly suspected for the Murderer; at length upon diligent Inquiry, it was found out (about Two Months after the Death,) that a certain Gentleman had sworn he would Murder the Deceased, if he could ever meet with an opportunity. Upon this suspition he was taken up, the Prisoner denies the fact, and in particular saith, that he could make it appear by two (then present) how that two days before this Murder he went to *Salisbury*; and tarried there till Ten days after, and such a day, he with his Two Friends return'd to *London*, (which Two Friends being then there, declared they were ready to Depose the same. A Gentleman just then coming in, who knew and was very well acquainted with the Prisoner, having been inform'd of his Defence, immediately reflected upon this Defence, and knew it to be false, for this Gentleman with three others, (all knowing the Prisoner) very betimes the very morning the Murder was committed, (which was of a remarkable day) were walking out in *Lambs-Conduit* Fields, there and then met the Prisoner, (with another Person a Stranger to them) to whom they spoke, and he to them; and a little after the Prisoner, was his Spaniel running with a Fringe Glove in his Mouth; this Gentleman being well known to the Dog, calls the Dog, and takes from him the Glove, puts it in his Pocket, and carries it home. This Gentleman therefore knowing this Defence to be false, concluded (as he naturally might) that the charge was true, and hereupon (though with some reluctancy, because the Prisoner was his acquaintance, but not dearer to him then his love to Justice,) declares what you have before heard, and fetches the Glove and his two Friends, and all depose (in contradiction to the Prisoners Defence what you have before heard related, and the Glove appeared to be the Glove of the Person Murdered, and Fellow to that found by the Body.) And now I desire to know of you what you think of this Gentleman (who thus falsified the Defence,) did he do the duty of an honest man.

G. Truly I believe he did, and was to be commended for so doing, though the Prisoner was his Acquaintance, for Justice obliged him to it, and Justice knows neither Acquaintance, Relation or Friend.

T. But do you not think that this Gentleman *(in foro Conscientiæ)* had been consenting to this Murder, had he suffered the Prisoner by such a forged Defence (which he well knew to be false,) to baffle the Prosecution,

G. By his silence he would have consented to the Murder, and (negatively at least) protected the Prisoner from that just Punishment which both the Law of God and Man justly inflicts for such an offence.

T. Upon the whole matter, I think you have rather lost then got any ground by those Depositions upon which you so much rely'd, to falsify *D. S.* Testimony; and that which you have brought to destroy, hath strengthened her Evidence, and consequently

sequently gives credit to the truth of that most Barbarous Murder.

L. For my own part I am very well satisfied, that *D. S.* hath depofed the truth; for how can it be thought that she should declare so long since that she knew of this Consult, if she had not indeed heard it; her very saying it, would have gone nigh (as it would then have been managed *per fas aut nefas*, to have cost her life; and to believe that she would hazard her life to a Lye, can't enter into my thoughts. And therefore I am verily perswaded that nothing but the power of truth made her speak in this matter.

G. It appears sworn by *Hewit*, that *D. S.* threatned Mrs. *Holmes* with Revenge when she was turned away.

L. For this you have the Oath of one who is sufficiently detected of a falsity in two other particulars; and therefore not in this or any thing else to be credited.

T. Had she designed any Revenge, she would have sworn more home upon Mr. *Holmes*, for when she was asked whether she did remember that Mr. *Holmes* was in the Room either of the Two Meetings before my Lord's Death, she declared she would not swear it, because she remembred not that she had heard him there; but all that she could positively swear against him, was what passed after my Lord's Death, (*viz.*) When Mr. *Holmes* came into the Room about Three of the Clock that day my Lord dyed, one strikes him upon the Back, and cry, we have done the feat; upon which Mr. *Holmes* said, *What is the Earls Throat cut, to which the other replied yea, and further said, he could not but laugh to think how like a Fool the Earl looked when they came to cut his Throat*; upon *Holmes*'s Question, it was plain he well understood the meaning of that expression, *the Feat was done*, or otherwise he could not so readily have hit the thing.

G. Can it be supposed Mr. *Holmes* would at Three of the Clock that day my Lord Dy'd, ask whether my Lord's Throat was cut, when it had been from Eleven of the Clock that day in every mans mouth; and consequently *Holmes* could not but believe without any further inquiry at that time of the day.

L. What *Holmes* here spoke by way of Interrogation, might be intended as a strong affirmation of what seemed to be asked, and this you can't wonder at; Have you forgot that common Figure? *Quærit Erotesis*, &c. *Is not this the Carpenters Son? Is not this he* (speaking of St. *Paul*) *that destroyed them which called on his Name at Jerusalem, &c.* in both these, the thing is most strongly affirmed. A Thousand such instances might be given. Or it's possible that *D. S.* might mistake; for whereas she saith, that *Holmes* said, What is the Earls Throat cut? which makes it an Interrogation, the Expression might be, What the Earls Throat is cut, and this makes it a positive Affirmation. Here the words are the very same, only in the first, the Copula is placed before the Subject, and in the last just before the Predicate.

G. I must confess if either of these have sworn true, or the dying man spoke truth, this truth is a very strong confirmation of her Testimony, and I cannot well disbelieve these Five, seeing they do all so well agree in their Evidence; for Five swear *Smith* was there about Peas time, which must be after *April*. I shall detain you no longer upon this particular, but desire you to proceed.

T. Secondly, the many reports in several parts of *England* (before the Earls Death) that the Earl of *Essex* had cut his Throat in the Tower. This is proved by Eight Witnesses.

L. Enough sure to one point.

G. If their credit be good, none ought to doubt what is attested by so many.

L. The Scripture saith, that in the mouth of Two Witnesses a thing shall be confirmed; he that will doubt the truth of a Fact attested by Eight credible Persons is not to be argued with.

T. Pray read these Eight Informations.

G. *W.T.*

(22)

'G. W. T. declareth, and is ready to depose, that *Wednesday* being the 11th of *July* 1683, the second day before the Death of the late Earl of *Essex*, one Mr. *H.* of *Froom* in *Somersetshire*, told this Informant, that the Earl of *Essex* had cut his Throat in the Tower. This Informant farther saith, that about the 18th of the same Month of *July*, in the Year aforesaid, meeting some Clothiers then newly come from *London*, the Clothiers declared to this Informant, that the Earl of *Essex* had cut his Throat in the Tower, *Fryday* before, about Nine of the Clock in the morning; upon which this Informant declared, he had heard it from Mr. *H.* the *Wednesday* before my Lords Death. This Informant farther saith, that meeting the said Mr. *H.* soon after, this Informant asked the said Mr. *H.* how he could inform this Informant the *Wednesday* before my Lord of *Essex*'s Death, that my Lord had cut his Throat in the Tower, when it appeared that my Lord of *Essex* did not dye till *Eryday* morning after, about Nine of the Clock. Upon which the said *H.* answered, that all concluded my Lord of *Essex* would either cut his Throat, or be an Evidence against his Friend my Lord *Russel*, and most believed my Lord would rather cut his Throat, then turn Evidence against his Friend.

'*J. B.* of *Marlborough* in the County of *Wilts*, Pinmaker, declareth, and is ready to depose, that he this Informant was at *Froom* about 8 in the morning, about 100 Miles from *London*, *Fryday* the 13th of *July*, in the Year of our Lord, 1683, and this Informant then heard at the *Dolphin* aforesaid, that the Earl of *Essex* had cut his Throat in the Tower; and the Person that informed this Informant then farther declared, that he much feared it might go the worse with my Lord *Russel* which that day was to be try'd.

'Mrs. *M.* declareth, and is ready to depose, that *Thursday* the 12th of *July*, 1683, going with her Daughter into *Barkshire*, her Daughter informed this Informant, that the night before being *Wednesday* night a Gentleman declared it was reported one of the Lords in the Tower had cut his Throat.

'Mr. *P. H.* Merchant and his Wife both declare, and are ready to depose, that these Informants were at *Tunbridge-Wells* about Thirty Five Miles from *London*, the day of the Death of the late Earl of *Essex*, and about Ten of the Clock that very morning, it was whispered nigh the Wells, that the Earl of *Essex* had cut his Throat in the Tower, but the same was soon contradicted and hushed up till Chappel was ended, which was about or a little before Twelve of the Clock, and then the same report was revived, and so continued without any contradiction.

My Lord was not known to be dead till after Nine.

'*T. F.* of *Andover* about 60 Miles from *London* declareth, and is ready to depose, that the 10th of *July* 1683, being the *Wednesday* next before the Death of the late Earl of *Essex*, this Informant heard it reported at *Andover* aforesaid, that the Earl of *Essex* had cut his Throat in the Tower, and it was that same *Wednesday* likewise declared, that the Earl cut his Throat for this reason, (*viz.*) the King and Duke coming into the Tower where the Earl of *Essex* was a Prisoner for High Treason, the Earl was afraid the King would have came up into his Chamber and have seen him; but his Guilt and Shame was such, that he could not bear the thoughts of it, having been so ungrateful an Offender against so good a Master; therefore his Lordship cut his Throat to avoid it. This Informant farther saith, that the same *Wednesday* night inquiring at the Coffee-house, whether the *London* Letters made any mention of this, he could hear of none that writ of it; upon which this Informant concluded it was false, though the same report continued at *Andover*. This Informant further saith, that by *Friday* Post he did expect a Con-

(23)

'Confirmation of the same, but could not
'(upon inquiry) hear of any *London* Let-
'ters that spoke of it; upon which this
'Informant concluded all was false. But
'*Saturday* being the 14*th* of *July*, the ve-
'ry next day after the Earl's death, this
'Informant was told that the Earl of *Essex*
'had cut his Throat in the Tower; upon
'which this Informant declared he had
'heard the same (repeating what he had
'as before heard) the *Wednesday* before;
'upon which this Informant was told that
'it was very strange, seeing the Earl did
'not cut his Throat till the *Friday* after,
'at or a little after Nine of the Clock in the
'Morning.

'*J. B.* Declareth, and is ready to De-
'pose, That he, this Informant, lay at
'*Andover* (about Sixty Miles from *London*)
'*Thursday* night the 12*th* of *July* 1683,
'the very next day before the death of
'the late Earl of *Essex*; and as this Infor-
'mant *Fryday* Morning about Four of
'the Clock, was going out with the Ostler
'to catch his Horse, the Ostler several
'times over-told this Informant, that the
'night before it was reported at his Ma-
'sters House, that the Earl of *Essex* had
'cut his Throat in the Tower. This In-
'formant further saith, That the very
'same day in the Afternoon he came to
'his own House in *Southwark*, in the
'County of *Surry*, and was then Inform-
'ed, that the Earl of *Essex* that very
'Morning, between Nine and Ten of the
'Clock, had cut his Throat in the Tower;
'upon which this Informant was much
'surprized, having, as before, heard the
'same at *Andover*, nigh Sixty Miles from
'*London*, above Four hours before the
'Earl's death.

'*J. S.* of *Bolt* and *Tun Court* is
'ready to Depose, That at or before Six
'of the Clock, that very Morning the late
'Earl of *Essex* dy'd in the Tower, (*viz.*
'*July* the 13*th* 1683.) there came
'into this Informants House, a Gentle-
'man, who, with much concern, told
'this Informant he had just before heard

'the Earl of *Essex* had cut his Throat in
'the Tower; but this Informant about a
'Eleven of the Clock the same day being
'informed that the Earl was not dead till
'about Nine of the Clock. This Infor-
'formant was much surprized at the Re-
'port of my Lord's having cut his Throat
'so many Hours before the Earl's death.

G. Have any of these eight been sworn
before the Lords?

T. I have been informed by all those
Eight Witnesses, that they have Deposed (in Substance) as you have before
heard.

L. I think no Man can well doubt the
Truth of this Report before my Lord's
death, thus Deposed by so many Witnesses.

T. Those Men wink hard, (that they
may not be convinced) who will not
reasonably conclude from those very Reports only, were there no other sort of
Evidence, that this Brave and Honourable,
but unfortunate Earl was indeed barbarously Murdered; for you may observe all those
Reports in many Places of *England*, Agree in
the Manner how, and the Place where; for
all said that the Earl had cut his Throat
in the Tower: One Report doth not say the
Earl had destroyed himself, which might
have comprehended any manner of death,
neither do any of those Reports say,
That my Lord had Poisoned, Stab'd,
Hanged or Pistolled himself; (all which
are common ways of Self-destruction,
and either might have been practiced by
any Gentleman under Confinement) neither do either of those Reports differ in
the Place where, (though all those Places where the Report was before my
Lord's death, that my Lord had cut his
Throat in the Tower, could not at the
time of this Report be presumed to have
been informed of my Lord's being in the
Tower) I say all these Reports jump in
one and the same manner of Self-murder, and all agree in the Place where,
(*viz.*) the Tower. This clearly proves,
that some days before my Lord's very
Commit-

This previous Report can be prov'd by many more; but if these eight will not satisfie, eightscore will not convince.

Note

Commitment to the Tower, it was concluded, not only that my Lord should be murdered in the General, but likewise the Particular manner how, and the Place where resolved upon. For how could *Froome*, (being a Hundred Miles from *London*) hear *Wednesday* Morning the 11th of *July*, of my Lords being Prisoner in the Tower; when his Lorship was not sent to the Tower till the day before(being the 10th in the Afternoon: Or how could this Commitment be well heard of at *Andover* (about Sixty Miles from *London*) on *Wednesday* Morning, (*Tuesdays* Post not being there till *Wednesday* in the Afternoon) when the Commitment was not till the *Tuesday* in the Afternoon ; and yet at both these Places, this very *Wednesday* Morning, was it reported that the Earl had cut his Throat in the Tower.

L. 'To me 'tis beyond all doubt from what before appears, that the Tower must be fixed upon as the place, where this perfidious Cruelty was to be acted, before my Lord was Prisoner in the Tower, and the particular manner concluded in, or otherwise the Reports as to the manner how, and place where, would have differed.

G. But how could it be supposed to be sent from hence the *Saturday* before my Lord's death, that my Lord of *Essex* had cut his Throat in the Tower, when it was well known throughout this Town, that my Lord was not then in the Tower, nor committed till the *Tuesday* following?

T. Upon the best Inquiry I could make, and the most probable reason I can give (how this came so reported in the Country, before it was indeed done) is this: It was resolved upon, as D.S. deposeth, Nine days before my Lord's death, that my Lord's Throat should be cut. Now those that were privy to the whole Secret, and were willing to oblige their Country Correspondents and Friends with this (to that bloody Party) grateful resolution, That the Earl's Throat was to be cut in the Tower, and laid to his own Charge ; and this to be done either soon after his first Commitment, or upon my Lord *Russell's* Tryal (which was put off some short time) such as had received so weighty Intelligence were likewise willing and ready, partly out of a desire to oblige their Friends in the Country, (to whom this Design might be as acceptable) and partly out of an Itch of telling News, and of being the first in the Country that gave Information of this (to them glad-tidings) not doubting but my Lord's Throat was indeed cut, when it was first resolved upon to be cut, (*viz*.) either upon his first Commitment (which they might suppose would have been before it was, all things being so resolv'd upon) or upon my Lord *Russell's* Tryal (which was to have been before it was, but put off, of which these Country Intelligencers might not hear.) These (I say) being informed that the matter was thus laid, concluded the thing was done as it was so designed to be done, and so reported the thing as done before it was indeed done.

G. I took more particular notice of F's Information, than of either of the Eight. If I mistake not, *F.* swears that the *Wednesday* before my Lord's Death, it was reported at *Andover*, That the King and Duke being in the Tower, the Earl was afraid the King would have come up into his Chamber, and have seen him, but his guilt and shame was such (in consideration of his great ingratitude to the best of Masters) that he cut his Throat to avoid it ; I desire to see this Information again. Note.

T. You are as to the Substance in the right.

G. This looks as though the Story were made after my Lord's Death, for the King and Duke went not to the Tower till *Friday* Morning, and their then going was altogether a surprize to the whole Town: And after the Earl's Death their being then there occasioned very gross reflections, seeing they had not been (as I have been credibly informed) above twice toge-

together in the Tower since the Restoration. Now that this unfortunate Action (the Earl's Death) should be cloathed in the very same circumstances, as afterwards pretended to be done, not only as to the Manner how, the Place where, but likewise the Reason wherefore; which Reason sets forth the King and Duke's being in the Tower when the Earl did it, and done to avoid seeing his Majesty; for the Earl (as was said) was afraid the King would have come up into his Chamber and seen him; but the King and Duke's being in the Tower could neither be foreseen nor expected; this, I say, makes *F*'s Evidence scarce credible.

T. Neither the Cutting the Earl's Throat, or the place where it was to be done, or who was to be there, (*viz.* the King and Duke) when it was to be done, could be either foreseen or expected by any but those who either laid this bloody Scene, or were privy by Information to its contrivance, and such as well knew, or had been informed how this matter was resolved upon, may well be supposed capable of giving a particular Information of this cruel Tragedy.

L. I do well remember that the very Morning my Lord dy'd there was a small Paper cry'd about of the Earl's Death, wherein it was so represented, and the common report of the Town then was, That the Earl cut his Throat, for the same reason so long before assigned by the report at *Andover.* I must confess this is very astonishing, and whosoever believes *F*'s Evidence only, must from such a belief be fully assured, not only that the Earl's Throat was designed to be cut; but likewise that it was contrived to be done in the same circumstances it was afterwards acted under, for else it could not possibly be so circumstancially reported before my Lord's Death; not only as to the *How* and the *Where*, but likewise the *Wherefore* given out before it was done.

T. Gentlemen, I perceive you are both extremely surprized with this particular Evidence of *F.* as what looks like

an after-made Story, seeing the Earl's Death was here so long before reported, as afterwards it was pretended to be acted, both as to the Circumstances of the King and Duke's being in the Tower, and the Consideration that (was pretended) then moved the Earl hereunto (*viz.*) fear of the King's coming into his Chamber, and seeing him, which his guilt and shame (as was pretended) would not bear the thoughts of: But to confirm this Deposition, you will hereafter hear others depose the same; in the mean time I desire you would compare this with that part of *D. S.* Evidence, which declares, That Nine days before the Earl's Death it was declared, that the *Duke* had concluded and ordered his Throat to be cut; And his *Highness had promised to be There* when it was done. Now it would have looked more directly upon his *Highness*, should he alone have gone into the Tower that Morning; and therefore as a colour to that pretended reason for the self-murther, and a Skreen to his *Highness*, his Majesty must be perswaded to go down likewise; so that if any should say the Earl was Murthered, it should be esteemed a Reflection upon his Majesty, who was then in the Tower, as though his Majesty had gone to the Tower that Morning to Murther the Earl. Thus we find the matter managed by the Lord Chief Justice and Attorney-General at Mr. *Braddon*'s Tryal, almost throughout the Tryal.

L. I perceive then that you do not think *Charles* the Second had any Hand in contriving this Murther.

T. I do not, I assure you; but rather the contrary, upon very good reasons; which you will hereafter be satisfied in, for I shall mention them in their proper place. But I do verily believe, that some short time before the King's Death, his Majesty was perswaded the Earl was Murthered; and had his Majesty lived six Months longer, it's very probable you might long since have seen this detection.

L. I have some reason for the same belief: For I do well remember about six Months after the late King's Death, I was credibly told this Story; my Lord Chief Justice *Jefferyes* not long after that King's Death was at some publick place, where he took an occasion to speak very largely in praise of his Majesty, then lately deceased; and after he had made a very long harangue in his praise, his Lordship turned about and whispered a Gentleman in the Ear (whom he thought his Confident) saying, *If the King had lived six Months longer, we had been all Hanged, notwithstanding what I have said.*

T. The measure of his Lordship's Iniquity was not then full.

L. It seems not; but every Man must believe his Lordship's measure was very large, or otherwise the great quantity of innocent blood therein powered by his vile Injustice, had long before his Death made it run over.

G. I do very much wonder (admitting the Earl was Murthered, which I am now almost brought to the belief of) how it should thus become generally reported in so many places before his Death.

L. This *almost* will shortly be an *altogether*, and you will in this be throughly perswaded of the truth of this barbarous Murther; for I have reason to think, much more will be said to prove it, because there are so many Witnesses of which we have as yet had no account.

T. The reason of its being so generally reported before it was done, you will not so much admire at, if you consider all the Circumstances of this Action. This Murther was not acted out of any private Motive, to some private End; it was not done for the satisfaction of Personal revenge: No, this was a branch of that Cursed, Arbitrary, and Popish Design against our Civil and Religious Rights at that time carried on with all the fury imaginable under colour of supporting the English Monarchy and Church of *England*, both which were then falsly said to be threatned with Ruin by that Party, of which that truly Noble, but unfortunate Lord, was marked (out) as one of the Chief: I say this was done to remove a Chief Obstacle to that Popish and Arbitrary end, the true Enemies of both Church and State were then carrying on; for you find it Sworn by D. S that several days before the Earl's Death, the Papists curs'd him as one who knew much of their Designs, (which he could not be ignorant of observing though with hatred) from those high Posts he had been imployed in) and was so very averse to their Interest, that unless he was taken off, *they should never carry them on.* The carrying on their Popish, Arbitrary, and Devilish Design you see was by themselves assigned as the reason of this most perfidious and barbarous Cruelty; so that this Murther was a branch of their Plot, and consequently might be supposed to be known to many; All which have not been Men of the greatest secrecy, witness their Reports of the Fire of *London* so long before it came to pass; and their giving an Account of Sir *Edmondbury Godfrey's* Death in the Country, before we could be assured of the same in Town, the Body not being then found. Several the like Instances might be given.

L. For my own part, I can wash my hands from the blood of any of those unfortunate Gentlemen which suffered for endeavouring to oppose those Arbitrary designs, which the Charitable opinion most men had in the then Court could not at that time believe to be true, but to our great Danger and Cost we have since seen them appear more bare-faced; and those very men who esteemed it Damnable to draw the Sword in defence of our Religious and Civil Rights, though never so grosly Invaded, have since altered both their Opinion and Practice, and could now weep over the Dust of those whose Persons they esteemed not deserving of life. But, blessed be God, our Common Danger taught us to unite against the Common Enemy of all true Religion and Liberty, and to joyn as one Man with that Hand from Heaven (our present Soveraign)

(27)

raign) fent to refcue us from what threat-ned the deftruction of whatfoever was dear to any of us. May God in mercy preferve us from thefe heats and animofi-ties which being (by our common Enemy) once throughly enkindled, may go nigh to end in the utter deftruction of all that which of late hath been miraculoufly fnatch'd out of the fire, inftrumentally by that hand which fome of us (ungrateful as we are!) by our actions feem, neither to thank as our Benefactor, nor acknowledge as our Sovereign, though he feems to have a double Title to the Crown, *Jure Divino,* (by that Miraculous fuccefs God was plea-fed to Crown him with,) and *Jure Huma-no* by that Election (in common Grati-tude) made by the States of the King-dom.

L. From all thefe reports, we may well conclude the Earl's Death was refolved up-on by that Bloody Party which Murdered him both in Perfon and Reputation, and the manner how, the place where, and the (forged) Reafon wherefore agreed in. Thefe Bloody minded men would (without doubt) from the fame motives, and to car-ry on the fame end, deftroy as many more, were it once again as much within their power as it then was, only they would do it with this difference, that whereas there-in they did act clandeftanly; we muft ex-pect that hereafter they would do it in the face of the Sun, and juftify it. But from their Cruel Power and Bloody Malice, Good Lord deliver us.

G. I defire not to detein you any longer on this particular, for I am herein well fa-tisfied, and therefore pray proceed.

T. I am now come to the fecond gene-ral head, (viz.) what paffed the day my Lord Died; you may obferve it was de-nied by Bomeny, Monday and Ruffel, the three that attended on my Lord at the time of his Death, the firft is his Servant, and the two others as his Warders, that there was any man let into my Lord's Lodgings be-fore my Lord's Death that Morning my Lord Died; the like did John Lloyd (the Senti-nel that Morning my Lord Died, at the

door of Major *Hawley*'s Houfe, wherein my Lord lodged.) I fhall now prove that there were fome Ruffians let into my Lords Lodgings a little before his Death to Mur-der my Lord.

Pray read this Information.

G. 'S.S. Linnen-Draper declareth, and is ' ready to depofe, that the 21*th* of *Ja-* ' *nuary* laft, this Informant was at the *Goat* ' Alehoufe in the *Minories*, where *John* ' *Lloyd* Sentinel upon the late Earl of *Effex* ' at the time of his Death, as this Informant ' then was informed, was that day brought ' Prifoner, being taken up as fufpected pri-' vy to the Death of the late Earl of *Eff x.* ' This Informant further faith, that he this ' Informant difcourfed the faid *Lloyd* con-' cerning the faid Earl's Death, and the ' faid *Lloyd* did for fome fhort time often ' deny that he had let in any men into the ' Earl of *Effex*'s Lodgings that Morning the ' Earl dyed; This Informant perfwaded ' the faid *Lloyd* to difcharge his Confcience ' to God and Man, and tell what he knew ' with relation thereunto, left by his denial ' or filence, he fhould draw the guilt of that ' Innocent Blood upon himfelf; but the ' faid *Lloyd* for fometime perfifted in his ' denial, and whilft the faid *Lloyd* was de-' nying his letting in any men into my ' Lord that Morning my Lord Died, before ' his Death, there was brought into the ' Room one Major *Webfter* (as this Infor-' mant afterwards underftood him to be,) ' then Prifoner for the fame matter. This ' Informant did thereupon ask the faid ' *Lloyd* whether he knew the faid *Webfter,* ' which the faid *Lloyd* denied, and faid, he ' never faw him before in his life; upon ' which this Informant faid, it was very ' much that the faid *Lloyd* fhould not know ' or remember to have feen the faid *Webfter* ' who was his Neighbour, and very noto-' rious in the place where he lived. But ' the faid *Lloyd* perfifted for fome fhort ' time in his denial of any knowledge of ' the faid *Webfter*; but foon after, the faid ' *Lloyd* took this Informant by the hand,

E 2 and

'and wringing this Informant's Hand, with
'Tears in his Eyes, spoke to this effect.
'Master I give you a Thousand thanks for
'your good Advice, and I do now remem-
'ber by special order of Major *Hawley* I
'did let in two or three men (but to the
'best of my remembrance three) into my
'Lord's Lodgings that morning my Lord dy-
'ed, and a very short time before his death;
'and that man (pointing to *Webster*) was
'one of the three Men I did so let in; upon
'which this Informant told the said *Lloyd*, it
'was very strange he should pretend that
'*Webster* was one of three Men he had let
'into my Lords Lodgings just before his
'death, when the said *Lloyd* had a little be-
'fore pretended that he never saw the said
'*Webster* before that time. This Informant
'further spoke to the said *Lloyd* to this
'effect, That as the said *Lloyd* was consent-
'ing to my Lords Death, in case he did
'endeavour to stifle any truth which might
'tend to the Discovery of my Lords Mur-
'der, so would the said *Lloyd* be guilty of
'*Webster*'s Blood, if he should charge him
'in this particular with a Lye; for what
'Jury soever should believe that *Webster*
'was one of those let into my Lord just
'before his Death (it having been by all
'deny'd that any were so let in,) would
'likewise believe that *Webster* was one of
'the Ruffians that Murdered his Lordship;
'and therefore this Informant advised the
'said *Lloyd* to be very careful in the mat-
'ter: Whereupon *Lloyd* replied, that he
'could be very positive in the Man, and
'if he were even then to dye, he could
'safely and truly charge him upon his
'Oath with it. This Informant further
'saith, that *Lloyd* did then further declare,
'that as soon as he had let in those men
'into my Lords Lodgings, he did hear se-
'veral (and he did suppose them to be
'those he so let in,) go up Stairs into my
'Lord's Chamber, where there immediate-
'ly ensued a very great noise and tramp-
'ling, and thereupon somewhat thrown
'down like the fall of a Man; not long after
'which, it was cried out that the Earl of
'*Essex* had cut his Throat. *Lloyd* did fur-

'ther declare, that he did not remember
'that he saw those men go out of Major
'*Hawley*'s House, but he did believe they
'might tarry some time in the House, till
'the Croud came in upon the Discovery of
'my Lord's Death, and then went out with
'the Croud.

L. Did any others besides Mr. *S.* hear
this *Lloyd* thus confess the letting in these
men.

T. Yes. Besides *Lloyd* before the Justice
confessed the letting in Two men into my
Lords Lodgings a little before his Death;
as appears by the Coppy hereof.

The Examination of John Lloyd *of* Good-
mans-yard, *in* Aldgate *Parish without, in*
London, *Clothworker, taken before* John
Robins *Esq; one of the Justices of Peace
for the County of* Middlesex, *the 22th day
of* January, Anno Domini 1689.

THis Examinant saith, on the day where-
on the Right Honourable the late Earl
of *Essex* was found dead, upon the suspition of having been Murdered in his Lodgings in the Tower of *London*, he then being
a Soldier, was standing Sentinel at the Door
of the said Earl's Lodgings, and had order
to let no body go up Stairs to the said
Lodgings without leave from Major *Hawley*
or the Warder then in waiting on the said
Earl; and that about half an hour after
Eight of the Clock in the Morning of the
said Day, two Men (to this Examinant unknown,) knocked at the Hatch-door belonging to the said Lodgings, and by per-
mission of the said Warder, entred the said
Lodgings, but when they came out, he can
give no account; and that about Nine a
Clock he heard a struggling on the said
Morning, and a little time after, heard a
Crying, my Lord is dead.

T. Read this likewise.

'*G. C. T.* of the *Minories*, Butcher, de-
'clareth, and is ready to depose, That af-
'ter *Lloyd* had lain about a Month in *New-*
'*gate*, he did desire this Informant (as he
'was informed,) to see him, who by per-
'mission of the Honourable Lords of this
'Com-

(29)

'Committee went accordingly; when this
'Informant came to *Lloyd*, the said *Lloyd*
'spoke to this effect, (*viz.*) Master, as you
'are my Neighbour, so I hope you will
'be my Friend and *True* to me, to which
'this Informant declared he would be a
'Friend to the said *Lloyd* as far as he could;
'whereupon the said *Lloyd* declared, that
'all the time he had been in *Newgate*,
'somewhat lay upon his Conscience, and
'troubled him night and day, upon which
'this Informant asked the said *Lloyd* what
'that was that was so troublesome to him,
'whereupon the said *Lloyd* after often pres-
'sing this Informant *to be True to him*, told
'this Informant, that when he the said
'*Lloyd* was first Prisoner at the *Goat*-Alehouse
'in the Minories, he did confess somewhat
'to a Gentleman, who was altogether a
'Stranger to him, which confession troubled
'him. This Informant then desired to
'know what that confession was which had
'been so troublesome to his mind; *Lloyd*
'hereupon renewing his request, that this
'Informant would be *true* to him, said he
'was troubled in Conscience night and
'day, because he had confessed to that
'strange Gentleman the letting in those
'Men into my Lord's Lodgings just before
'his Death. This Informant then told the
'said *Llyd*, the like he had confessed to
'this Informant and several others; and
'even before the Justice of Peace had
'owned it under his Hand; but if it
'were false, he ought to retract it,
'and be sorry for having said it; *Upon*
'*which the said* Lloyd *declared it was*
'*indeed very true that he did let in those Men,*
'*but it was what he should not have said.*
L. 'You say that the Sentinel pretends he re-
'members not when these Ruffians came out
'of the house; but I have been informed that
'a Servant Maid (who then lived in the
'Tower) came that morning into *Leaden-*
'*hall*-Market, and wrung her hands, and cryed
'out, *The Earl of Essex was Murdered, The*
'*Earl of* Essex *was Murdered*; upon which
'the People gathering about her, advised
'her to silence, telling her she would bring
'her self into trouble by such Expressions.

'The Maid thereupon declared she was
'sure it was true, for she saw the men
'that murdered him just as they came down
'out of his Chamber, and one of them al-
'most pushed her all along.
G. Do you know who this Maid is.
L. No but I spoke with several that saw
her the same Morning in the Market, and
heard her declare as above related.
T. There hath been great diligence used
to find out this Maid, but neither of those
who heard her, knew her name.
L. I am sure it's the duty of those who
knew her, (or of any other that could testify any thing material in this matter) to
give Information to the Gentlemen by this
Honourable Family engaged in this Prosecution.
T. Mr. *Braddon* a little after my Lord's
Murder, was informed of a Person (if I
mistake not, he was said to be a Waterman) who likewise saw those Ruffians as
they came out of the house, just before my
Lord's death was known, and observed
some Blood upon one of their Cloaths, but
having been often search'd in the King's
Bench Prison, and in a hurry forced to
convey away his Papers, he lost the name
and place of abode of this man.
L. That's a great misfortune; but if this
discourse comes to the hand of that Person,
or any that have heard him declare what
is above related, or any thing else material
in this matter, they are desired to send notice to Mr. *Braddon*, from whom a letter
being left at *Richard's* Coffee-house nigh
Temple-Bar, it will come safely and speedily to his hands.
T. It would be no little assistance to a
farther discovery of this matter, (though I
am sure every man that believes what is
here related, as proved or ready to be attested, must be well satisfied in this Murder,) if every man that is not in the least
accessary to this Murder, would but be so ingenious and free as to send Mr. *Braddon* and
give him an Account hereof. It's not desired that any should declare more than
what is true, and what he would answer at
the dreadful day of Judgment; for whose.

ever

ever doth in this case attest a Lye; or what to him is such, endeavours to commit by such his Perjury, the worst sort of Murder.

L. Did either of the Warders or my Lords Servant publickly confess the letting in those.

T. No, nor this Soldier before he was seized the 21th of *January* last.

L. Seeing then they did all deny that any Men were let into my Lord that morning, I can't but suppose these Men so let in, were let in to Murder my Lord; for had any Persons been innocently let in, it might have been innocently confessed and owned, but being admitted into the House with this Villanous and Bloody design, those waiting on my Lord, thought it neither convenient nor safe to confess the letting in of any.

G. This *Lloyd* expressed himself very odly to *T.* whom having often desired and enjoyned to Secresy, to him pretended he was much troubled in conscience for what he had confessed, but nevertheless declared such his confession to be true, but it was what he should not have owned. This looks as though there were some cursed Confederacy entred into for the suppression of truth.

L. I thought you would be brought over.

G. I were never so wedded to the belief of a Fact through prejudice or misinformation, but upon a full and clear discovery of my mistake, did readily renounce my first belief, and cleave to the best Information, or at least that which to me seemed the truest; and to deal plainly with you, I did not think so much could be said to prove what many Industriously endeavour to perswade me was false. But there comes even now into my mind, an objection against this *Lloyds* confession, which will I think destroy it's credit with all Men. If I mistake not, you told me this *Lloyd* at Mr. *Braddon*'s Tryal upon Oath denyed the letting in any Men before my Lords death.

T. 'Tis very true.

G. How then can any man give credit to this confession, which is a point blank contradiction to his former Oath. Nay if *Lloyd* upon Oath asserted what before he had forsworn, I could not barely upon the credit of his Oath believe it.

T. Barely upon the credit of *Lloyd*, I should hardly believe any thing; only consider that the Confession of every man though ten times perjured, is to be admitted against himself. But farther, pray reflect on the Circumstances of *Lloyd*'s first Oath, and you will find in several respects he stood prejudiced, so that his first Oath could not be of equal credit with his now Confession. For admitting my Lord was Murdered by those men so let in, either *Lloyd* was privy to the Murder, or he was not; if he was privy, then he swore to save himself; if he was not privy to the designed Murder, or knew any thing of it, till after the fact was done, then could he not but expect, that the same principles backed with the same power which Murdered my Lord, would have likewise destroyed him, should he have declared what he knew in the matter; therefore the fear of being hanged in the one case, and the danger of a stab or the like in the other, were powerful Arguments with this Sentinel. I do grant no man (upon any consideration whatsoever,) ought to be influenced to Perjury, but yet I desire never to fall under so strong temptations. You can't therefore but confess this Sentinel at the time of Mr. *Braddon*'s Trial was under a strong prejudice to deny what he might in this case know, and that for the reasons before alledged; wherefore compare the circumstances of his Confession with what he afterwards declared, under a great Injunction of Secresy; (*viz.*) *That he was troubled night and day, he had confessed the letting in these men, for though it was indeed true, he should not have confessed.* Consider truth becomes not a Lye by being deny'd, (though upon Oath,) nor a Lye a Truth by being sworn. Wherefore all circumstances considered, you have much stronger reasons to believe *Lloyd*'s now Confession, than his former Oath. But that there were some Men let into my Lord, and were bustling

bustling with his Lordship just before his Death, appears more clearly from this Information following, which I desire you to Read.

G. 'M. B. Declareth, that a little before
'the Death of the late Earl of *Essex* was
'discovered, this Informant was walking
'up before the Earls Chamber Window,
'and hearing a very great trampling and
'bustle in my Lords Chamber, this Infor-
'mant stood still, and looking to the Win-
'dow of the said Chamber, saw Three or
'Four Heads move close together; and
'heard one in the Chamber, which seemed
'to be one in this bustle, cry out very loud
'and very dolefully, 𝔐urder, 𝔐urder,
'𝔐urder; This Informant not then
'knowing it to be my Lord's Lodging, nor
'thinking any other of this Cry, than
'what might be occasioned by some acci-
'dental quarrel, walked up towards the
'Chappel, but not out of sight of the
'Lodgings; and about a quarter of an hour
'after (or less,) it was first cry'd out in
'the house, that the Earl of *Essex* had cut
'his Throat, upon which this Informant
'went down to the House, and being
'shewed the Chamber where the Earl lay,
'she found that was the Chamber where
'she saw the Men, and heard the bustle,
'and *Murder* thrice cry'd out as before
'related. This Informant further saith,
'that some few days after this, telling Mr. P.
'and his Wife, (whom she then kept in
'her lying in) of what she had seen and
'heard as before declared; the said Mr. P.
'advised her not to speak of it, for her
'divulging it, in all probability would
'prove her ruine.

L. Is this Woman Sworn.

T. Yes, and as she hath Informed me, deposed the same.

G. But what is become of this Mr. P.

T. His Information is ready, which you may read.

G. 'A. P. declares, that within a Week
'after the Death of the late Earl of
'*Essex*, *M. B.* did give this Informant
'and his Wife the same Account as above
'related by the said *M. B.* and this Infor-
'mant did then caution and advise the said
'*M. B.* not to reveal it, lest it should prove
'her ruine.

L. Is this Mr. P. sworn?

T. Yes, as he hath informed me, and deposed the same.

T. This Mrs. B. was very unwilling at first to declare in this matter what she knew to be true.

L. Why there was no danger in the discovery, upon this Revolution.

T. It's true; and it was not danger, but (what she thought her) interest that would have deterred her.

L. Interest! Is she a Papist?

T. No, nevertheless she thought it not for her Profit this Murder should be discovered.

L. Certainly it's both the duty and interest of all true Protestants, that this Murder should be fully detected; and I can't well foresee wherein it could be inconsistant with this Womans Interest (if she were indeed a Protestant,) that this Barbarous cruelty should be laid open.

G. It may be she was afraid some Friend or Relation might be concerned.

T. That's very true, it was to save a Relation, but not of Blood or Affinity, but a Civil Parent, the cruel Father of us all, the late K. I mean. For the case stood thus; this Mrs. B. had been Nurse to some Papists of Quality, and others where that Infamous *Madam Midnight*, *Madam* Wilks had been Midwife; and this Mrs. *Wilks* had pretended a great kindness to this Nurse, and had assured her she would get her into the Court to be Nurse to several Persons of Eminent Quality, which this Woman thought might be much for her advantage; and therefore when Mr. *Braddon* first spoke to her, and asked her whether she was in the Tower that Morning the late Earl of *Essex* died, she answered (seeming under some surprise and disorder,) Yes. Mr. *Braddon* then desired to know
what

what she either heard or saw with relation to that unfortunate Lords death; she very shortly replied Nothing; whereupon Mr. *Braddon* (who before had discoursed Mr. *P.*) told her either she was a Liar or Unjust, a Liar if she did not see and hear that which was material with Relation to my Lords Death, seeing she declared the contrary just after my Lords Death to Mr. *P.* and his Wife; or very unjust, if what she had formerly declared were true, and would not now reveal it; she said she would have nothing to do with it, and so flings up Stairs. But Mr. *Braddon* being shortly after informed that this Woman had declared it was against her Interest this Murder should be discovered and prosecuted, *because it would be fixed upon King* James, whose return and settlement she desired, for Madam *Wilks* had promised her as before declared; and therefore seeing Mrs. *Wilks* would have no interest in case this Murder were discovered, and so she should loose a very great Friend. She was resolved not to tell what she knew, nor would have any thing to do in the matter. Mr. *Braddon* being thus informed, desired once more to see this Nurse; when he saw her, he told her he did understand that there was somewhat which stood as a prejudice against her revealing what she knew, but he declared that he would move the Honourable Committee of Lords, that she might be brought to the Bar of the House of Lords and Sworn, where she should either perjure her self in the concealing of what she knew, in doing whereof, she would not only be guilty of Perjury (when sworn to discover the truth,) but to that Perjury would add Blood, (for which at the last day she must expect to answer;) for could she reveal any thing with relation to this Murder, and stifled it, she by such her silence consented to the Blood of my Lord; and how clear soever she might escape the punishment of our Law, she could not but expect she must answer it before him who positively requires Blood for Blood, and that all Governments should make diligent Inquisition for the Blood of the slain, or otherwise he would require that Blood (thus buried through neglect) at the hands of such Majestrates as were difficient in their Inquiry, and more strictly would he one day reckon with those that could detect the Murder, but refused to reveal it; for upon such more especially would the guilt lye, because the Majestrate can make no discovery but by Information; and therefore those that refused or neglected to give their Information, would most certainly one day severely answer for such their silence. Such Discourse as this Mr. *Braddon* had with this Woman before several others; after which Mr. *Braddon* desired to know whether she would go voluntarily or upon motion, be brought to the House, for he was resolved she should be Sworn. Hereupon she declared, seeing she must be sworn, she would rather go willingly than through such compulsion; and then went accordingly, after which she declared what you have before heard, whereas before she was sworn she would reveal nothing.

L. This is a great Argument both of the truth of her Evidence, and the Integrity of the Woman, who rather than sacrifice her Conscience by Perjury, would sacrifice (what she really believed to be) her Interest.

T. Would no Person in this Case be guided by Interest or Affection, but all ingeniously reveal what they know, you would soon find that discovered which now lies buried in silence, but may sooner be detected than some imagine.

L. If it shall hereafter appear, that any Person knows any thing material of this Villany, and hath not revealed it, he may be most justly esteemed consenting to this Murder; and how far our Law may extend in its punishment, there may be an occasion hereafter to try.

G. This

G. This Evidence of *M. B.* doth very much agree with *Lloyd*'s Confeſſion, for *Lloyd* declared, That upon the three Mens going into my Lord's Room, there was immediately a very great Noiſe, and this *M. B.* heard; But *Lloyd* declares nothing of Murder cry'd out, which *M. B.* declared ſhe heard. It's ſtrange *Lloyd* ſhould not hear it as well as the Trampling, if indeed there was any Murder cry'd out.

L. It is very probable that *Lloyd* did hear Murder cry'd out; for it's hardly poſſible to be otherwiſe, becauſe it ſeems Murder was cry'd out thrice very loud, and very dolefully; but ſhould *Lloyd* have confeſſed that he let in theſe three Men, and that upon their going into my Lord's Room, he heard a very great trampling and buſtle, and my Lord cry out (Murder ſeveral times) as before depos'd; by this he ſhould have accuſed himſelf as privy to the Murder; for ſeeing *Lloyd* did not immediately cry out to the next Guard, ſo that theſe Ruffians might be ſecured, and if poſſible the Murder prevented, or at leaſt theſe Cut-throats taken, one of which he might eaſily have done. Nay, in all probability theſe Men would have ſoon deſiſted, had they heard the Sentinel cry out. But *Lloyd* lets them go, and inſtead of a Diſcovery, by Perjury endeavours to conceal it; and therefore may well be ſuppoſed prepared to permit this execrable Tragedy.

G. Permit! What could a Sentinel do, who is placed at his Stand, but could not leave his Poſt?

L. Two things are required of ſuch Sentinels; firſt, to ſee the Priſoner be kept cloſe, without any Communication by Word or Papers thrown into his Window; and ſecondly, to preſerve him from Violence.

G. 'Tis very poſſible that this poor Sentinel might know nothing of the Matter till after the Perſons were let in, and then he perceiv'd, by their buſtling with my Lord, and his Lordſhip's crying out Murder, that they came with an intent to murder my Lord; yet the Power and Authority that ſent theſe two Men, might tie both the Tongue and the Hands of this Sentinel, from endeavouring either to prevent the Action, or ſecure the Actors; that he thought it might coſt his Life to oppoſe with either. So that this poor ignorant Souldier, is as much to be pitied as blamed.

T. Had he made a full and ingenuous Confeſſion upon his being now ſeized, and given this Reaſon for his Silence, he had deſerved great pity for falling under ſo great a Temptation as the fear of Death. But when inſtead of this Ingenuity, which might be naturally expected from ſuch Innocence as you here repreſent this Souldier under, you find the contrary; and inſtead of being ſo free as to tell the whole Truth, he ſeemed much troubled that he had revealed any part, as appeared by that Expreſſion to *T.* when he declared, 'That tho' it was indeed true what 'he had confeſſed, he ſhould not have con- 'feſſed it; this, I ſay, is ſo far from arguing this Souldier that Man you would now ſeem to repreſent him, as it rather concludes him a Confederate in the Fact.

G. 'I muſt confeſs, his retracting what he 'had owned to be true, and declaring he was 'very ſorry he had confeſſed it, tho' it was 'indeed true, ſeems to argue him not ſuch a 'Stranger to the Fact as I could wiſh he 'were.

L. Have you any thing more as to this Point, for I perceive we are very tedious to you?

T. Not in the leaſt; But I rejoice in this Occaſion, of giving you Satisfaction in this Matter. Here are ſome other Informations, with relation to this Point, which I deſire you to read.

G. E. G. and *S. H.* declare, 'That the 'day of the Death of the late Earl of *Eſſex*, '(*viz.*) The 13*th* of *July* 1683, about ele- 'ven of the Clock the ſame day, one *R.* in 'the hearing of theſe Informants, did declare, 'that he was in the *Tower* that Morning, where 'it was reported, That the Earl of *Eſſex* had 'cut his Throat; *but he was ſure he was mur-* '*dered, and that by the Order of his Royal High-* '*neſs*; for the ſaid *R.* then declared, that he 'did obſerve his Majeſty and Royal Highneſs 'part a little from thoſe that attended them,

F and

'and discoursed (to the best of these Infor-
'mants remembrance, the said R. declared it
'was) in French, concerning the Prisoners
'then in the Tower; and his *Highness* declared,
'That of all the Prisoners then there, the
'Earl of *Essex* ought to be taken off: but his
'Majesty said he was resolved to spare him
'for what his Father had suffer'd; upon which
'his Highness seemed very angry, and a little
'before the Death of the said Earl, his
'Highness parted a little way from his Ma-
'jesty, and then two Men were sent into the
'Earls Lodgings to murder him, which having
'done, the same two Men did again return to
'his Highness. *This the said R. declared with*
'*great Earnestness and Passion, and, protested he*
'*thought no Man was safe which was against the*
'*Popish Interest, if once they began thus bare-*
'*faced to cut Throats.*

T. R. proceeded farther, which you shall hear in its proper place.

G. How very improbable is it, that the King and Duke should talk so loud concerning the Earl of *Essex*, as that a Souldier should hear them? This seems to carry its own Confutation.

T. If you consider it I think there is very little if any probability in this Evidence; for you may observe that *R.* declared the King and Duke stood a little way off from those who attended them, and they discoursed in *French*. Now there is not one common *English* Souldier of a thousand who doth understand *French*, the Odds was then so great that this Souldier knew not what they said; therefore it's not so improbable as at first you may think it.

G. Can it be thought that the Duke (admit he was so wicked as to be concerned in such a Fact) would be so very foolish as to send the Ruffians so that any People might see their Mission and their Return.

T. Pray consider this Murder in all its Circumstances; and then tell me whether those bloody Varlets had not all Reason in the World to have all the Security could be expected or desir'd; you well know that my Lord of *Essex* was deservedly very popular, and therefore a Parliament that

should have had the least Information of this treacherous and bloody Murder, would have prosecuted the Matter with all the Diligence and Vigor, that such a piece of Barbarity deserved. Now should they in such their Inquisition have detected those treacherous Villanes, these bloody Men must have expected no Mercy. And should the Duke have imployed them in his Closet only; and they could not by any Circumstance have given Satisfaction that they were his hired Journey-Men, in this piece of great Service, their Evidence against him had not been the tenth part so credible as it would have been, could they have proved that they were sent by his Highness towards the Earl's Lodgings just before his Death, and soon after returned to his Highness, before others knew that this cruel Tragedy was finished. This Circumstance, I say, would have so corroborated their Evidence against their Master, that none could in the least have doubted of the truth of their being so imployed, that were once satisfied they were as before sent by, and returned to his Highness. This then obliged his Highness under no less Obligation than Self-Preservation to skreen those his faithful and ready Servants from any Prosecution, well knowing that his own Interest (and indeed Life) was wrapt up in theirs.

Wherefore I think this matter was very cunningly managed (as to the Security of these Cut-throats from the Hands of Justice, either in their Punishment or Prosecution) and it could not possibly have been done with greater Safety to the Persons of those that did it.

L. What is become of this honest brave *English* Souldier?

T. We have reason to believe he was taken off by way of Prevention, as you will hear in its proper place.

L. I have heard of others that have fallen Sacrifices to the damned Secrecy of this Villanous Murder.

T. I shall immediately inform you of one: here is the Information of two, much of the same with the former.

G. J.

G. J.B. and his Wife both declare, 'That about one of the Clock the very day the late Earl of *Essex* died in the *Tower*, one *R.M.* that Morning (a Souldier in the *Tower*) came to these Informants House, and these Informants desired the said *M.* to give them the best Account he could how the Earl of *Essex* cut his own Throat? to which the said *M.* (with some Earnestness and Passion) answered, that the said Earl did not cut his own Throat, but was barbarously murdered by two Men sent for that purpose by his Royal Highness to the Earl's Lodgings just before his Death.

T. What *M.* did further declare, and what was since his Fate, you will hear in its proper order.

G. These four are but hear-say Witnesses.

T. It is very true; but seeing we have great reason to believe that the addition of more Blood was the occasion of the Removal of these two, especially the latter (as you will hereafter find) I think such Informations ought not to be slighted; for after that rate it's but taking off such as knew any thing with relation to a Murder, and you are very secure from any Discovery, tho never so many upon Oath give an Account of what those Men (whose Mouths have been by bloody Men stopt from giving their own Relation) have declared in the Matter, these two Souldiers related the same as to the sending the Men into my Lord's Lodgings in two Houses as far distant as *Dukes-place* and *Baldwin's Gardens*, and I am verily perswaded that neither *H.* nor *G.* ever spoke to *B.* and his Wife in their Lives; for neither two remember to have seen or heard of the other Informants.

L. Who could imagine that two Souldiers should declare with such Concern and Earnestness, that which was so very dangerous to be spoken, if their love to Truth, and their hatred of such a Treacherous and Bloody Murder, had not even forced it from them, to the hazard of almost their Lives by such their Relation.

G. No Man in particular ought to suffer upon hear-say Evidence:

T. 'Tis true, no Man ought to suffer barely upon a hear-say Evidence; but such Testimony hath been used to corroborate what else may be sworn, and of it self may (in some Cases) be enough to give Satisfaction in the general of the Truth of a matter, and no further is it here used— But the next Account of these two Mens being sent, as before, by his Highness, shall be from the first hand— Read this.

G. Mr. *P.E.* declareth, 'That he, this Informant, was in the *Tower* that Morning the late Earl of *Essex* died, and about a quarter of an hour before the said Earl's Death was discovered, this Informant observed his Highness to part a little way from his Majesty, and then beckned to two Gentlemen to come to him, who came accordingly; and this Informant did observe his Highness to send them towards the Earl's Lodgings, and less than a quarter of an hour after this Informant did observe these very two Men to return to his Highness, and as they came they smiled, and (to the best of this Informant's hearing and remembrance) said, The business is done: upon which his Highness seemed very well pleased, and immediately thereupon his Highness went to his Majesty, soon after which News was brought to the King that the Earl of *Essex* had cut his Throat.

L. This is no hear-say Evidence, and, compared with what the two poor unfortunate Souldiers, the day of my Lord's Death (as before) related, I think is very material, and *ad Hominem*.

G. P. must confess that Expression, *viz. The business is done*, looks with an ill face, especially considering the Glee with which it was spoken. Vile Imps of Hell that shall rejoyce in having done the most Treacherous Murder this Age or Nation ever heard of!

T. You find by *D. S*'s Evidence, 'That after they had cut my Lord's Throat, they were extreamly over-joyed, and one of them striking the Master of the House upon the Back with great Joy, cried, The Feat was done; and he could not but laugh to think 'how

(36)

'how like a Fool the Earl of *Essex* looked
'when they came to cut his Throat.

L. Thefe bloody Villains are the greateſt
Fools (morally ſpeaking) for ſuch horrid
barbarous Cruelties, is the higheſt degree of
moral Folly ; and how like Fools and
Rogues will ſuch Blood-ſuckers look, when
they come to receive the Reward due to
ſuch Barbarity?

G. God's Judgments commonly overtake
(even in this Life) that heinous and
crying Sin of Murder, for which the Penalty of Blood was by him expreſly required, in that Ancient Statute, wherein it was
poſitively enacted, that, *Whoſoever ſheds Man's
Blood, by Man ſhall his Blood be ſhed.* I believe
the Law in this Caſe will be fully executed
upon all concerned, or ſome eminent Judgments inflicted almoſt, if not altogether as
bad as the Penalty.

T. May no Character whatſoever be ex-
cuſed from ſome remarkable Puniſhment or
other?

L. Amen.

T. You did object againſt what was ſworn
to be ſaid by *M.* and *R.* becauſe they, (*viz.*)
B. and his Wife, and *H* and *G.* were but hear-
ſay Evidence; but I deſire you to reflect upon
the many ſuch Teſtimonies produced to
prove the high ▬▬▬ Plot in 1683. Nay,
read but the Evidence of Mr. *Blaithwait*,
(Clerk of the Council, in 1683.) in Mr.
Braddon's Trial, *pag.* 22. you will there find
Mr. *Blaithwait* being ſworn on the behalf of
the King, againſt Mr. *Braddon*, gives an Account to the Court what the young *Edward*'s
Siſter declared to the Council-Board, (*viz.*)
That Braddon *compelled the Boy to ſign it*, (the
Paper the young *Edward*'s ſigned) this you
ſhud to be only hear-ſay Evidence, and the
Author (the Siſter) then in Court, but teſtified no ſuch thing; therefore this hear-
ſay Evidence ought (if any ought) to have
been rejected ; and yet this hear-ſay Evidence (tho' not confirmed by the Author
then upon Oath) was not only admitted, but
ordered to be printed in the Trial in large
Capital Letters; how much ſooner ought
the Evidence of *B.* and his Wife (as to

what *M.* declared) and of *H.* and *G.* as to
R's Account, be particularly remarked, ſeeing *M.* and *R.* we cannot now produce in
Court (as that Author was, but eſpecially
the firſt) being preſumed to be murdered,
by way of prevention, by that bloody Party
that murdered my Lord.

L. We have a Maxim in our Law, *That
no Man ſhall take an Advantage of his own
Wrong*; but the Papiſts will totally deſtroy
this Maxim, for by the Murdering of thoſe
who know their Offences, they totally ſup-
preſs and deſtroy their Evidences, and then
will not admit of an Account, tho' upon
Oath, of what theſe Men ſo murdered (by
way of prevention) declared, becauſe it's
but an hear-ſay Evidence; certainly if there
be any Wrong, Murder is ſuch, and of all
Advantages (by that Wrong) the ſaving
one's Life is the greateſt.

T. Lloyd upon his firſt Confeſſion could
not be poſitive whether Major *Hawley*, or
Monday, opened the Houſe Door to the Ruffians.

G. It could not be Major *Hawley*, for you
ſaid he declared, That he went out of his
own Houſe at five in the Morning, and returned not till after my Lord's Death ; ſo
that between Five and paſt Nine (till after
my Lord's Death) Major *Hawley* was not
in his Houſe, and therefore could not open
the Door to thoſe that went in a little before
Nine.

L. If Major *Hawley* did indeed 'let in
thoſe Ruffians, I ſuppoſe you don't think
he'l own it. And therefore *Hawley* may deny his being at Home after Five, till my Lord
was dead, to avoid being ſuſpected to be
the Man that let them in.

T. Major *Hawley*'s denial in this Caſe, is
as true as his other Denials, of which you
will hereafter hear, to prove this denial
falſe. It is poſitively ſworn by *N.* 'That
' he ſaw the ſaid Major *Hawley* go into his
' Houſe, as my Lord *Ruſſel* was carrying to the
' *Old-Baily*. Now this was not above half an
' hour before the Murder committed; and then
' whereas *Hawley* pretends he did not go nigh
' his own Houſe after five of the Clock in the
Morning,

'Morning, till after my Lord's Death. It's
'contradicted by the positive Oath of one,
'who swears, That he saw Major Hawley se-
'veral times, a little before my Lord's Death,
'run up thro' that Gate which is nigh, and
'leads to his House; and he would immedi-
'atly come in haste down to the Gate, and
'peep on both sides, as tho' he would see the
'way clear; and because the Warder let in
'but one Man to the Tower, Hawley came run-
'ning to him in great fury, chiding him for
'admitting that one.

L. Major *Hawley's* denial of what is so
sworn, looks as tho' he had not been thus
careful in keeping all clear, but for some
Design which was to be done, with as great
secrecy as the Time and Place would admit.

T. You may remember, that *Bo. Mo.* and
Ru. declar'd, That there was a Razor delivered to my Lord wherewith to pair his Nails;
which his Lordship having done, he retired
into his Closet, and there cuts his Throat;
the Closet Door being afterwards opened, all
these three (as they depose and declare)
saw the Body there lie in its Blood, and the
Razor, as before, delivered to my Lord to
pair his Nails, lying by him.

G. This is in short their Relation; and
how can you possibly disprove it, seeing
there was none with my Lord but these
three? and therefore how can it be contradicted by any?

T. I will disprove this Relation in every
part.

First, I will convince you, that there was
no Razor delivered to my Lord to pair his
Nails.

Secondly, That my Lord did not lock
himself into his Closet, nor was there first
found lock'd in, as is sworn by these Men.
And,

Thirdly, That the Razor was not lying
by the Body, when these three first saw the
Body dead.

G. I can't imagine how. (in these Particulars) you can falsify their Relations.

T. I shall prove *Bomeny's* Relation to be
false by what *Russel* swears, and *Russel's* De-

position forged by what *Monday* declared
the day my Lord died.

L. As soon as my Lord was found dead,
Bomeny, Monday, and *Russel,* ought to have
been secured.

T. 'It was so order'd by his Majesty: for as
'soon as News of my Lord's Death was
'brought to King *Charles* the Second, then in
'the *Tower,* his Majesty sent my Lord *Alling-*
'*ton,* Sir *C———* and *Thomas*
'*Howard* Esq; to my Lord's Lodgings, with
'Orders, That all who were attending upon
'my Lord at the time of his Death, should be
'secured and examined, with relation there-
'unto. His Majesty did further order, That
'all things should remain (as to the Body)
'in the same Circumstances it was first found,
'till the Coroner's Inquest had seen the Bo-
'dy.—Before Sir *C———* had pro-
'ceeded far in the Examination of any about
'my Lord's Death, a Gentleman came (as
'from his Majesty) with Orders, That Sir
'*C———* immediately should go to the *Old-*
'*Baily,* (where the Right Honourable the
'Lord *Russel* was then upon his Trial) and
'give the Attorny General notice of my
'Lord's Death: But Sir *C———*
'(by the same Gentleman) desired his Ma-
'jesty to permit him to finish the Exa-
'minations (he was then upon) before he
'went; but the same Gentleman came the se-
'cond time, and declared, his Majesty had
'expresly ordered Sir *C———* to go forth-
'with, and leave the Examinations to such
'others as were there, (which Sir. *C———*
'accordingly did). Sir *C———* further
'saith, That he remembers not who this Gen-
'tleman was, which thus twice came with
'Orders from his Majesty.

L. Forgot who this Gentleman was! this
seems somewhat strange, for within a Week
after my Lord's Death, Mr. *Braddon* appeared
publick in the search after it; and the very
next Week after my Lord's Death, he was
before the Council-Board, and this caused
the Matter to be publickly discoursed; all
the Circumstances attending the Action,
were used as Arguments of this Murder;
not the least whereof was the malicious and

extravagant Application which the Court at the *Old-Baily* made against that Honourable Prisoner the Lord *Ruſſel* then upon his Trial. Now Sir *C────────* having been that Meſſenger that was ſent with the News of my Lord's Death, immediately ſaw, and could not but well obſerve, with what induſtrious Malice and Injuſtice Sir *George Jefferies*, and the then Attorny, applyed that ſad Accident to the taking off that brave, but unfortunate Perſon, whom they were then, by their ſtrained Conſtructions and Miſapplications, villanouſly haranguing out of his Life. For this Reaſon Sir *C──────* muſt immediately reflect upon his being the Meſſenger of ſuch ſad Tidings, and therein upon the Perſon that brought the Orders as from his Majeſty, for his ſuddain going to the *Old-Baily*; which Reflection would have ſo imprinted this Perſon in his Memory, that Sir *C──────* w**ẛ** he not well known, would be thought to have had that happy Faculty of retaining, or forgetting, at pleaſure.

T. I thought no Man could have forgot what he would; and that the more a Man did endeavour to forget, the more fixed would the thing to be forgotten, have remained in his Mind. But I now find my miſtake, and I will likewiſe learn this Art of Forgetfulneſs, which in ſome Caſes may be of uſe.

G. Gentlemen, I know this Gentleman of whom you ſpeak, and am very ſorry for his Forgetfulneſs, which I am very well ſatisfied is real, for I do think him a Man of Honour, and conſequently one that would not lie, much leſs upon Oath declare his forgetfulneſs of what he remembred. It's very poſſible Sir *C.* upon reflection, may call to mind that Gentleman who brought thoſe Orders, and then, I dare ſay, he will, if after that called upon, freely diſcover him, ſeeing by his ſilence, he would likewiſe by Perjury, conceal what might be of no ſmall uſe in this Detection.

L. By this Meſſenger we ſhould ſoon know whether his Majeſty's Name was not uſed without his Authority, for which there is no ſmall reaſon.

T. For my part I am well ſatisfied the Hand of treacherous *Joab* was in this Meſſage, and that the King's Name in this, as in other Things, was uſed by him, who not long after is thought to have removed both Name and Thing from him that then poſſeſſed them. But *Bomeny*, *Monday*, and *Ruſſel*, ſhould have been immediatly ſeparated upon the firſt Diſcovery; and they ſhould have been kept apart till the Jury ſat; and the Jury ought to have examined theſe Men apart, and neither to have known what other had ſaid, ſeeing it was very natural to ſuppoſe, if my Lord fell by treacherous and violent Hands, theſe Men could not be ſtrangers to it; and therefore by their croſs Examinations apart, they might the more eaſily be detected of Falſity; for ſeeing theſe Men were to give a falſe Relation of the Matter, (to hinder the diſcovery of the Truth) their ſeparate Examinations might the more eaſily have detected the Story, it being very difficult for three Men (upon ſeparate and croſs Examinations) ſo to agree, as to Time, Place, Perſon, Manner, *&c.* of an Action as not to be detected; Truth is ſtill the ſame, but Lies are almoſt infinite. Did not the Jury obſerve this method?

T. No; theſe Men were ſuffered to come together that morning they were examined, and for ought I can hear, each heard what other ſaid. Nay, which is more, after *Bomeny* had been upon Oath examined by the Coroner, and given this Information following, taken in the Coroner's own Hand.

The Information of Paul Bomeny, *&c.*

Saith, "That the Earl of *Eſſex*, on the "13th. Inſtant, did ſpeak to this Informant to bring him a Penknife to pair his "Nails, but this Informant could not then "get one; the Earl of *Eſſex* called to him "again on *Friday* the 13th. Inſtant, about "eight of the Clock in the Forenoon; did "again ſpeak to this Informant to bring him "a Penknife to pair his Nails; but this Deponent telling him that he had not one, "his Lord commanded him to bring him a "Razor,

" Razor, which he accordingly did, and then
" his Lordship walked up and down the
" Room scraping his Nails with it, and this
" Informant then left him, and coming a-
" bout half an hour afterwards up into the
" Bed-Chamber, found his Closet-Door fast,
" whereupon this Informant knocked at
" the Door, and called, My Lord, my Lord,
" but he not answering, *pushed the Door a
" little open, where he did see his Lord lying all
" at length on the Ground in his Blood, with
" the Razor near him on the Ground.* And further
" deposeth, That he hath not any Papers
" of his Lord's, nor doth know where any
" of his Papers or Writings are; *and also,
" that on Thursday Night last was very merry at
" Supper, and did not seem to be discontented
" the next Morning.*

This Information is Verbatim as the Coroner took it from *Bomeny*'s own Mouth.

The Coroner proceeding to ask further Questions, *Bomeny* began to hesitate extreamly.

L. Truth to all Questions had been ready at hand; but Lies were first to be forged before they could be given in Answer.

T. You are in the right: But to proceed. Upon this Hesitation, *Bomeny* desired he might write his own Information.

G. I suppose the Coroner and Jury were not so indiscreet as to suffer this.

T. Indeed they did, and I am very charitably inclined to believe favourably of both Coroner and Jury, as to their Honesty, tho they themselves can't justify their Indiscretion when they gave *Bomeny* this Liberty, there being not a convenient place for to write his Information where the Jury were sitting he retired into another Room.

L. To his Instructors (I suppose) that were to be assisting to him in contriving, or rather remembring him of that Story which they thought might most easily deceive: Gross Folly of both Coroner and Jury,!

T. Their Folly in this, themselves condemn, but any ill design in either I believe not. When he had been about an hour wanting, he brings into the Coroner and Jury this following Information, viz.

The Information of Paul Bomeny, &c.

Saith, " That when my Lord came to Cap-
" tain *Hawley,* that was the 11th of *July*
" 1683, my Lord of *Essex* asked him for a
" Pen-knife to pair his Nails with, as he was
" wont to do ? to which this Informant an-
" swered, being come in haste, he had not
" brought it, but he would send for one,
" and accordingly sent the Footman with a
" Note for several things for my Lord, a-
" mong which the Pen-knife was inserted,
" and the Footman went and gave the
" Bill to my Lord's Steward, who sent him
" the Provision, but not the Pen-knife, and
" he told the Footman he would get one
" the next day; when the Footman was
" come, my Lord asked if the Pen-knife was
" come ? this Informant answered, No, but
" he should have it the next day, and ac-
" cordingly he on the 12th Instant in the
" Morning, before my Lord of *Essex* was up,
" this Informant sent the Footman home
" with a Note to the Steward, in which,
" among other things, he asked for a Pen-
" knife for my Lord, and when the Foot-
" man was gone, about, or a little after
" Eight a Clock my Lord sent one Mr. *Russel*
" his Warder to this Informant, who came,
" and then he asked him if the Pen-knife
" was come ? this Informant said, No, my
" Lord, but I shall have it by and by ; to
" which my Lord said he should bring him
" one of his Razors, it would do as well ;
" and then this Informant went and fetched
" one and gave it my Lord, who then went
" to pair his Nails; and then this Infor-
" mant went out of the Room in the Passage
" by the Door, and began to talk with the
" Warder, and a little while after he went
" down Stairs, and soon after came the
" Footman with the Pen-knife, which this
" Informant put upon his Bed, and thought
" my Lord had no more need of it, because
" he thought he had paired his Nails; and
" then this Informant came to my Lord's
" Chamber [*about Eight or Nine in the
" Forenoon on Friday the* 13th *Instant*] with

" *a little Note from the Steward, where
" *there were three Lines writ* ; but not find-
" ing his Lord in the Chamber, went to the
" Close-stool Closet-door, and found it shut,
" and he thinking his Lord was busy there,
" went down and staid a little, and came up
" again, thinking his Lord had been come
" out of the Closet, and finding him not in
" the Chamber, he knocked at the Door
" with his Finger thrice, and said, My Lord,
" but no body answering he took up the
" Hanging and looked through the Chinck,
" and saw Blood, and part of the Razor,
" whereupon he called the Warder *Russel*,
" and went down to call for help; and the
" said *Russel* pushed the Door open, there they
" saw my Lord of *Essex* all along the Floor
" without a Perriwig, and all full of Blood
" and the Razor by him. And this Depo-
" nent further deposeth, That the Razor
" now shewed unto him at the time of his
" Examination, is the same Razor which he
" did bring unto my Lord, and did lie
" on the ground in the Closet by my
" Lord.

You find some of *Bomeny*'s printed Informations writ in *large Capital Letters*, and
likewise some of this so writ.

L. I perceive it.

T. The first was inserted by my Lord
Sunderland's Order, the then Secretary of
State, or some under him. And the third
omitted, for it was in the Original, which
you have just now read; and the second was
interlined by the Coroner after *Bomeny* had,
as before, brought this Information to him:
what the Coroner interlined was, as himself
saith, with *Bomeny*'s Consent, and truly I
think very favourably of him.

G. I perceive that by comparing the Relation printed by Authority, that next Monday after my Lord's Death, with what you
here declare to be the Original, it materially differs, for they added to it, and took
from it as they pleased; so that this is (in
strictness speaking) a forged Information
that was printed.

L. As in a Deed or Bond, the adding to,
or taking from either, in Construction of
Law, is forging the whole: So in an Information, once signed and sworn to, nothing
can be added to it, or diminished from it,
without being in Law a Forger of the whole.

G. What reason had the Secretary of
State to print *Bomeny*'s Information different from the Original.

T. My Lord *Sunderland*, or some under
Confident, perceiving *Bomeny* had sworn
the Delivery of the Razor, and what thereupon happened to be of the Thursday,
the day before my Lord's Death, which
was not only contrary to his Instructi-
ons, but a point-blank Contradiction to his
Confederate *Russel*; it was thought convenient, either by my Lord *Sunderland*, or
such Confident under him, that these two
Informations should be reconciled in the
Print, how contradictory soever they were
in the Original (which could not be seen
and compared with the Print by any but the
Coroner, in whose Custody they were)
and therefore on Friday the 13th Instant was
to be (by way of Forgery) added to *Bomeny*'s Informations, but this done (as hath
been observed by an ingenuous Author on
this occasion) without the least Congruity
either to Sense or Grammar; for nothing
can be more apparent than that the fore-
going part of the Information relates wholly
to Thursday; but at last, without any regard
to what *Bomeny* had before sworn, on Friday
the 13th Instant is foisted in, contrary to all
Rules of Grammar, and common Measures of
Sense as well as Justice, which justly esteems
this printed Information forged. This forged Reconciliation is done with the greatest
Incongruity and Absurdness as well as False-
ness imaginable; and I know not whether
the Folly of the Suborner (for without
doubt the Suborner and Reconciler in this
case are the same, or of the same stamp)
or the Perjury of the suborned in this Information be most conspicuous.

G. Sir, I now perceive what was the
reason of this Alteration (or rather Forgery) in this Information; but as you have
often observed, God Almighty allots to the
Knave

Knave such an Allay of the Fool, that the Fool hangs the Knave up half way; and in this that Observation is so Notorious, that I never saw more of the Fool in the Knave in my Life. Certainly this Gentleman that villanously (in protection of the Murder) thus turned Reconciler, either did not understand Sense himself, or else did believe none would read this Information that did, &c.

T. Pray read these two Papers.

G. J. W. Painter saith, That the very day the Earl of *Essex* died, he went with one (*George Jones* since dead) to the *Tower*, to discourse *Nathaniel Monday* concerning the Death of the said Earl: and when they came to the *Tower*, meeting with the said *Monday*, he gave them this Account; That as soon as the Gentleman Jaylor had opened my Lord's Chamber Door; that very morning, he the said *Monday* (by Order) went in to my Lord's Chamber, and tarried there, because their Orders were, that one of the Warders should be in his Lordship's Chamber, and the other at the Stair's Foot. And that they had this farther Order, not to suffer his Lordship to have a Knife, or any thing like it, but whilst he used it in cutting his Meat; and that being done, all Knives, and such-like, were to be taken from him: To which his Lordship answered, He should take nothing ill in them in observing their Orders. This Informant further saith, That the said *Monday* did then declare, that he tarried with my Lord in his Chamber two hours, or better, that very morning; and that whilst he was with my Lord in his Chamber, he did observe his Lordship paired his Nails with the Heel of a Razor. This Informant further saith, that the said *Monday* did further declare, Before he left his Lordship, and went down Stairs to stand below, he called up *Russel* his fellow-Warder, to stand in the Chamber; and as he went down Stairs, he lighted his Pipe and sat at the Stairs foot; but before he had half smoaked his Pipe, he heard it cried above Stairs, that my Lord had cut his Throat. Hereupon he, the said *Monday*, ran up Stairs, and pushed the Closet Door open, and there found my Lord dead. This Informant further saith, that the said *Monday* did further declare, That when he came up Stairs, he asked Mr. *Bomeny* and *Russel*, where they were whilst my Lord was in the Closet? The said *Bomeny* answered, he was sitting upon the Bed in my Lord's Chamber; and the said *Russel* declared, he stood at my Lord's Chamber Door, just without the Door: whereupon he, the said *Monday* (as the said *Monday* declared) check'd the said *Russel* for not keeping in the Chamber, according to Order. *Richard Jordan* declareth, That on the day Mr. *Braddon* was tried, (upon the account of the late Earl of *Essex*) this Informant heard *Nath. Monday* declare, That the very morning the late Earl of *Essex* died, as soon as the Gentleman Jaylor open'd the Chamber Door, which was about seven of the Clock, the said *Monday* first stood as Warder above Stairs upon the said Earl; and at the first opening the Door, did observe the said Earl have a Razor in his Hand, pairing or scraping his Nails with it; and this the said *Monday* declared he saw a long time before *Russel* stood Warder above Stairs upon the said Earl.

T. By these two Informations you may perceive what *Monday* declared, My Lord had this Razor in his Hand about seven a Clock in the Morning, long before *Russel* came up Stairs to stand Warder upon my Lord; and that my Lord pared his Nails with the Heel of the Razor.

G. I find it as you say.

L. Monday I perceive tells *W.* the very day my Lord died, that the very same morning, about seven of the Clock, *Monday* told my Lord that they (his Warders) had Orders not to suffer his Lordship to have a Knife, or any thing like it, whilst he was cutting his Meat; and that being done, the Knife was to be taken from his Lordship. This looks as tho there were some Jealousies that my Lord would cut his Throat, — for otherwise why would they not suffer him to have a Knife?

T. It looks more like, either a Suggestion of *Monday*'s own Invention, or a Lesson taught him to make others believe that there was such a Suspition; for *Monday* now denies it.

I desire now to compare these three Mens Relations, as to the Time of delivery of the Razor; by doing which, you will have reason to believe no Razor at all was delivered to his Lordship. For the clearer understanding hereof, I suppose *Bomeny* under Examination with the Jury, and answering according to what he hath sworn.

☞ *Jury.* Did you deliver this Razor to my Lord?

Bomeny. Yes.

Jury. When did you deliver this Razor to my Lord?

Bomeny. About eight of the Clock that morning my Lord died.

This according to what he first swore: but he then withdraws to write his own Information, which point-blank contradicts this his Oath in that particular, for he is then examined, and answereth as followeth.

Jury. Do you remember the very Time that you delivered this Razor to my Lord?

Bomeny. Yes.

Jury. When did you deliver this Razor to my Lord?

☞ *Bomeny.* About eight of the Clock on *Thursday* morning, being the day before my Lord's death.

This, as you observe, he swears in the Information himself writ, and brought to the Coroner.

T. Bomeny then to withdraw, and let *Russel* answer to this particular.

Jury. Mr. *Russel*, do you know when this Razor was delivered to my Lord?

Russel. Very well, for I saw it delivered to my Lord by *Bomeny.*

Jury. When did you see this Razor delivered?

Russel. Less then a quarter of an hour before we found my Lord dead. I stood Warder at my Lord's Door; and I heard his Lordship ask for his Penknife to pair his Nails; and *Bomeny* said, it was not brought: upon which ☞ my Lord required a Razor, saying, it would do as well; and I saw *Bomeny* give my Lord the Razor, it being then about nine a Clock.

Jury. Who first stood as Warder at my Lord's Chamber Door, or in my Lord's Chamber, yesterday morning, before my Lord dy'd, was it you or *Monday*?

Russel. Monday, upon my Lord's Chamber Door being opened, first stood at the Door; and after he had been there as long as we use to stand, he called me up, and then went down and stood at the Stairs-foot, at the House Door, where I did before stand.

Jury. Then this Razor you saw delivered to my Lord, after *Monday* went down Stairs, and whilst you stood as Warder at my Lord's Door?

Russel. It's very true, for I am sure I stood by *Bomeny* when he delivered the Razor, and saw it delivered to my Lord.

Jury. What distance of Time do you say there might be, from the time this Razor was delivered, to the time of my Lord's death?

Russel. I am sure it could not be half an hour from the time of the delivery of the Razor, to the time we found my Lord dead in the Closet.

T. Russel withdraws, and *Monday* is examined.

Jury. Mr. *Monday,* did you see my Lord have any Razor in his Hand yesterday morning before his death?

Monday. Yes, I did.

Jury. What time was it when you saw my Lord have the Razor in his Hand?

Monday. About seven of the Clock, as soon as the Gentleman Jaylor opened my Lord's Chamber Door; for I first stood Warder above Stairs, and as soon as the Door was opened, I saw my Lord have the Razor in his Hand, and observed him to pair his Nails with it.

Jury. Was this before *Russel* came up to my Lord's Chamber door to stand Warder there?

Monday. Yes, almost two hours.

T. This is according to their own Informations and Relations. Now can you believe that this Razor was delivered by *Bomeny* at eight of the Clock *Friday* morning, according ☜ to his first Oath, and yet not delivered till eight of the Clock *Thursday* Morning, according

cording to *Bomeny*'s second Oath? And can you also believe that the Razor was not delivered till about nine of the Clock *Friday* Morning, according to *Ruſſel*'s Information? and at the same time give Credit to *Monday*, who declared, my Lord had the Razor by seven of the Clock, two hours before *Ruſſel* came up to stand Warder at my Lord's Chamber Door.

L. These Three are of equal Credit, and consequently you have as much reason to believe *Bomeny*, as *Ruſſel*; and *Monday* deserves equal Credit with either of the Former: But all can't be credited, neither can *Bomeny*'s Contradictions be reconciled, or can one of these be thought true, without giving the Lie to the other two; therefore upon the whole Matter, you can't reasonably believe there was any Razor at all delivered.

G. I find all three in the main agree, that my Lord had a Razor delivered him to pair his Nails, and their Contradiction is only in point of Time.

T. 'Tis true, it's a Circumstantial Contradiction in point of Time, and the Contradiction of the two Elders in the History of *Suſanna*, was a Circumstantial contradiction in point of Place; for the first swore they took *Suſanna* in Adultery under a Mastick Tree, and the second under an Holm Tree: Both these agreed in the main (as you call it) *Viz.* that they found her in Adultery; But by this contradiction as to the Place, where, *Daniel* convinced all then present, that these two Elders were perjur'd in their Evidence (and consequently *Suſanna* Innocent of her Charge) and thereupon these Two Accusers justly suffered, what by Perjury they would have unjustly caused to be inflicted upon the Innocent. Did you ever hear any deny *Daniel*'s Wisdom in this Detection; or arraign his Justice in the punishment those two false Accusers thereupon suffered?

G. I must confess, these Contradictions look as tho neither was true; for Truth would have been the same to all.

T. Besides, you find all three agree in this, That my Lord pared his Nails with the Razor, which appears to be false by this Information, which I desire you to read.

G. John Kettleheater, one of the Jury upon the late Earl of *Eſſex*, sweareth, That the Nails on the Fingers and Feet of the said Earl were very long, and not scraped or pared as he could discern.

L. Being proved perjur'd in one Part, believed in Nothing.

T. Whereas it was sworn and declared by all, that my Lord's Body was locked into the Closet; I will now suppose that *Bomeny*, *Ruſſel*, and *Monday*, were to answer as to the opening this Door, according to their former Informations, and you will find their Contradictions, as to this, as gross as the former.

Bomeny first appears.

Jury. Mr. *Bomeny*, Was my Lord's Body locked into the Closet when he was first found dead?

Bomeny. Yes.

Jury. Who opened the Door?

Bomeny. When I had knocked at the Closet Door, my Lord not answering, I did open the Door, and there saw my Lord lying along in his Blood, and the Razor by him, and I then call'd the Warders.

This according to his first Information, taken (as before) by the Coroner.

About an hour after this, the Jury do again examine him as to this Point, and he answering according to the Information, which (as before) he writ in the Room next the Jury, and then you will find it as followeth.

Jury. Mr. *Bomeny*, Did you first open the Closet Door upon my Lord's Body?

Bomeny. No, I did not, but *Ruſſel* did, for after I had knocked at the Door thrice, calling my Lord; my Lord not answering, I took up the Hangings, and peeping thro' a Chink, I saw Blood, and part of the Razor; whereupon I called the Warder *Ruſſel*——and the said *Ruſſel* pushed the Door open.

T. At Mr. *Braddon*'s Trial, *Bomeny* being ask'd who did first open the Door? upon Oath answered, He knew not who opened the Door.

L. Here *Bomeny* is twice against himself; first he swears that he himself opened this Door before he called either of the Warders.

Secondly,

Secondly, swears that he did not first open the Door, but *Russel* pushed it open; and thirdly, deposeth, that he knew not who opened the Door.

T. I desire the other two, *viz.* *Russel* and *Monday*, may in this particular answer, and then compare them altogether.

Jury. Mr. *Russel*, Did you find the Closet-Door locked upon my Lord's Body?

Russel. Yes.

Jury. Who first opened this Closet-Door?

Russel. When *Bomeny* saw my Lord's Body through the Chink, he cried out, My Lord was fallen down sick, whereupon I went to the Closet-Door and opened it, the Key being on the outside.

T. Here *Russel* makes no difficulty in opening the Door: But observe *Monday*'s Answer. *Russel* withdraws and *Monday* is called.

Jury. Mr. *Monday*, where were you when my Lord was first found dead?

Monday. I was standing at the foot of my Lord's Stairs, and hearing a great Noise of my Lord's Death, I ran up Stairs and found *Bomeny* and *Russel* endeavouring to open the Door, but the Body being so close and strong against the Door neither could.

Jury. Who then opened the Door?

Monday. I being much stronger than either of these two, put my Shoulders against the Door, and pushing with all my Might, I broke it open.

L. Upon the whole matter, I find first *Bomeny* opened the Door before he called either of the Warders, according to *Bomeny*'s first Information taken (as before) by the Coroner; and secondly, that he did not open the Door, for *Russel* opened it, according to *Bomeny*'s second Information (which himself writ) and *Russel*'s Deposition: And thirdly, that neither *Bomeny* nor *Russel* could open the Door, because the Body lay so close against it, and so *Monday* broke it open: This according to *Monday*'s account of the Matter.

T. Which of these three do you believe?

G. Their Contradictions being such, I can believe neither, but conclude this is a contrived Story throughout, and yet so ill laid together, as I never saw a worse-made Story in all my Life.

L. So gross Contradictions in so short a Relation I never yet met with.

G. 'Tis very much they should so thwart each other had they agreed upon a Story; and yet it's more improbable they should so differ, had they designed to reveal the Truth; for the true Relation of a Fact is still the same, whereas false Relations are almost infinite; but these three are the greatest Fools I ever heard of, in not laying their Story better together.

T. I have often heard a very ingenuous Gentleman say, that God in Mercy to Mankind allotted such an Allay of the Fool to every Knave, that the Fool hangs the Knave up half way.

L. It's indeed a Mercy that the Knave and the Fool go together; for were it not for the latter, the former would do much more Mischief.

G. It was a common saying of Sir *H. B.* That no Man was known to be a Knave, but he that was a Fool.

T. If you don't believe the Closet-door was locked upon my Lord, you can't believe this was sworn for any other end but to stifle the Truth, and consequently to hinder the true Discovery of the manner of my Lord's Death.

G. As I can't believe their Relations true, so neither can I comprehend to what end they should invent this Story of the Closet's Door being lock'd upon my Lord, seeing my Lord might as well have been said to have cut his Throat without locking the Closet: What Service could they propose by this part of their Story of the Closet-door's being locked upon the Body.

T. The use they afterwards made of this, was the end they proposed by this their Invention; they strongly argued to the Truth of my Lord's self-Murder from this very Circumstance; for they say, Can it be thought possible that my Lord should be murdered by others, when it was impossible that

that any should do it in the Closet and come out of it, leaving the Body so close against the Door, which opened inward, and there was no other way but the Door out of which they could come? Had this Relation therefore been true, it would have been as strong an Argument of my Lord's being a Self-Murderer, as the contrary (appearing by the many and gross Contradictions before observed) is of his being treacherously murdered by others. But as a further Argument of the Closet-door's not being locked, I desire you to observe the Closet, and how the Body was first seen by such as were some of the * first that went up into my Lord's Chamber after my Lord's Death was known. At the beginning of this Book is the Room and Closet drawn, and how the Body was first found: By this you may perceive how my Lord's Legs were lying on the Threshold of the Closet-door, and you find the Closet-door could not (whilst the Body lay thus, and it was not then pretended to be moved) be locked; this appears by what *William Turner* and *Samuel Peck* declare, and they have deposed before the Lords.

William Turner and *Samuel Peck* declare that these two Informants were Servants to the late Earl of *Essex* at the time of his Death, and bringing in some Provisions into the *Tower* just upon the first Discovery of my Lord's Death, of which as soon as they heard, these Informants ran up stairs and found my Lord's Legs lying upon the Threshold of the Closet-door.

G. I am now satisfied how they proposed to argue from it on their own side; but the Edg of the Argument (through their Disagreement and Contradictions in their Evidence) hath been turned against them, and wounded them to the quick.

T. In the third and last place, I shall disprove that part of these three Mens Relations, which saith, that the Razor was locked into my Lord's Closet when he was first found dead: Those three have all deposed, or often declared, That the Razor was found by my Lord's Body locked into the

* *Before any that came from the King saw the Body.*

e

Closet, and all three denied that there was any bloody Razor thrown out of my Lord's Chamber-Window just before my Lord's Death was first discovered to those out of the House.

L. If the bloody Razor was thrown out of the Window before my Lord's Death was discovered, then it's most certain it could not be found lock'd in (with the Body) in the Closet upon the first Discovery, as by these Treacherous Varlets is deposed.

Pray read these Papers.

G. William Edwards, aged about Eighteen Years, declareth, "That being in the "*Tower* that Morning the late Earl of "*Essex* died, and just before the Discovery "of his Death, viz. about Nine of the "Clock the same Morning, as this Infor- "mant was standing almost over against "the Earl of *Essex* his Chamber-Window, "he saw a bloody Razor thrown out of "the said Earl's Chamber-Window, and "fell just without the Pales that stood "before the Door, which this Informant "was going to take up; but just as this "Informant came to take up the Razor "(which this Informant found very bloo- "dy) there came a Maid out of Major "*Hawley*'s House and took up the Razor, "and then ran in with it into Major "*Hawley*'s House immediately after disco- "vering my Lord's Death.

Thomas Edwards, Father to the said *William Edwards*, *Sarah Edwards*, and *Ann Edwards*, and *Elizabeth Edwards*, all declare, and are ready to depose, That the said *William Edwards* the very Morning of my Lord's Death, when he came home, did give the same Account in substance to these Informants.

G. Was not this *William Edwards* sworn at Mr. *Braddon*'s Trial?

T. Yes.

G. If I mistake not, he did there upon Oath deny it.

T. 'Tis very true.

G. How then can there be any Credit given to what one swears in Contradiction to what he hath before deposed? When upon Oath he declared, he saw no such

such Razor, but it was a Story that he invented to excuse his Truanting.

T. I desire that you will consider when this Story was first told by the Boy (*viz.*) about ten of the Clock that morning my Lord died. Now it was not then known it would be sworn, that this Razor lay by my Lord's Body, locked into the Closet when the Body was first found, as did appear the Monday after, when the Coroner's Inquisition, and *Bomeny's* Deposition were printed; and therefore there could not be any use made of this Story, when first told, against the Truth of my Lord's (pretended) Self-murder, for that was possible to be true, what was suggested in answer to this by a certain Gentleman, who as soon as he saw what *Edwards* declared, asked, What use could be made of it, and how this did appear to argue that my Lord was murdered? for he further said, That it might be when *Bomeny* came and found that Razor, which he had before delivered to my Lord, proved the Instrument of his Death, he took it up, and with great indignation threw the Razor out of the Window, as we many times throw away what we have hurt our selves with. To this it was answered, It appeared sworn before the Coroner, That as soon as *Bomeny* saw my Lord, and part of the Razor, thro' a Chink of the Closet-Door, he called out to *Russel,* that my Lord was fallen down Sick; so that there was a Noise of this in the Room before ever the Closet Door was opened, and consequently before *Bomeny* could have any opportunity to take up the Razor: Whereas it here appeared, by what *Edwards* said, that all things were very quiet in the House till the Maid had taken up the Razor, and the Maid first discovered my Lord's Death; Upon this the Gentleman urged this no further, but what he herein declared was so ready at hand, as tho' he had before heard of the Razor's being thrown out, and thought this the best Salve for it. As for the pretence, that this Lie was invented to excuse his truanting, this is very ridiculous; this Boy, in very great earnestness, as soon as he returned from the *Tower,* told his Mother and Sisters, that the Earl of *Essex* had cut his Throat, and thrown the Razor out of the Window; this argued his simplicity.

Now the material part of the Story was then (generally believed to be) true, (*viz.*) That the Earl had cut his Throat, and that he should add the throwing out of the Razor, when (as before observed) there could be no use thereof made towards the proof of my Lord's Murder, is such a Suggestion as can't be supposed.

But as a clearer Answer to this, I will now tell you how the Boy came first to deny that he saw the Razor thrown out; and, secondly, what made him forswear it.

As for the first; What occasioned the Boy's first denial. When Mr. *Braddon* went first to Mr. *Edward's* House, (which was *Tuesday* morning next after the Earl's Death) he asked Mr. *Edwards,* Whether his Son had seen a Bloody Razor thrown out of my Lord's Chamber-Window, just before the discovery of my Lord's Death? Mr. *Edwards* at first was surprised with the Question, and wept, saying, He was undone if he should be turned out of his Place in the Custom-House; but being pressed to speak according to the Truth, he did declare what you have before heard; the like did the Mother, and two of the Sisters: Upon this Mr. *Braddon* desired to see the Boy, (for before this Mr. *Braddon* never saw Mr. *Edwards,* or his Son, or any of his Family to his knowledg); the Father answered, He was gone to School; but if Mr. *Braddon* would come in the Afternoon, the Boy should be kept at Home, and he might then discourse him, which Mr. *Braddon* promised to do.

And accordingly about two of the Clock in the Afternoon went. When he came to Mr. *Edwards,* he was told by the Mother and Sisters, that the Boy had denied he ever saw any Razor thrown out. Upon which Mr. *Braddon* inquired, Whether the Boy had ever deny'd it before he (the said Mr. *Braddon*) had been there that morning? To which it was answered, He had not. Whereupon Mr. *Braddon* did further enquire, Whether

ther. the Boy voluntarily deni'd it, or what made him do it? Upon which the Mother delared, That his Eldeſt Siſter (being a-fraid of the Conſequence of this Story) as ſoon as the Boy that day came from the School, ran to him in great fury, and in a threatning manner told him, That ſeveral People would be hanged for what he had ſaid, and that he himſelf might be hang'd likewiſe. Upon which the Child came running to her, and cried out, The King would hang him; and immediately thereupon denied what he had before declared, and ſo often repeated, without any the leaſt Contradiction.

Hereupon Mr. *Braddon* deſired the Boy might come into the Parlour, where, before his Relations, and others preſent, he might diſcourſe the Boy. At firſt the Child could not be perſwaded, being afraid; but at laſt came into the Room, where Mr. *Braddon*, before ſix or ſeven then preſent (none of which before that day he had, to his knowledg ever ſeen.) before ever he did ask the Boy, whether what he had as before declared, were true or falſe, ſpoke to the Child to this Effect, (*viz.*) *Mr. Braddon*; Can you read? *William Edwards*; Yes. *Mr. Braddon*; Did you ever read the 5th Chapter of the *Acts of the Apoſtles* ? *William Edwards*; Yes. Don't you there find that there were two ſtruck dead upon the Place for telling a Lie. *W. Edwards*; Yes. *Mr. Braddon*; God is ſtill the ſame God of Truth, and a God of the ſame Power likewiſe; and he knowing all things, knows better than you your ſelf, whether what you declared were True or Falſe. Wherefore if it be indeed a Lie, (notwithſtanding you have ſo often declared it to be true) now deny it, and never more own it, leſt for your ſaying that which is falſe, God execute the ſame Judgment upon you, and immediately ſtrike you dead: But if it be true, be neither afraid or aſhamed to own it. Immediately hereupon the Boy confeſſed it was true; and then declared as before related. Being asked, what made him deny it? he anſwered, His Eldeſt Siſter threatned him, and ſaid,

the King would ha
then likewiſe confe
You have here
Boy came firſt to
the Reaſon thereof
Arguments he retr
to his firſt Confeſſi
proved by many v
comes under a Juc

G. I am herein
it to paſs that th
Braddon's Trial?

T. That is the
ed. This Boy wa
of the King, as
And as *William Ed*
minſter-Hall, that
tried, and before h
ly (at whoſe Ho
him, and in a th
'That if he had th
'would have him
'on *Monday* mor
'gether for what
not being then abo
extreamly frighte
being ſo very yo
the Pain of ſuch a
Sacred Obligation
what was true, to
might otherwiſe l

L. It's very na
his Age might be
being of ſuch Y
ſuppoſed to have
which People of
to have. But thi
be a very ill Man,
out of his Evidenc

G. I have hear
a very honeſt Man
fore eſteemed very

T. I have reaſo
Loyalty, *and ſomtn*
ſuch Service, as
Character ſome v
and of my Opini
have heard what
this Caſe.

But as a farther Argument of this Razor's being thrown out of my Lord's Chamber Window, Pray read this Information.

G. J. L. aged about 18 Years declareth, "That as she was standing upon the high "Ground almost over against the Earl of "*Essex*'s Lodgings that Morning the Earl "died, and a little before the Discovery of "his Death, she saw a bloody Razor thrown "out of my Lord's Chamber Window, and "just before the Razor was thrown out she "heard two Shreeks."

T. That this Girl discovered this to her Aunt the very Morning my Lord died, proved by Mrs. *G.* and others are ready to attest the same. At Mr. *Braddon*'s Trial the Girl's Aunt, and one Mr. *G.* then a Lodger in her Aunt's House, deposed the same.

L. You have here three Witnesses sworn, that this Child related this Story to her Aunt as soon as she came from the *Tower*. Do you doubt the Truth of what these three Persons have sworn?

G. I am very well satisfied these three depose the Truth; but it may be this Boy might tell the Girl what he saw, and so it is but one Evidence.

T. It will be proved as far as a Negative can be proved, That this Boy and Girl never spoke to each other till some time after the Earl's Death, and the Relations of the Boy and Girl were altogether strangers to each other, having never (to their Remembrance) heard or seen one another, which might be well supposed, for their Habitation was some distance from each other: Mr. *Edwards* and his Son and Family living in *Mark-Lane*, the Girl and her Relations at St. *Katherines*; besides, you may observe the Girl stood upon the high Ground over against the Earl's Chamber Window, and the Boy in the lower Ground; where the Girl stood she (being but short) could hardly see the Ground where the Razor fell, but she declared she saw the Maid in the white Hood come thereupon out of Major *Hawley*'s House: which Description agreed exactly with that Description the Boy gave of the Maid.

L. Their Evidence thus agreeing, can't well be doubted.

G. I have been informed this Maid is now reputed of a loose Character.

T. Admit it true, she could not be so thought when she was but just past twelve Years of Age, and it was then she first declared it, and six Years since and more swore it: Therefore her now Character can't in common Reason prejudice her then Testimony given in her innocent Childhood, and her now Testimony is but a Repetition of her former Oath. Besides, had this Fact been told by Persons of never so great Infamy (that did appear to be altogether strangers to each other) their Agreement in their Relations had given Credit to their Testimony, being first reported when (as is before observed) there could be no end proposed by telling this Lie, seeing when it was first declared, it appeared not in the least inconsistent with the (pretended) Truth of my Lord's Self-Murder, because this Razor after the Discovery, out of Indignation, might have been thrown out of the Window by some attending on my Lord. Now had this been sworn the next day after my Lord's Death, which at the time it was first told by this Boy and Girl, could not appear otherwise, then this Story of the Razor's being thrown out of my Lord's Chamber Window had fallen to the Ground, and no way useful to prove the Murder. But this I have already more at large insisted upon.

L. It's an old and true Proverb, Children and Fools tell Truth; the Reason of this saying is, because Children and Fools not being capable of that Invention, which such as are of Years and Understanding may be supposed to have, speak without design the naked Truth of the Fact.

T. A farther Argument of the Truth of this is the Relation of *R.* and *M.* (the two Souldiers before mentioned) both which the very day of my Lord's Death declared in this particular the same with the Boy and Girl, as appears by these Informations following. Pray read them.

G.

G. E. G. and *S. H.* further declare, 'That about 11 of the Clock, the very day 'my Lord dy'd, the aforesaid *R.* did further 'say, That my Lord was murdered; but be-'fore his Death was discovered to any out 'of the House, there was a bloody Razor 'thrown out of my Lord's Chamber-Win-'dow; and that a Maid took it up, and car-'ry'd it into my Lord's Lodgings.

J. B. and his Wife do both further declare, 'That the aforesaid *R. M.* the very day of 'my Lord's Death, did further say, That 'after my Lord's Murder, and before his 'Death was known, there was a bloody Ra-'zor thrown out of my Lord's Chamber-'Window, which a little Boy endeavoured 'to take up; but there came a Maid out of 'Capt. *Hawley's* House, and took it up, and 'run with it into Capt. *Hawley's* House, and 'then the Maid was the first that discovered 'my Lord's Death.

L. These two Witnesses agree with the Boy, not only in the Main (as you call it) but in several Circumstances of the Story, with the Boy's Relation: First, in the Main, that there was a bloody Razor thrown out of my Lord's Chamber-Window before his Death was known. Secondly, *Meaks* agrees with the Boy, that the Boy did endeavour to take up this Razor, but was prevented by the Maid, who forthwith carried it into Major *Hawley's* House. And, Thirdly, that this Maid was the first discovered my Lord's Death.

G. I must confess, their Agreement in their Relations gives great Credit to the Truth of their Testimony.

L. Was it ever yet known, that four Persons, some very Young, and others of Riper Years, and all Strangers to one another, should give the same Account of a Fact, in all its Circumstances, and the Fact not True?

T. For the farther Confirmation of this Truth, I shall prove (by three Witnesses more) it was a general Report in the *Tower* that morning my Lord died, That the Razor was (as before related) thrown out of my Lord's Chamber-Window. Pray read these three Papers.

G. I. S. declareth, 'That this Informant 'was a Souldier in the *Tower* that very mor-'ning the late Earl of *Essex* died in the '*Tower*; and about eight of the Clock in 'the same morning, this Informant was 'sent as one of the Guards upon the Honora-'ble Lord *Russel* to the *Old Baily*; and as 'this Informant was returning to the *Tower* '(with several of this Guard) one in great 'haste from the *Tower* met them, and said, 'the Earl of *Essex* had cut his Throat, and 'thrown the Razor out of the Window. 'Upon which it was Answered, the Earl of '*Essex* had great Courage, first to Cut his 'Throat, and then to throw the Razor out 'of the Window.

This Informant further saith, 'That after 'he came into the *Tower*, that very morning 'he heard it declared by several, that there 'was a bloody Razor thrown out of my 'Lord's Chamber-Window before my Lord's 'Death was known.

R. G. Declareth, 'That he was a Souldier 'in the *Tower* that very morning the late Earl 'of *Essex* dy'd, and after the Earl's Death, 'this Informant heard it discoursed (that 'very morning) in the *Tower*, that there 'was a bloody Razor thrown out of my 'Lord's Chamber-Window before my Lord's 'Death was known: and it was further 'said, That the Razor was much broken and 'notched, which some then attributed to 'the fall out of the Window, but others 'said it might be against the Neckbone.

L. Against the Neck-bone! That's a pretty Business indeed, that my Lord should so hack the Neck-bone, as to break the Razor, according to the description you have before given us of the Razor.

T. So Ridiculous as you make this, it was the very same that the Surgeon the next day said to the Jury, as you will anon find.

L. A Surgeon, either Knave or Fool; a Knave if he told them what he did not himself believe, and nevertheless endeavoured (when upon his Oath to speak the Truth) to impose upon the Jury; and a Fool if
H he

he did believe it: But pray read the Third Information.

G. R. B. declareth, 'That he, this Informant, was in the *Tower* that very morning 'the late Earl of *Essex* died; and immediately, upon the first discovery of my Lord's 'Death, this Informant went to Major *Hawley's*, (where my Lord then lay) and by the 'Door of the said Major *Hawley's* House, this 'Informant heard several then and there declare, That there was a bloody Razor thrown 'out of my Lord's Chamber-Window, before 'my Lord's Death was known, some then and 'there asserting, that they saw the Razor so 'thrown out.

L. Who now can doubt this Truth thus attested and confirmed?

T. But to put the Matter beyond all colour of contradiction or doubt, read the farther Testimony of Mr. *S. S.*

G. S. S. farther saith, 'That the very 'day Major *Webster* and *Lloyd* were taken up, '(*viz.*) the 21st of *January* last, as suspected 'concerned in the Death of the late Earl of *Essex*, this Informant was in the Goat-Ale-house in the *Minories*, where the said *Webster* and *Lloyd* were then in the Constable's 'Custody, and this Informant did then and 'there hear the said *Webster* declare, That 'he did nothing (with relation to my Lord) 'but pull off his Cravat, and took the Razor 'up from the Floor, and threw it out of the 'Window: Upon which this Informant asked 'the said *Webster*, What hurt the Razor had 'done him, that he should throw it out of the 'Window? To which the said *Webster* replied, That when he did it, he was under 'such a consternation as he knew not what he 'did. This Informant farther saith, That upon this Confession of the said Major *Webster*, '*Lloyd* the Sentinel then sitting by this Informant, did declare, That it was indeed true, 'that the Razor was thrown out, for it was 'thrown out of my Lord's Chamber-Window, just over the said *Lloyd's* Head, and 'the Razor fell just without the Pales. The 'said *Lloyd* did further say, That he did observe a little Boy, and the Maid of the 'House, to struggle for the Razor; but the 'Maid took it, and ran in with it into Major '*Hawley's* House, soon after crying out, My 'Lord of *Essex* hath cut his Throat: and the 'said *Lloyd* declared, the said Maid was the 'first discovered to him my Lord's Death.

T. As a confirmation of this, (*viz.*) that this Maid was the first that discovered to the Sentinel my Lord's Death, read this Information.

G. J. N. declareth, 'That he, this Informant, went into the *Tower* that very morning 'the late Earl of *Essex* died; and just before 'the knowledg of my Lord's Death, this Informant went to the Sentinel that then stood 'at my Lord's Lodgings, and asked the said 'Sentinel, how the Earl of *Essex* did? to which 'the said Sentinel answered, Very well—

T. Observe, the Sentinel at this time pretended, my Lord was very well, and confessed not any knowledg of his Death. But proceed,

G. '—Just as this Informant had asked 'this Question, and been thus answered, he 'did observe a Maid run in great haste into 'Major *Hawley's* House; and as the Maid was 'come to the Stair-foot, and going up Stairs, 'he did observe a tall black Man, a Warder, 'and another Gentleman, come down Stairs 'from my Lord's Chamber-Wards, and neither of these two spoke one word of my 'Lord's Death, as this Informant heard, who 'stood about six foot from the Door; but 'the Maid ran up in great haste, and immediately, in as great, came running down 'Stairs, wringing her Hands, and crying out, 'My Lord of *Essex* had cut his Throat, which 'Discovery was the first this Informant heard 'of my Lord's Death, who stood (as before) 'very nigh Major *Hawley's* House. And this 'Informant did observe the said Maid to have 'a Razor in her Hand, either as she ran up 'Stairs, or as she came running down as aforesaid.

L. I wish we could but know who this Warder and another Gentleman was, that came down Stairs as the Maid ran up, for they could not be ignorant of what was done.

T. By description it must be *Monday*, for there was but two Warders in the House at

that

that time; and this description agrees not with the other; as for the other Gentleman a short time may discover him.

G. This Confession of *Lloyd*, as to the Boy's endeavouring to take up the Razor, but the Maid's taking it up, and carrying it into the House, immediately upon which my Lord's Death was discovered, I find agrees with the Boy's Relation, and with what *M.* and *R.* declared the very day my Lord died.

L. If you will not be convinced of the Truth of a Fact, attested by such positive and circumstantial Relations, (agreeing in their several Accounts, as to the material Circumstances of the Fact, as was before observed) and confirmed by two of the Persons accused; the last whereof, in his Relation, gave the same representation of the Fact, as was before related by so many; I say, if such Evidence as this will not convince you in in this Particular, it argues you are under an invincible prejudice, which moral Testimonies will not remove.

G. I can't but acknowledg my self in this Particular satisfied, as to the truth of this Razor being so thrown out, as before deposed; but I am altogether to seek of the Reason of this Action, what should make these Ruffians to throw it out.

L. You have the Reason, *Webster* himself assigned for doing it; for he was asked, What made him throw it out? he answered, He was under such a consternation, that he knew not what he did.

T. You did before observe the scituation of the Room and Closet, and how the Chamber-Window (out of which the Razor was thrown) was about 17 foot distant from the Closet where the Body lay; therefore it's very probable, after this bloody Ruffian had murdered my Lord, and blooded the Razor, as the pretended Instrument of his Death, they having not finished the whole Scene, and laid the Razor by the Body, as was intended; but this *Webster*, who threw it out, standing not far from the Chamber-Window, with the bloody Razor in his Hand, was surprised when a Person came up Stairs (of whose coming he was not aware); and under this consternation (as is natural to a surprise in such horrid Villanies) threw the Razor out of the Window, but discovered nothing of my Lord's Death; and then the Maid (who it's possible was the occasion of this surprise) went out and took it up; and as soon as she returned into the House, discovered my Lord's Death, as you have before at large heard related.

G. This seems to be probable enough.

L. It may shortly prove more than probable.

G. What is become of this Maid that carried up the Razor?

T. She is under Bail.

G. Doth she deny it?

T. Yes, and saith, she went out of her Master's House almost half an hour before my Lord's Death was known, and returned not until my Lord's Death was publick, and several People in the House to see my Lord: For she tells this Story, 'That about half an 'hour before my Lord's Death was known, 'my Lord's Footman came to her, and told 'her, the Warder would not open the Wicket 'to let in my Lord's Provisions that were 'brought; and therefore begged her to go 'to her Master, (Mr. *Hawley*, the Gentleman-'Porter) to desire him to go to the Warder 'that kept the Gate, and order him to let in 'the Provisions.

L. It's much the Footman himself could not go to Major *Hawley*, for certainly the Major (well-knowing whose Footman he was) would soon go and give Orders to let in the Provisions upon the Footman's request as his Maids, unless the Maid had some collateral consideration (besides that of a Servant) which might influence her Master.

T. There was no need of eithers going, as you will immediately hear. Upon this she declares, 'She did accordingly go to her Ma-'ster, who thereupon ordered the Warder to 'let in my Lord's Provisions; and as they, '(viz.) my Lord's Footman, *Will. Turner*, and 'one *Sam. Peck*, and a Porter, were bringing 'the Provisions, a Sentinel told them, They 'were come too late; upon which this Maid 'declares she was surprised, and asked *Will.* '*Turner* what should be the meaning of that

H 2 Ex-

'Expreſſion, *You art come too late*; for ſhe
'did not underſtand it: Whereto *Turner* an-
'ſwered, that he did ſuppoſe the Sentinel
'believed thoſe Proviſions to be my Lord
'*Ruſſel's*, who being gone to his Trial, this
'Souldier might think he would never re-
'turn again to the *Tower*, and ſo the Provi-
'ſions were brought too late: This (ſhe
'declares) ſhe then believed; but as ſoon as
'they came in ſight of her Maſter's Houſe,
'they admired to ſee ſo great a Croud a-
'bout the Door, but were ſoon too well
'ſatisfied in the occaſion, for it was juſt
'before diſcovered that my Lord of *Eſſex*
'had cut his Throat.

G. This looks as a made Story: for, can it be thought that the Warder would not let in my Lord's Proviſions?

T. It is indeed a forged Lye throughout; for *William Turner, Samuel Peck*, and the Porter do all three declare, that the Maid was not with them whilſt they were bringing in the Proviſions, neither did the Warder that kept the Gate in the leaſt ſcruple the letting in my Lord's Proviſions; this they all ſay they are ready to depoſe.

G. Then this Maid is a Confederate; for otherwiſe ſhe would ſpeak the Truth.

T. Surely ſhe that endeavours by ſuch a falſe villanous Invention to evade the Truth, becomes conſenting to my Lord's Murder, and at the laſt day ſhall anſwer it.

L. Nay, ſhe may anſwer it before, if it be once plainly made appear that ſhe did carry up the Razor, and was the firſt that diſcovered my Lord's Death; for by what ſhe then ſaw, and hath ſince heard ſworn by thoſe who attended on my Lord, ſhe could not but be well ſatisfied my Lord was murdered, and endeavouring thus to ſtifle it by her falſe Evaſions—

T. To which, ſhe ſaith, ſhe did ſwear before the Secretary of State.

L. That adds Perjury to the firſt Guilt. Without doubt her endeavouring by Perjury to conceal and ſtifle the moſt perfidious and barbarous Murder our Nation ever knew, ſhall render her culpable in no ſmall degree.

T. Juſt as the Maid cried out, My Lord had cut his Throat; one Mr. *B.* (then an Enſign) ran into the Houſe, and was the firſt Man in my Lord's Chamber, after my Lord's Death was known, the Blood then ſeeming almoſt reeking hot; this Mr. *B.* declared, that as he ran in he did obſerve (this Maid whoſe Name he knew to be *Alice*) ſtanding at her Maſter's Door wringing her Hands and crying; and *N.* (who ſaw the Maid run into her Maſter's Houſe and up Stairs, and then heard her cry out, Murder, and likewiſe in her hand the Razor) declares, that was the very Maid which ſtood at the Door when Mr. *B.* went into the Houſe.

L. By all Circumſtances this muſt be the Maid; for had not this Wench been ſome way concerned, ſhe would never have invented this Lie; for Innocence flies not, nor needs a Lie for its Defence, but is always ſupported by Truth; and Innocence it ſelf becomes juſtly ſuſpected for Guilt when it makes uſe of a falſe Defence; the Law, and the natural Reaſon of the thing preſuming that every one will uſe the beſt, and conſequently the trueſt Defence in Protection of his Innocence. Pray proceed.

T. The Circumſtances of the Razor in the top's being ſo broken, and the many other Notches, as before appears by the Razor, are natural ſelf-Evidence of the Truth of the Razor's being thrown out of the Window; for my Lord in cutting his Throat could not ſo do it, notwithſtanding an old Chirurgion to the Jury declared otherwiſe; for the Jury asking him, Whether my Lord in cutting his own Throat could ſo break and notch the Razor? The Chirurgion anſwered, that it was poſſible for my Lord to do it againſt his Neck-bone, occaſioned by the Tremefaction of my Lord's Hand when the Razor came to the Neck-bone.

L. Certainly there was a Tremefaction in the Chirurgion's Underſtanding or Honeſty, when upon Oath he gave this Anſwer, for I do ſuppoſe he was ſworn.

T. He was ſo.———As a further Argument againſt my Lord's cutting his Throat

in

(53)

in the Closet, the Circumstances of the Closet (as found when my Lord was first found dead) appear in Evidence. You may observe the Closet is but three Foot and one Inch wide, and seven Foot long in one side, and about five Foot long in the other; now it's declared by those attending on my Lord, that there was no Blood against the Wall a foot higher than the Floor, nor any upon the Cloose-stool, or any of the Shelves of the Closet; whereas had my Lord cut his Throat standing on the Closet, the Blood would have immediately gushed out of so large an Orifice five Foot at least, wherefore that part of the Wall over against his Throat must have been very bloody; but in this case there was none at all, and therefore it could not be done standing: neither did his Lordship do it kneeling; for there was no Blood as high as his Throat, as in that Posture would have then been: and that his Lordship did it not lying along, appears from the Position of the Razor; for the Wound beginning on the left side, and ending on the right, the Razor must have been on the right side of the Body, whereas it lay about fourteen Inches or more from the left.

G. All these self-Evidences might have appeared to the Jury upon their view; and it's very much they did not observe them.

T. What the Jury did, and how they were managed, you shall soon hear. But I shall,

First, take notice of the many Irregularities, with respect to the Management of my Lord's Body, the Chamber and Closet after my Lord's Death.

Secondly, The false and malicious Suggestions by Major Hawley to the Jury, to hinder the Discovery of the Truth, and to influence them to the belief of my Lord's self-Murder: And,

Thirdly, The Oppressions, Threats and Severities since used to avoid a Detection of this unparalled bloody Treachery.

First, The Irr[e]
the Body, Room
Death, these wer[e]
Jury from makin[g]
say were natural
the Body was [found]
the Clothes carri[ed]
Chamber and the
the Jury saw the
ry the next day [found]
stripp'd and was[hed]
covered with a S[heet]

L. This was ve[ry contra]
ry to all Practi[ce]
dead, especially u[pon]
Murder, I say, u[pon]
seeing none could
ter to give any A[ccount]
came dead, but
ding on my Lord
to be suspected
(if my Lord wer[e]
taken off) the
relation to it, tho[ugh]
the Circumstance[s]
Persons thus atte[r]
apart, in order t[o]
that they might
and agree in a
the Discovery [of]
Villany.

T. This had b[een]
according to Ki[ng's]
express Order;
matter was mana[ged]
heard declared.

The next day
the Jury met, a[t]
Major Hawley's H[ouse]
stances before rel[ated]
were adjourned t[o]
the Tower to con[fer]
When the Jury h[ad]
Examination, Mr.
demanded a sight
which the Coron[er]
next Room, and
said, It was the B[ody]

they were to fit upon; the Body was there, and that was sufficient.

L. Who was it that called the Coroner into the next Room? and to whom did he there go? for it's probable this was what these Gentlemen (who ever they were) then in the next Room, would not have inquired into so strictly; I desire to know their Names.

T. The Coroner protests he hath forgot who called him, or to whom he there went.

L. Forgot! I must confess I have heard of the Art of Memory, but never of the Art of Forgetfulness: as none are so deaf as those that will not hear, so none so forgetful as those that will not remember.

T. You are very sharp upon the Coroner, of whom I have a more charitable opinion.

L. Your Charity ought not to blind your Judgment; Can you believe this Gentleman forgets, what he hath had all the reason imaginable to remember? for seeing my Lord's Death was so soon after his Death questioned, this must naturally put the Coroner upon reflecting on what passed, which might argue either for or against the Murder. I am sure these Reflections would have naturally brought to, and imprinted in his Mind this particular Passage: but, peradventure, should the Coroner true Answer make to this Point, and confess that such Gentlemen in the next Room advised him to check the Jury for their too great Inquisitives, this would have look'd like making himself an Accessory (*in Foro Conscientiæ* at least) after the Fact; and therefore self-preservation makes him forget what otherwise he might well remember.

T. I must confess you have some Reason on your side; but seeing the Coroner is fair in his Answers to other Questions, and hath, (by his ingenuity in discovering what we could not have otherwise known) been assisting to a Detection; I do from such his fairness and readiness argue for his Innocence.

L. He is fair, I find, in his Answers to such Questions as touch not himself, but when Self lies at stake, he prevaricates.

G. It's very probable he may at present forget what hereafter may come into his Mind; and I dare say he will be ingenuous in what he knows when his Memory serves, for I have heard a very fair Character of the Gentleman.

L. When his Memory doth serve (as you call it) I shall believe his Forgetfulness to be real, but till then pardon me if I think otherwise.

G. In the mean time forbear your Censures.

T. From what Circumstances of the Cloaths could the Jury have had any sight into the Matter?

L. Had the Body lain in its first posture, the Jury would have seen the print of a bloody Foot on my Lord's Stocking, coming out of the Closet, which would have argued, that some had before been with the Body in the Closet, though the contrary was then pretended by those three attending on my Lord.

Secondly, They would have found my Lord's Cravat cut in three pieces, as the two Women that strip'd my Lord have often declared, proved, as followeth, (*viz.*)

Philip Johnson, and *Miriam Tovy,* have both deposed, That *Mary Johnson* (Wife of the said *Philip Johnson*) hath often declared, That she help'd strip the Body of the late Earl of *Essex,* by the command of Major *Hawley,* at whose House my Lord died; and that the Neck of my Lord's Cravat was cut in three pieces.

T. W. Gentleman, saith, ' That *Alice Car-*
' *ter,* the very Night she was first seized,
' (as suspected privy to the Murder of the
' late Earl of *Essex*) did declare, That she
' help'd strip the Body of my Lord of *Es-*
' *sex,* by the command of her Master, Ma-
' jor *Hawley,* and that my Lord's Cravat
' was cut in three pieces.

G. It's

G. It's very much my Lord had not put off the Cravat, or cut above it, had he done it himſelf.

T. Thoſe that attended on my Lord, ſay, my Lord had put off his Periwig, and laid it upon the Shelf of the Cloſet, that the Hairs of the Periwig might not hinder the Action.

L. Sure the Neck of the Cravat was a far greater Impediment, and ſuch as would have effectually hindred my Lord from doing it with a Razor, the pretended Inſtrument of his Death. This alone is a ſtrong Argument that my Lord did not cut his own Throat, as is ſworn by thoſe Treacherous Villains that attended on my Lord; neither do I believe it was done at all by any Razor, but with a more convenient Inſtrument for that purpoſe.

G. Did you ever hear with what Inſtrument it was done?

T. Yes, and who (beſides any before named) is ſaid to be one of the Actors in this curſed Tragedy; pray read this Information.

G. The Information of R. D. of the Pariſh of St. Mary-Somerſet, London, Schoolmaſter, taken before me James Cardraw *Eſq; Juſtice of the Peace for the County of* Middleſex.

'THis Informant ſaith, That a little af-
' ter the late Duke of Monmouth was
' routed in the Weſt, one Mr. *J. E.* (to the
' beſt of this Informants remembrance) told
' this Informant, that it was almoſt Univer-
' ſally whiſpered amongſt the acquaintance
' of Mr. *John Holland,* (formerly Servant to
' the Earl of *Sunderland*) that the ſaid Mr.
' *Holland* had confeſſed to one Mr. *D.* of his
' intimate acquaintance, (and afterward
' concerned with *Holland* in the Robbery of
' Mr. *Gatford,* for which both were condem-
' ned, and the ſaid *D.* executed, but *Holland*
' pardoned) that the ſaid *Holland* was con-
' cerned in the murder of *Arthur* late Earl of
' *Eſſex,* in which he was employed by the
' Earl of *Sunderland,* upon this occaſion,

'(*viz.*) The ſaid Mr. *Holland* one day waiting
' on my Lord *Sunderland,* his Lordſhip ſeem-
' ed much diſturbed with Paſſion: upon
' which the ſaid *Holland* told his Lordſhip,
' that if his then coming to his Lordſhip had
' ſo diſcompoſed him, he would withdraw and
' wait on his Lordſhip ſome more conveni-
' ent time; whereupon my Lord ſaid, that
' he ſhould tarry, for it was not with him
' (the ſaid *Holland,*) that he was angry, but
' with others; and that he was concerned
' to think, that of ſo many Servants his
' Lordſhip had made, and been ſo very kind
' to, he had not one he could truſt, or would
' ſerve him (or words to that effect): Upon
' which the ſaid *Holland* replied, He was
' then ready faithfully and punctually to ob-
' ſerve his Lordſhip's Commands, in any
' thing. My Lord then diſcovered to the ſaid
' *Holland* the deſigned Murder of the ſaid
' Earl of *Eſſex,* and would have the ſaid
' *Holland* therein to be engaged; to which
' the ſaid *Holland* readily conſented; and
' that the ſaid Earl's Throat was cut with a
' large Knife, and not with a Razor. And this
' Informant was then further informed, That
' the ſaid *Holland* had further declared to
' the ſaid *D.* that ſome People were after-
' wards made away for blabbing what they
' knew concerning the ſaid Earl's Death, and
' that the ſaid *D.* had charged the ſaid Mr.
' *Holland,* before ſeveral of their Acquain-
' tance, one day drinking together, with
' what the ſaid *Holland* had confeſſed to him
' the ſaid *D.* as aforeſaid; and that he the
' ſaid *Holland,* upon his being ſo charged,
' ſeemed much dejected, but could not deny
' it. This Informant further maketh Oath,
' That one *D. P.* about three Years ſince, did
' give this Informant almoſt the ſame Ac-
' count, with relation to *Holland* and *D.* And
' the ſaid *D. P.* did further tell this Infor-
' mant, that when the ſaid *Holland* and *D.*
' were committed to *Newgate* for Robbing
' Mr. *Gatford,* the ſaid *D. P.* went to ſee
' the ſaid *Holland* in *Newgate,* to condole his
' Condition: But the ſaid *Holland* was very
' cheerful, and told him, the ſaid *D. P.* he was

ſecure

'secure of his Life, and likewise not to want
'Mony as long as the Earl of *Sunderland* was
'-living. The said *D. P.* did likewise then
'further tell this Informant,—That the said
'*Holland* (as soon as he was committed to
'*Newgate* for the aforesaid Robbery) sent to
'my Lord *Sunderland* for some Mony, and
'that his Lordship sent him the said *Holland,*
'16 *Guineas*. And this Informant hath been
'told by several, that the said Lord *Sunder-*
'*land* hath many times supplied the said
'*Holland* with Mony.

L. I doubt not but *Holland* was well rewarded. for. this eminent Service, and my Lord *Sunderland* obliged to stand his Friend under all Exigencies.

T. Sometime after my Lord's Death, *Holland* drew in this Mr. *D.* (a very ingenuous young Gentleman, but infortunate in such his Company) to be concerned in the Robbery; of one Mr. *Gatford*, for which both were condemned; *Holland* of the two seemed far the greatest Criminal, and therefore, according to the reason of the thing, had least hopes of Life; but contrariwise, he was very chearful, and my Lord *Sunderland* extreamly kind to him, beyond a common Degree of Favour; insomuch as Major *Richardson* taking particular notice of his extraordinary Kindness to this profligate Fellow, told one of my Lord's Gentlemen, ' That it was not for his
' Lordships Honour to appear so much for one
' of the most villanous Character imaginable.
To which it was Answered, that his Lordship had a great kindness for *Holland*, upon the Account of my Lord *Spencer*, to whom this *Holland* had formerly been a Servant.

L. There was certainly some further Reason.

T. His Lordship's Favour still continued to this *Holland*, who afterwards being in Prison, often writ to my Lord for Mony, which was accordingly sent, and sometimes would procure the liberty to go to my Lord *Sunderland*, and some others, for Mony, of which the Person, (*viz.*) one *I. W.* that went with him, taking particular notice, asked the said *Holland*, How it came to pass that he could go with that freedom and assurance to my Lord *Sunderland* and those others, and be so generously supplied with Mony at all times? To which Mr. *Holland* made Answer, Damn him, he had done that Service for them that they durst not do otherwise.

L. Durst not do otherwise! a very becoming Phrase for a Man of his Character to use with relation to a Person of my Lord's Quality. This argues either some extraordinary secret Service done for his Lordship, the Discovery whereof would tend highly to his Prejudice, or else this *Holland* is a very impudent Lier; but the first seems most probable, considering my Lord's extraordinary kindness to *Holland* in *Newgate* (as was before observed) and his constant supplies upon all application.

T. I have been credibly informed, by a Gentleman that was once a fellow-Prisoner in the *King's-Bench* with *Holland*, that *Holland* did use to bring Letters he writ to my Lord *Sunderland*, and desired this Gentleman to direct them in French, pretending, that if my Lord saw his hand, he would not open the Letter.

L. I rather believe the Direction was to cheat my Lord's Servant (who carried the Letter from the Messenger, or Penny-post Man) than to influence my Lord to read it.

T. This looks most likely, I must confess, this *W.* (once about three Years since) saying to *Holland*, it was much whispered, that my Lord of *Essex* did not cut his own Throat, but was by others taken off; *Holland* said, Damn him, it was not a Farthing matter if twenty such were taken off.

L. A very fine Fellow for such Service; he who declares, *It is not a Farthing Matter if twenty such were taken off,* (by which he meant Murdered, for 'twas in Answer to the same he spoke it) would not boggle much at the doing that villanous Murder, especially considered that hereby he secured himself from punishment in his after-Villanies.

T. I remember very well, a Gentleman told me that it was some Years since discoursed fed in *Wales* (of which Country *Holland* is), That *Holland* being asked how he escaped Punishment for Mr. *Gatford*'s Robbery, (before taken notice of) he Answered, with his usual Phrase, Damn him, they durst not take him off, for at the place of Execution he would have discovered how my Lord of *Essex* came by his Death: but the Gentleman either really hath, or pretends to have forgot who told him of it.

L. I find many Mens Memory in this Case, *ad placitum*, to remember or forget as they think fit.

G. I have heard of a Letter writ by *Holland* to the Earl of *Feversham*, (if I mistake not); which Letter was read in the House of Lords, and therein it was said, that Mr. *Braddon* would have suborned *Holland* to swear in this Case; and as I have heard, Mr. *Braddon* offered a considerable Reward to Mrs. *Holland*, and a Friend of *Holland*'s, to prevail with *Holland* to come in, and take upon him this villanous Crime. This, if true, was a very foul practice.

T. Yea, if true, it had been villanous, and had deserved (before God) as great Punishment as the Murderers themselves: For as in the Old Law, (*Deut.* 19. 16, &c.) 'If any false Witness rise up against his 'Neighbour, the Person forsworn (when 'detected to be so) was to receive the same 'Punishment the Man accused should have 'undergone, in case the Charge had been 'true; whether Tooth for Tooth, or Life 'for Life, *&c*. This Law hath an innate universal Reason; and it were not amiss if the same were with us enacted. Now as the Witness himself doth deserve this Punishment, the like (*in Foro Conscientiæ*) doth the Suborner: For if in our Law, he that hireth another to poison, stab, or any other ways to murder a Man, is justly esteemed Accessory before the Fact, and shall undergo the same Capital Punishment, the Principal shall suffer: So do I think it reasonable that whosoever suborns a Person, to take away the Life of any, is (before God) guilty of the Murder of the Person accused, equally with him that commits the Perjury; and both are indeed, according to the universal Reason of the Thing, guilty of a more heinous Murder, than he that cuts another's Throat; seeing in this he corrupts Justice, and by Perjury makes Justice (which by God is designed, and by Man used as a protection to the Innocent) a Means to destroy, whom in its own Nature it should acquit and protect. If that Physician, who to destroy his Patient, maliciously poisons his Physick, (designed by Nature for the preservation of the natural Man) deserves the worst sort of Death, because he becomes so vilely treacherous; how much more heinously criminal is he, who by Subornation or Perjury, corrupts Justice, which Heaven enacted, and Mankind flies to for a Security to the Moral Man. Wherefore with you I should concur in this Particular, that Mr. *Braddon* deserves the worst Death could be contrived, were he guilty of this (indeed False and Malicious) Charge. But the truth of the Case, I can in great part attest, which is this, (*viz.*)

Mr. *Braddon* having some reason to believe *Holland* one of the Ruffians, he did use all means possible for his Apprehension; but he found that *Holland* lay very private; and, as he had reason to believe, designed to fly beyond-Seas, (as his own Letter before-mentioned declared); hereupon Mr. *Braddon* applied himself to some of *Holland*'s Acquaintance, and by them being brought to Mrs. *Holland*, Mr. *Braddon* told her, That he had reason to believe her Husband was concerned in this villanous Murder; and herein he was confirmed by Mr. *Holland*'s absconding; for Innocence desires a Trial, but Guilt still flies from Justice. Mr. *Braddon* then told her, That if her Husband were really guilty of this Fact, and would immediately surrender himself, ingenuously declaring how, by whom, and with whom, and for what hired to do this barbarous Murder, her Husband would have a general Pardon, and both him and her provided for.

for. But if her Husband was innocent, (notwithstanding whatsoever was said to the contrary) and should take upon him a Crime (for any advantage whatsoever) of which he was not guilty, he did deserve to be hanged here, and damned hereafter, seeing by his Perjury he would make Justice an Instrument of executing the worst of Murders.——— But if he were indeed the Man, and should surrender himself, and discover the whole matter, he must be sure to keep within the limits of Truth; for should he be detected in the least Perjury, no Man was more vigorously prosecuted, nor any more severely punished than he (for such his Perjury) must expect to suffer.

These were the Arguments with which Mr. *Braddon* would have suborned (as that Letter calls it) *Holland* to a full Discovery: and I do appeal to all the World, whether, admitting this to be true (as it will be proved when occasion serves) Mr. *Braddon* deserves this Villanous Charge; for the Truth of this I do (on Mr. *Braddon's* behalf) appeal to the Consciences of Mrs. *H.* Mr. *P.* and Mr. *S.* with whom Mr. *Braddon* several times treated in this Affair.

G. If the Case were as you have represented it, Mr. *Braddon* did nothing herein but what was consistent with a good Conscience, and for which he deserves not the least Censure. If I mistake not, you said *Holland* did also go to others for a Supply, as well as my Lord *Sunderland*; Pray who were these?

T. Pardon me (Sir) if I name them not, you will hear of them in convenient time.

G. Sir, pardon the Question, if the Answer be a secret.

T. It is enough that I give you Satisfaction in the General, and I desire not to be press'd to answer all Particulars, for it may not be proper.

G. I desire to know nothing which may either prejudice you to reveal, or the thing it self by being revealed, but esteem it as a great Favour you have been already so large and particular in the Discourse,

which hath given me great Satisfaction, and will convince such as shall hear it from me.

L. A Convert!

G. Sir, a Convert to Truth I rejoyce in being; tho at the same time it's not only mine, but every good Man's Duty to grieve for these ill Men, who are any ways concerned in this Villany, especially considering to whom this looks related.

L. We see how it looks related *ad Hominem*, and *ad Rem*, and we are very glad this Author hath Abdicated, and his Design is frustrated. His Highness hereby thought to have made one great step towards the Accomplishment of what Heaven in Mercy hath delivered us from; I think we can never for this be grateful enough, either to God the chief Author, or to our Soveraign, his Instrument, and those Right Noble and truly worthy Lords and Gentlemen, that to the hazard of Persons and Estates, embarqued on this Glorious Design, which Heaven, to a Miracle, blessed with such a sudden (and as to the manner, without Blood) unexpected Success.

T. But to return to the Jury from whence we digressed in pursuit of *Holland*, and the Instrument of Death.

And to the second Particular, *viz.* *Hawley's* unfair Practice, with relation to the Jury, to corrupt them into a belief of the (pretended) self-Murder.

Mr. *Fisher* did then further declare, that he had been informed my Lord of *Essex* was a very pious good Gentleman: to which *Bomeny* answered, My Lord was indeed a very pious good Man; upon which *Fisher* reply'd, it was then very improbable he should be guilty of this the worst of Actions.

Major *Hawley* perceiving that the Jury were like to be influenced with my Lord's true Character (for such indeed his Lordship was, as he was to *Fisher* represented) and thereby made believe that my Lord did not cut his one Throat; (▬▬▬ to what Majoy *Hawley* may be reasonably presumed to desire they should find) therefore to remove this, and corrupt them into a belief

lief of a Lie, viz. The pretended self-Murder; *Hawley* tells *Fisher* that it was his Mistake in my Lord, that made him believe his Lordship such a Man; for all those that knew his Lordship well, knew this of him, That it was a fix'd Principle in my Lord, that any Man might cut his own Throat, or otherwise dispose of his Life, to avoid a dishonourable and infamous Death: so that this Action was not unlike his Lordship, but according to his avow'd and fix'd Principles. This false and malicious Suggestion of Major *Hawley* (which the Jury then did suppose to be true) did very easily incline them to believe that my Lord had (pursuant to this Principle) cut his own Throat, to avoid that Dishonourable and Infamous Death, which his Circumstances seem'd to threaten.

L. What is this *Hawley?* Could his Condition pretend to any Intimacy with his Lordship, that he seemed so well to know my Lord's Principles in this matter?

T. *Hawley* now denies all, and protests to their Lordships of this Committee, that he was not nigh the Jury in the Victualling-House all the time of their Inquisition, nor ever heard it said to be my Lord's Principle, That any Man might cut his Throat to avoid an Infamous Death, till their Lordships in this Committee told him so.

L. Sure the Major's Memory must be very short, for there is hardly any Man of conversation in Town, but must have often heard it so said, it being a general discourse, immediately upon my Lord's Death, that such was his Lordship's Principle.

G. This I have been very often credibly informed, and have heard it reported in all Coffee-houses, and used as one, and not the least Argument of my Lord's having indeed cut his own Throat. I do much wonder the Major should pretend that he never heard of it, especially when he himself did suggest the same to the Jury, and press'd it as an Argument of my Lord's Self-Murder; I do not well understand this.

T. Gentlemen, to me the reason of this is plain; For when Major *Hawley* found that such a Suggestion was used as an Argument of his Guilt, to avoid this Charge, he doth not only deny his suggesting it, but, as a good Reason (had it been true) that he could not, declared, he never heard it by any said (before their Lordships charged him with it) that such was my Lord's Principle.

L. Major *Hawley*'s denying that he did suggest this to the Jury, or ever heard it said to be my Lord's Principle, when the Matter is positively sworn against him, naturally argues that this was a false, forged, and maliciously-invented Story, by that bloody Party; and *Hawley* the Man by them pitched upon, as the most proper Person to corrupt the Jury, (the then proper legal Judges of the Manner of my Lord's Death) with this treacherous and villanous contrived Suggestion; so that the Jury might be more easily inclined to believe my Lord's Self-Murder upon evidence as inconsistent as false.

G. I do much admire Major *Hawley* should deny he was with the Jury at the Victualling-house, if he were indeed there; seeing his being with them there was no Crime, and therefore needed no denial.

T. His bare being there, needed neither denial or excuse; but to avoid the Charge of what he falsely and treacherously did whilst he was there (which he could never excuse) he thought best, in general, to deny that he was with the Jury at all in the Victualling-house.

G. But this was very Foolish, because the Major being so well known, (and it may be to all the Jury) his being there could not but be remembred by many of them.

T. Almost all the Jury do remember him there, and likewise the Coroner, and Surgeons can't but know he was there.

G. The Major's denial therefore looks ill: for if he had been there, upon any lawful or indifferent Account, he might have lawfully and innocently justified the same; but his denial (when proved so very false) looks as though his Charge were too true.

T. The Jury had another Reason to remember the Major's being there with them at the Victualling-house; for when some of the Jury moved for the Adjournment of their Inquisition till some further time, and in the Mean while notice to be given to my Lord's Honourable Relations, that they might bring what Evidence they thought good.——

L. This had been proper, and it's very customary; for sometimes the Jury do not bring in their Inquisition in many days.

T. It had been both proper and practised in this Case, had not Major *Hawley* prevented it.

G. How could the Major hinder it?

T. Hawley enters a *Caveat* by another villanous and false Suggestion: for upon this Motion of the Jury, *Hawley*, with great earnestness, assures the Jury, they could not adjourn their Inquiry, but must immediately dispatch; because his Majesty (*Charles* the Second) had sent an Express for their Inquisition, and would not rise from Council (where he was then sitting) till their Inquiry was brought him; wherefore they must make all haste possible. This the Jury believing, they made more haste than good speed, and so, sooner than otherwise they would, finish'd their Inquisition.

G. Doth Major *Hawley* remember this, Messenger sent by his Majesty?

T. Hawley totally denies this likewise, and in answer, saith, (as before) that he was not nigh the Jury at the Victualling-house, and so could not thus hasten them.

L. Denies it! is it not sworn?

T. It is.

L. Certainly the denial of a Criminal, shall not ballance the Testimony of the Accuser.

T. Especially when the Person accusing is of a much cleerer and better Reputation (in all things considered) than ever the Person Accused can justly pretend to.

G. I am sorry for the Major, whom I did ever think very Loyal.

L. His *Old Court-Loyalty* [Obedience without reserve] qualified him as a fit Instrument in this perfidious and villanous, though then Court-Loyal Service. I remember that a Popish Captain, about two Years since, declared, 'He looked upon 'himself, bound to obey (without reserve) 'his King in all Commands; and swore, his 'Loyalty was such, that he would cut his 'Confessor's Throat, when under confession, 'if his Prince should so command him.

T. A thro'-paced Loyalist upon my word.

G. A Loyalist! a Loyalist for the Devil.

L. Even such Loyalty those Men had, which were imployed in my Lord of *Essex* his last Service.

G. I have been informed, that Major *Hawley* hath declared, 'He would go forty 'and forty Miles bare-foot to discover this 'Murder, if my Lord were indeed mur-'dered by others.

L. Verba Credam cum facta Videam; Shew me thy Faith by thy Works.

T. That this *Hawley* was a Man who still thirsted for the blood of those brave true *English* Champions that opposed the late Court-Arbitrary-Designs, and could afford those honourable Lords, and truly worthy Knights and Gentlemen, no better Titles than *Rogues*, appears by what he declared the very day, that a great Number of Honorable Lords (amongst which this unfortunate Lord I hear was one) and worthy Knights, Gentlemen and Citizens dined together at *Mile-end-Green*; for, sometime that Afternoon, *Hawley* told Mr. *Bunch*, then a Warder, that above 200 Rogues that very day dined together at *Mile-end-Green*, but he did wish that he had forty of the biggest of them there in the *Tower*, that they might be made the shorter by the Head, for till then the Land would never be at quiet.

L. What is become of this Major *Hawley*?

G. He is Major of the *Tower*, and likewise is (as I think) Gentleman-Porter, his Place worth some hundreds a Year.

L. What, is he now intrusted in the *Tower*?

G. Yes with almost (if not altogether) the greatest Trust (next under the Honorable Governour) that is now in the *Tower*, and he is even my Lord *Lucas*'s Right-hand in the management of the *Tower*-Affairs.

L. Is this which is here said to be sworn against *Hawley*, known to the Lord *Lucas*?

T. I believe not.

L. It

L. It were well his Lordſhip were acquainted with it; for moſt certain (if what be ſworn againſt him be true, which it's reaſonable to believe) *Hawley* is very deep in this Matter; and then we well know for what intereſt he muſt cordially act, tho' in appearance he ſeem otherwiſe.

T. The 21ſt of *January* laſt, when his Wife (or ſome Gentlewoman in his Houſe when he was taken) heard of the *Major's* being ſeized upon as ſuſpected concerned in, or privy to this Fact, ſhe cry'd out, 'God 'ſend us our good King again, for he will 'ſoon put an end to this Matter.

L. And without doubt an End to thoſe that inquired into it.

G. I muſt confeſs, theſe falſe Suggeſtions (for I can't believe them otherwiſe, ſeeing Major *Hawley* denies his being with the Jury) reflect upon the Major as too officious in this Matter; and I fear this great officiouſneſs of the Major, was in order to a very ill End; I can think no otherwiſe, and am heartily ſorry for him, becauſe I have heard many Loyal Men ſpeak very well of him, and to me he hath appeared no otherwiſe. Some Men of our *late Loyalty* will ſpeak the better of him upon this very account, and that which would make him odious in the ſight of honeſt Men, in the eſteem of theſe renders him the more acceptable; but as for theſe worthy Gentlemen who have had good Thoughts of this Man, as ſoon as they find theſe things, (and ſomewhat elſe) ſworn againſt him, they muſt either believe him not Innocent in this, or diſcredit the Evidence; to do which, would argue Prejudice, when the Accuſer is of a clearer Reputation than ever this Gentleman can pretend to; and beſides, in this ſtands *Rectus in Curia,* neither his Perſon or Eſtate depending upon the Iſſue of this Cauſe; nay, if he ſtand under any Prejudice, it is, that my Lord ſhould ſtill appear a Self-murderer, becauſe, ſhould it prove otherwiſe, the Coroner's Inqueſt (of which this Gentleman is one) muſt expect the laſh of ſome Mens Tongues; though I do think them to blame in nothing but ſome indiſcretion; for I am verily perſwaded, that theſe Gentlemen (for the moſt part, at leaſt) did not rejoice in that unfortunate Accident, but did heartily wiſh they had received any Information to find it otherwiſe than their Evidence moved them to; but nothing of that appearing from any Perſons who came in to depoſe on my Lord's behalf, and theſe Gentlemen being obliged to go according to *Evidence,* they are not ſo much to be blamed, as pitied, for being ſo hurried into their Inqueſt.

L. I find you are an Advocate both for the Coroner and his Jury: Think you they ought to be juſtified in all Particulars?

T. It's one thing to juſtify, and another to mitigate; As I do not think them altogether excuſable, ſo neither do I believe them ſo Criminal as ſome would repreſent them; and as far as in Juſtice I may, I think it my Duty to clear them, and all Men, from any Aſperſion.

L. You ſay the Jury ought to have proceeded according to *Evidence :* Ought they not under that Notion to have comprehended the ſeveral Irregularites in the total Change of the Circumſtances of the Body, Room, and Cloſet, from the State in which they were when the Body was firſt found? Ought they not to have conſidered, as *Evidence,* the palpable and groſs Contradictions, (before at large obſerved,) between thoſe attending on my Lord, which argued the Falſity of the Evidence, and that, the truth of my Lord's being murdered? And ought they not to have conſidered, as *Evidence,* the ſeveral Cuts before obſerved to be in my Lord's Right-hand, which argued his Reſiſtance to put off the Inſtrument of Death? Ought they not to have conſidered as, *Evidence,* the Gentlemens tampering with the Coroner in the next Room (for I can believe theſe Gentlemen there for no other purpoſe) and 'till the Coroner's Memory ſerves him to name theſe Men, and their Buſineſs with him, I ſhall not think the beſt of him:

ey ought to have
he Circumstances
nded) Instrument
the length of the
the Wound, and
nd an Inch diffe-
appears by your
b Razor, and not
ill, this Razor, in
ould be held by
de, and not less
must be held in
with that steadi-
aking this large
ed; so that the
ound not above
Hand to make a
s deep: this must
Mathematical Im-
ve been compre-
t self had been
the (pretended)
To all which, to
same, let us add
se three attend-
ut suffering them
Examinations, so
their Story; and
erein, to permit
n he began to
which alone gave
he was telling a
readily occurr'd)
om (to his Tu-
l write his own
er all, their Re-
nd contradictory.
Men have, in all
vidence, have they,
it they observed
d not, it argues
ty, or somewhat

do confess to have
disown to have
ticular (they say)
ve observed any
nd.
mber not! These

Gentlemen, I perceive, have likewise learn'd the Art of Forgetfulness, so that they will remember nothing which may seem to reflect upon their Discretion or Integrity: I would have some of these you have before mentioned set up a School to teach this Art never before found out by any.

T. I have heard of one of these Jury-Men, who being asked, what Cuts he did observe in my Lord's Right-hand? answered, Should he confess any, it would reflect upon them.

L. And therefore this Gentleman was resolved to forget, to reflect upon them! I perceive this Gentleman doth not consider how his stifling (in not owning what he can't but remember) the Truth makes him, *in Foro Conscientiæ*, accessory after the Fact, to my Lord's Murder: For whosoever there is that knows any thing, which he believes in its Discovery might tend to the Detection of this most perfidious Murder, and by his Silence endeavours to stifle it, therein (before God) becomes consenting to that Fact, as accessory to which at the last day he shall answer. Our Law makes him accessory after the Fact, that endeavours to conceal and convey any from Justice, whom he knows guilty of such a Villany; and for such his Crime he shall answer with the Forfeiture of his Life. Now the reason of this Law I take to be this; because such an Offender (endeavouring to defraud Justice of its due, by protecting his Life, which by his Transgression became forfeited to the Law) becomes consenting to the Fact, and shall in his own Life become subjected to that Punishment, the Person by him so conveyed away would have suffered, when taken; nay, the Crime becomes not excused by the Person's being apprehended, after he is so concealed or conveyed away, but the Person guilty hereof shall suffer the same Capital Punishment that is inflicted upon the Principal.

T. I wish all Men were such Casuists, as to understand this; and so good Men, as to put it in Practice: for you would then soon hear
of

of new Evidence in this Cafe.

L. A Man needs not much Cafuiftical Learning to know fo plain a Cafe.

T. In all your Heat, you do not confider thofe Circumftances that might influence the Jury, and deter them from doing what they ought in this Cafe.

L. What can plead their Excufe?

T. The great danger they had been under in finding my Lord murdered by others, pleads for your and all Mens charitable Pity towards Men under fuch a Temptation.

L. Nothing ought to deter Men from an inviolable Obfervation of that Maxim before mentioned, *Fiat Juftitia, & ruat Cœlum.*

T. The Obfervation of this, is, I muft confefs, every Man's Duty; but we find the fear of Death hath prevailed with the beft of Men to fwerve from their Duty, to the higheft degree. He of the Difciples who (in all appearance had the beft natural Courage, for he only wore the Sword, and * ufed it in the greateft Dangers) had the † higheft degree of Faith; was the ‖ *firft* that explicitly owned our Saviour, and declared (when fore-warn'd of his Denial) that *tho all Men deny'd our Saviour, he would not; nay, tho he were to die, he would ftick clofe to his Faith*; this very Man once under all thefe Advantages, in the midft of his Prefumption, was at laft hector'd out of his Faith by a poor filly Kitchin-Maid, thrice denying the Lord of Life, tho' even then, before his Face, and after his Reflection upon his Fault, and his weeping bitterly, he had not Courage enough to appear, own, and fuffer with his Mafter, as before he declared he would do, rather than deny him. Such Inftances as thefe fhould teach us all Pity towards thofe that fail in their Duty under the like Temptations; and likewife thofe that ftand, fhould take care left they fall.

G. I have been often told by a Merchant, who many Years lived in *Genoa,* 'That when fome young Noblemen (upon a fmall provocation) in the midft 'of the Street, have murdered others, 'they have upon the Spot immediately aloud

* *John* 18. 10.
† *Mat.* 14. 29.
‖ *Mat.* 16. 16.
Mat. 26. 55.

'declared, *That whofoever fhould fay they did* 'it, *fhould not long remain their Debtor.* By ' which the ftanders-by were given to un- ' derftand, that whofoever fhould difcover ' them to be the Men, muft expect to fall ' Sacrifices to their Revenge, or the Re- ' venge of their Party; and they fail'd not ' to perform what was fo threatned.

T. Little lefs in this Cafe was done, as fome have felt by woful Experience, who by their Expreffions in dereftation of this Murder, had expofed themfelves to the malicious fury of thofe Men, who never ftuck to add Blood to Blood, to prevent a difcovery of the firft, and carry on their devilifh Intereft.

And this brings me to the laft general Confideration, (*viz.*) The Backwardnefs of the then Government, and the many Threats, great Oppreffion, and barbarous Cruelty that hath been ufed to prevent a Difcovery of thofe barbarous and bloodyminded Men, with other Particulars, which feem to argue my Lord's being villanoufly murdered.

I fhall firft, fpeak to the Backwardnefs and Oppreffion of the Government in this Cafe. And,

Secondly, To fuch other Particulars as may be ufed as Arguments of this treacherous Cruelty.

For the firft, (*viz.*) The Backwardnefs of the then Government, and the many Threats, great Oppreffion, and barbarous Cruelty that hath been ufed to prevent a Difcovery of thefe barbarous and bloodyminded Men.' When Mr. *Braddan* went to the Earl of *Sunderland,* then Secretary of State; the very next *Thurfday* after the Death of the late Earl of *Effex,* and carried with him the Information of *William Edwards* and his Mother, (ready writ, but not fworn) my Lord *Sunderland* feemed much furprifed upon reading of them, (and indeed he had reafon to be furprifed, if he ftands fo related to the Matter as he is now fufpected to be); and then, in fome heat, asked Mr. *Braddon,* Who bad him bring thofe Things to him?

To

To which it was anſwered, That Sir *Henry Capel* had deſired it. Upon which my Lord ordered Mr. *Braddon* to come the next morning, and bring the Parties concerned, ſaying, *If it were proper, he would take them.*

L. I can't but here obſerve, that Anger and Heat you ſay my Lord *Sunderland* was in, when theſe Informations were (as above) delivered, as though it had been a Matter which did not *properly* belong to him, and therefore unleſs it were *proper*, he would not take them: The Secretary is angry that he was troubled with the Buſineſs; and yet the Court of *King's-Bench*, at Mr. *Braddon*'s Trial, ſaid, 'That Mr. *Braddon* had done well, if he had firſt gone to 'the Secretary of State.

G. But Mr. *Braddon* firſt tried ſeveral Juſtices of the Peace.

T. That did not then appear to the Secretary of State; wherefore the Secretary thought that an Impertinency in Mr. *Braddon*, which the Court of *King's-Bench* called his Duty.

L. If it *were proper*, my Lord *Sunderland* would take them! Certainly the Inquiry after a Murder is *proper* for the Magiſtracy; and the Murder of a Perſon of ſo great Quality, a *State-Priſoner* in the *State-Priſon*, by virtue of a Secretary of *State's* Warrant, is *proper* for a Secretary of State to inquire into, eſpecially conſidering the Relation that this Murder might be ſuppoſed to bear towards Perſons not of the leaſt Quality, nor Matters of the meaneſt Conſideration.

T. This holds good in the General; but there is never a General Rule, but hath an Exception; and this fell as an Exception under the General Rule for the Quality of the Guilty made this Exception, when otherwiſe there had been none; and therefore that Reaſon which you gave for the Secretary's Inquiry, (*viz.*) the relation of this Murder to, Quality and Matter of Conſequence, was the only Argument that balked the Inquiry.

L. Arguments! curs'd be ſuch Arguments as are thus grounded upon nothing but Deviliſh Policy, and are altogether inconſiſtent with, and repugnant to that Moral and Common Juſtice which ought to rule over all Quality, and all Matters whatſoever. Recommend me to that Miniſter of State which ever rejects ſuch Arguments; and with Courage and Integrity inviolably obſerves that brave Moral Maxim, *Fiat Juſtitia, & ruat Cœlum.*

T. May we be ever bleſſed with ſuch a Soveraign, and ſuch Miniſters of State, and Judges under him.

L. Did my Lord *Sunderland* think it *proper* to take thoſe Depoſitions next morning?

T. You will ſoon hear how they were taken; The next morning Mr. *Braddon* carri'd the young *Edwards* and his Siſter (who could teſtify the ſame with the Mother, then ſick in Bed) to my Lord *Sunderland*'s Office. His Lordſhip being then in Council, Mr. *Mountſtephens* gave his Lordſhip notice of Mr. *Braddon*'s coming; immediately upon which, Mr. *Atterbury*, the Meſſenger, was ſent to take Mr. *Braddon* into Cuſtody.

L. This I ſuppoſe was after the Boy and his Siſter had been examined.

T. No, before either of theſe had been ſeen by my Lord, or examined by any.

G. What colour of Commitment was there, when nothing had been ſworn, or ſo much as declared, againſt this Gentleman?

L. He was Committed, becauſe the matter, all Circumſtances conſidered, declared, (almoſt *ex Rei Natura*) againſt one who (in this reſpect) was troubled with a *Nolo me tangere*, which this Gentleman would have had ſearched and lanc'd, a thing by no means to be indured. Pray Proceed.

T. Mr. *Braddon* was called in before the Council, (before either the Boy or his Siſter) and in ſome heat, asked, What made him ſtir in that Buſineſs?

L. I never before thought the Diſcovery of a Murder, had been the Diſintereſt of the Crown, in whoſe behalf all Criminals are proſecuted,

T. As

(65)

T. As there hath been heretofore a great Difference between the Church of *Rome* and the Court of *Rome*, so have we lately seen the day when the Crown and the Crowned Head have been Diametrically opposite. The Crown [the legal Prerogative I mean] could do no wrong, but the Head that wore it hath done a World of mischief. The Judges did not obey the Crown [the Rightful Sovereignty] when they illegally destroyed Charters; nor were those vile Varlets that suborned Witnesses, truly Loyal; or those Mercenary Judges, Council and Jury, who (in contradiction to their own Consciences) seemed to believe those State-hired-Hackney-thorough-paced-perjured-Caitifs, who judicially murdered Men: 'Twas not the Crown, but he who possessed it, that dispenced with all Law by an unjust usurp'd Prerogative, the Peoples Rights being ravished from them, and sold to *James* the Second by the Corruption of that Bench, who (as an Honourable Brave English-Liberty-Property-Martyr truly said) had before been Scandals to the Bar. It was not the Crown, but the Crowned Head, that by an Illegal Arbitrary Power (and not Authority) sent those worthy brave true English Spirits, the most Reverend his Grace, and the Right Reverend the other Six Bishops, to the Tower, for humbly offering their Reasons for their Non-compliance with what in Consequence would have levelled all Fences to Property, Liberty and Life, neither of which (had that power in its largest Extent been compli'd with) could we have possessed but by such a precarious Right as a Royal Arbitrary *Ipse Dixit* at all times would have bar'd; and had not the Crown [the uncorrupt Regal Authority] as truly stated by those Learned Councils in this Eminent Tryal, acquitted these ever-to-be remembered Pillars from any Violation, Reflection upon its Just Rights, the Head that wore it would soon *Gradatim* have rob'd those Noble Couragious Church and State Confessors of their high Characters, Liberties, Priviledges and Immunities, whe (for I believe an Conviction and is no farther di and Grave) and the Chief of that their too great C not only secured cession, (when oth not their Judgme foreclosed his Ti fixed and settled that storm which gratefully requit In this the comm *Perset quod facies*

L. What othe give for his stirrin by the Family?

T. That was on but it was not the him; and there Mr. *Braddon* told That he was alt unobliged by tha that there lay n ment in him first Man whatsoever, the same Informa his love to Truth first moved him; he thought him what he had done of God) his Du though Death sta step he made.

L. May the lik in him.

T. Mr. *Braddo* Pocket the Coroni mation of *Paul B* you have before nourable Board, T herenciés, and ind before the Coron endeavoured to pr being attending o that they seemed ons to confirm

argued for, and thereupon made his Obfervations upon fome of thofe Incoherencies you have before at large heard related.

G. What was faid in anfwer to this ?

T. As foon as Mr. *Braddon* had made thefe Obfervations, His Royal Highnefs called for the Informations, which were accordingly delivered him, and *Mr.Braddon* expected His Highnefs would have faid fomewhat in anfwer to what was fo obferved.

L. Truly I thiuk His Highnefs might be the leaft Stranger to what thefe men had Sworn; for from what I have heard, I do believe that the fame Power and Intereft that hired thofe perfidious Villains to permit what was fo barbaroufly executed, had likewife given them Inftructions what to Swear, to give colour to the pretended Self-murder, and therefore His Highnefs might be the beft prepared to anfwer all Objections againft thefe mens Depofitions. But I long to hear how His Highnefs endeavoured to reconcile them.

T. His Highnefs could not then turn Reconciler, and therefore faid nothing to this matter, but delivered them to his then Majefty, who faid as little; whereupon the then Lord Keeper *North* took thofe Informations, and endeavoured to reconcile what was indeed irreconcileable : Whereupon *Mr. Braddon* objected againft his Lordfhip's Reconciliation, and urged the former Objections further ; upon which his Lordfhip feemed (though not much by his words, yet by his very pale changed Countenance) highly difpleafed with *Mr. Braddon* for making thofe Reflections.

L. What were thefe Depofitions Printed for, but to be obferved? did his Lordfhip think that every man would Twallow fuch grofs Contradictions as his Lordfhip's Corruption (againft his Judgment) would have reconciled?

T. After a long Examination, too tedious here to repeat, *Mr. Braddon* was ordered to withdraw ; and then the Young *William Edwards* was called in, the Child (being then not Thirteen years of Age) was very much afraid (having, as before, been foplifhly frighted by his Eldeft Sifter, as though the King would Hang him) and cry'd ; whereupon (as the Sifter hath reported) the Child was ftroaked upon the Head, and bid not to cry, and then asked, Whether he had not invented that Lye, to excufe his Truenting that day ?

L. A proper Queftion by way of Inftruction, for fuch a Child to anfwer. I fuppofe the Boy then anfwered, as by this queftion he was in effect bid:

T. You are in the right, for the Child to this queftion anfwered, Yes: The Sifter was examined, and fhe gave the fame account you have before at large heard, as to what the Boy had declared, and how *Mr. Braddon* had difcourfed them ; and then *Mr. Braddon* was the fecond time called in, and by the Lord Keeper *North* told, that he had inftructed this Boy in a Lye, and would have fuborned the Child to Swear it. To which Mr. *Braddon* anfwered, It was impoffible he could inftruct him to fay what the Boy had declared feveral days before he had ever feen the Boy or any of his Relations, as appeared by what his Sifter and the Boy himfelf muft own.

L. Had not his Lordfhip's Honour and Intereft fuborned his Confcience in this matter, he would have dealt more fairly.

Mr. *Braddon* then told his Lordfhip, That being well fatisfied in his Innocence and Integrity, he feared not any Profecution, but would readily give whatfoever Bail his Lordfhip fhould require; and accordingly that Afternoon gave Bonds with two Friends in 2000 *l.* a piece for his Appearance ; and hereupon continued the Profecution with all Vigor imaginable, for he was now obliged in Self-Juftice to endeavor in what he could, to corroborate the Boy's Evidence, which my Lord Keeper *North* corruptly called a Lye, and to which his Lordfhip (without any ground) pretended that Mr. *Braddon* would have fuborned the Boy to Swear; for at the fame time it appeared to his Lordfhip, as far as Negative could appear, that Mr. *Braddon* had not given,

(67)

given, offered or promised to the Boy, or any for him, or to any of his Relations, one Farthing or Farthings-worth, but did as you have before at large heard, use such Arguments as might most naturally Influence the Boy to truth: After Mr. *Braddon* had been about a month hurried up and down in both Town and Country upon several Inquiries, and all People (except Mr. *Crag.* one Gentleman who was ever ready to go with Mr. *Braddon* upon all occasions) very unwilling in the least to concern themselves.

L. It is very natural for men to be deter'd from engaging in that which was so roughly managed by the Council-Board, and threatned the Ruine of him who first appeared; for few men are for living a State-Confessor caged up within Iron Grates, or dying their Countries Martyr, but think themselves obliged to mind only their private Affairs, leaving all Affairs of State to those that have the Command and Steerage of this great Vessel [the Government] lest by their Intermeddling in those ticklish matters; themselves should have followed the unjust misfortune of those brave men, who couragiously, though to their Ruine, opposed themselves to the usurpt Prerogative, and Tyranny of the Times.

T. Had all men been like those men of Prudence (as they falsly term their Cowardices) what would long since have become of this Vessel, wherein all (with all we have) are imbarqued? The Commander in Chief, with most of the Chief Officers, had by a corrupt perjured Agreement amongst themselves, resolved upon the Sale of both Men and Cargo to that Corrupt and Arbitrary Will, which in a short time (if not providentially prevented) would have claimed all we are and have; as though we had held neither Property, Liberty or Life, but as those Corrupt Judges did their places, *Durante bene placito Regis.* But to return.

About the 16*th* of *August.* 1683. Mr. *Braddon* went down into *Wiltshire* to *Marlborough*, to enquire after a Report before my Lord's

Death, of my Lord's cutting his Throat: From *Marlborough* he was riding to *Froom* in *Somersetshire*, and at *Bradford* (about six Miles short of *Froom*) he was stopt, (there being then strict Watching and Warding, throughout that Country) by a Vile Persecuting Fellow, one Captain *Beach* an Attorney, who was ever Zealous for the Ruine and Destruction of those that stood firm to the True English Interest, and yet now pretends to be Zealous for his present Majesty and Government, though he declared when His Majesty first Landed, he did hope to see most of those Hanged that went in to him) being here Examined, and having given the Justice Satisfaction (a Gentleman then there, knowing Mr. *Braddon*, and assuring the Justice he knew him to be the same man he declared he was) the Justice was taken aside by *Beach*, and (as others declared who had heard this *Beach*) told, that he did not so strictly as he ought examine this Gentleman, for the Gentleman was certainly Disaffected to the Government, as might be seen by his wearing a Band and Cuffs.

L. A very strong Argument upon my word.

T. Hereupon the Justice came to Mr. *Braddon*, and told him he must search him, upon which Mr. *Braddon* (before ever the Justice saw his Papers) ingeniously declared the cause of his being then in the Country, where he was going, and upon what occasion; upon which the Justice Commits Mr. *Braddon* to *Wiltshire* Goal, by such an illegal Warrant (in its conclusion) as you never saw.

The Warrant ran as followeth, *viz.*

Wilts ss. **T**O the *Keeper of His Majesties Goal of* Fisherton-Anger *in this County, or his Sufficient Deputy, These: I send you herewithall the Body of* Lawrence Braddon, *apprehended in the Town of* Bradford *in the County aforesaid, this present Two and*

K 2 *twentieth*

twentieth day of August, taken upon Suspicion of being a dangerous and ill-affected Person to the Government, and for refusing to give an account of his business in those Parts, and for having Letters of dangerous Consequence about him. Those are therefore in the Kings Majesties Name to will and require you, that upon sight hereof, you receive him the said Lawrence Braddon into your Gaol, and him there safely keep, (not permitting him to have Pen, Ink or Paper, or Person to converse or speak with him) until you shall receive further Orders from His Majesty and Privy Council: Hereof you are not to fail at your peril. Given under my Hand and Seal at Bradford this 22th day of August aforesaid, Anno Regni Caroli Secundi Angl. &c. 35. Anno Dom. 1683.

Mr. Braddon told the Justice, the Warrant was illegal; for should the Goaler never hear from the King and Council, he must be kept a perpetual Prisoner: Warrants of Commitment ought to conclude, *Till he be discharged by due Course of Law*. But the Justice having Mr. *Beach* and some Attorneys of his own Judgment, declared he would justifie the Warrant; and under this Warrant Mr. *Braddon* lay in *Wiltshire* Goal about a Fortnight, and was then removed by *Habeas Corpus* upon the Statute to be bailed. All the Judges being out of Town, he was (according to the Statute) carried before my Lord Keeper *North* then in Council; when Mr. *Braddon* was first brought before his Lordship, my Lord Keeper smil'd, (thinking he had got such a hank upon Mr. *Braddon* and his Friends, as would ruine both) and told Mr. *Braddon*, notwithstanding Self-respect might weigh but little, he thought that he would have had such just regard to his Bail, as not to

have ruin'd them by those things then to be laid to his Charge. To which Mr. *Braddon* answered, That the only thing required of his Bail, was his Appearance the next Term, which he should (God willing) do, and thereby Indemnifie his Bail. No, replied my Lord Keeper (smiling) the Good Behaviour in the mean time was likewise required, and that hath been notoriously broken by this new Offence. To which it was answered, That there was no Good Behaviour at all required; and for the Truth thereof, Mr. *Braddon* appealed to the Bonds themselves, taken (as you have heard) before the Secretary of State; upon search it appeared his Lordship was in the wrong, upon which my Lord Keeper *North* seemed very Angry with Secretary *Jenkins*, that the Good Behaviour was here omitted; but the Secretary said it was the Omission of his Clerk, and it was, I believe, the only Omission of that nature that had happened in those times; for the Bonds then taken by the Secretary of State, in their Condition concluded, *And in the mean while to be of the Good Behaviour*; but in Mr. *Braddon*'s Bond this Clause was intirely left out.

L. Why could they make that a breach of the Good Behaviour, which a man was naturally bound to do for his defence?

T. Without doubt the then times would have made Mr. *Braddon*'s going into the Country, &c. to be a Breach of this Clause, because they did at his Tryal charge him with it as a Crime, and therefore most certainly would have adjudged it *Contra bonos mores*, and so a Forfeiture of the Bonds. Mr. *Braddon* desired my Lord Keeper, that such Persons might be sent for out of the Country, as had heard the report of my Lord of *Essex* having cut his Throat, before his Throat was indeed cut. Upon which an * Eminent Lord then said, This is just as it was in the Case of Sir *Edmond-Bury Godfry*. My Lord Keeper demanded of Mr. *Braddon* Bonds ████ in 12000 *l*. himself, and his Bail for

* Marq. of H--x to the best of Mr. Braddon's remembrance.

for his Appearance, and other Bonds (himself and Sureties) in the like Sum for his Good Behaviour; saying, He would have as good men Bound, as though he were to lend the Money out of his Pocket. These Demands being so very unreasonable, Mr. *Braddon* desired his Lordship, that his Lordship would be pleased to consider the Statute upon which he came to be Bailed, and that his Lordship would (according to the Statute) take such Bail as the Quality of the Person and Nature of the Offence required. Mr. *Braddon* did farther declare, That he was a Younger Brother, his Father living, and his Relations and Friends almost two hundred Miles from *London*. To which my Lord Keeper answered, That as the Statute required, so he did consider his Quality; for his Crime was such, that had he been an Alderman of *London*, for every 6000 *l*. he would have demanded 20000 *l*. so that his Lordship would then have had 80000 *l*. Bonds in Bail and Suretyship, twice as much as ever was given for any Noble-man in *England*, for any Offence whatsoever.

L. What was this Heinous Offence? Is the bringing Murderers to Justice, a Reflection on the Government? Certainly the Government's becoming a Skreen to such perfidious Villanies, and thus prosecuting and punishing him that would have detected them, is a Case without President, and so Notorious a Breach of the Rules of all Common Justice, that I knew not a more Impudent, Bare-fac'd, and Villainous Instance.

T. Mr. *Braddon* not being able to comply with these high Terms, was remanded by my Lord Keeper to *Wiltshire* Goal; but before the next Morning, advising with some Lawyers, he was told the Good Behaviour could not be required, and that Bail to answer the Cause of the then Commitment was all that could be demanded: Upon which the next Morning Mr. *Braddon* desired his Keeper to carry him to my Lord Keeper's House in *Great Queen-street*, for he did hope his Lordship would not continue to insist upon the Good Behaviour, which the Statute required not. Mr. *Braddon* was accordingly carried, but the Goaler went first to his Lordship, and informed my Lord Keeper upon what account he had brought Mr. *Braddon* once more before his Lordship; my Lord then said, *he neither had or could demand the Good Behaviour*; and then sent for Mr. *Braddon*, and declared as before: Whereupon Mr. *Braddon* (perceiving his Lordship in a better Humour than the Night before) desired his Lordship to accept of such Bail as he could give; which, with what he was before under, (by Bonds before the Secretary of State, for the same Offence in Effect) would amount to 10000 *l*. my Lord Keeper declared, he could not at his House alter what was agreed upon at the Council; but the Goaler should bring him down to the Council that Afternoon, and if it could be done, he should be then Bailed. About Eight of the Clock that night, Mr. *Braddon* did accordingly go before the Council, where his Lordship was so far from Bailing him upon the Terms by him offered, *That his Lordship renewed his Demand of his former Bonds in* 12000 l. *for the Appearance, and* 12000 l. *more for the Good Behaviour, notwithstanding that very Morning he had expresly declared, That he neither had or could demand Sureties for his Good Behaviour*.

L. My Lord's memory was very short, his Judgment soon changed, or his Conscience very Corrupt, to demand (against his own opinion which he declared that morning) what by Law could not be required.

T. My Lord Keeper told Mr. *Braddon*, he had a mind to be made Infamously Famous, and thereupon Sarcastically repeated out of *Juvenal*:

Aude aliquid brevibus Gyaris, & carcere dignum,
Si vis esse aliquis.

L. I do very well remember his Lordship was made a Lord, about that time King *Charles* the Second issued out a Proclamation against

against Petitioning, to which it was then said, my Lord Keeper *North* advised, and for that and other such good Services to the Publick, he was made a Lord: Whereupon that Saying of *Juvenal*, *Carr* in his Currant apply'd to his Lordship, and in his Translation render'd it thus;

Dare once but be a Rogue upon Record,
And you may quickly hope to be a Lord.

Probatum est.

But Blessed be God for this happy Change, which will (I hope) bestow nothing but grinning Honour on such vile perjured Services (in acting contrary to their Oaths) as *Jefferies* and *North* were advanced by.

T. Mr. *Braddon* having thus suffered in the defect of this Act, I cannot but here take notice of one great Omission in this Statute. This Act inflicts a Penalty of 100 l. upon the Goaler that denies the Prisoner, or any on his behalf, a Copy of his Warrant, and 500 l. Penalty on every Judge that refuses to grant an *Habeas Corpus* upon the Statute, for the removal of such Prisoner; but inflicts no certain Penalty upon the refusal to Bail the Prisoner, as shall upon this Act be brought before them, so that if the Judge either demand Ten times more than the Quality of the Prisoner, or the Nature of the Offence requires, or refuseth to take any Bail whatsoever, there can no Action of 500 l. for this refusal be brought, for no Penalty in this Case is Enacted. It's very strange that the Statute should lay so great Penalties upon the denial of the Means of Bail, (viz.) the Copy of the Warrant and *Habeas Corpus*) and yet not Enact an express Penalty for refusal of the End, (viz.) Bailing the Prisoner; for what signifies either a Copy of the Commitment, or an *Habeas Corpus* thereupon, if Bail be not procured? This is putting the Prisoner to a very Fruitless Expence.

L. Seeing the Statute requires the Judge shall Bail the Prisoner, taking such Recognizance with one or more Sureties, according to the Quality of the Person, and Nature of the Offence, a special Action of the Case lyes against such Judge upon his refusal, wherein it is to be supposed, not less than 500 l. Damages will be given.

T. Upon refusal, if there be little Damages sustained (as it may happen, for though one Judge refuse, another may grant the Prisoner his Liberty upon Bail) and consequently so proved, the Jury (being Sworn to go according to Evidence, as well in the Damages, as in the matter directly in Issue;) must go according to Proof, unless they think the Extravagant Verdicts of the late Times (which found 100 Thousand Pounds where not one Farthing was proved) will excuse them, in giving Fifty times more than was Sworn to be sustained. Few words more in the Statute, would, I humbly conceive, have sufficiently provided in this case; for in the Statute, where it is said, That if the Judges shall deny any Writ of *Habeas Corpus*, by this Act required to be granted, being moved for as aforesaid (it had been added; (Or *shall refuse such Bail as the Quality of the Prisoner, and Nature of the Offence required*) *they shall severally Forfeit to the Prisoner or Party grieved, the Sum of 500 l. to be recovered in manner aforesaid*. These few words would have given the 500 l. for refusal of Bail, as well as denying the *Habeas Corpus*; whereas without the like Clause, the Statute may (in Effect) be dayly evaded. But to return, Mr. *Braddon* was hereupon turned over to *Atterbury* the Messenger, where, for about five Weeks, he lay at no less Charge, than Four Pounds and odd Money *per* Week directly, besides other collateral Expences; this being too great for his Fortune to comply with, he (after some opposition) removed himself to the *Kings-Bench* (having before by a Friend agreed with Marshal *Glover* upon 2000 l. Security, and 5 s. 3 d. *per* Week Chamber-Rent, to have the Liberty of the Rules; but when he came over, the Marshal insisted upon two men in 10000 l. a piece, and

10 s.

10 *s*. 3 *d. per* Week Chamber-Rent, and then Mr. *Braddon* was to have Liberty of the Rules; but when Mr. *Braddon* had complied with these high Terms (so much above the first Agreement) the Marshal ordered him to be kept a close Prisoner under this Security at no less than 2 *l*. 5 *s*. 3 *d. per* Week Charge, and refused (whilst Mr. *Braddon* was thus close Imprisoned) to deliver up the Security-Bonds for this close Confinement; the Marshal pretended the Order of the then Lord Chief Justice *Jefferies*.

L. From the Crown of the Head, to the Sole of the Foot, our Government hath been corrupted.

T. After Mr. *Braddon* had lain some time under these hard Terms, he was Bail'd out by the *Kings Bench*, and then renewed his Prosecution with all possible Industry and Diligence; but about the 12*th* of *November*, 1683, he was taken up in *London*, by a very strange Warrant granted against him, by the then Court of Aldermen, or Sir *Henry Tulse*, the then Lord Mayor; the Warrant was against Mr. *Braddon*, as a Person *suspected to be disaffected to the Government*.

L. Suspected to be disaffected! Sure those who granted the Warrant, were very disaffected to the Laws, or otherwise they would never have issued out so strange and illegal a Warrant.

T. Upon this Warrant Mr. *Braddon* was carried before Sir *James Edwards*, and after that, the then Lord Major, and last of all, before the King and Council, where he was falsely and maliciously charged with being the Author of the *Protestant Flail*; many hundreds whereof (it was then suggested) he had bespoke about the time of *Colledge's* (pretended) Plot, as a fit Instrument to Massacre the King's Friends; King *Charles* then shaking one in his hand, declared it was a much more dangerous Weapon than the Popish-Dagger; but after Mr. *Braddon* had answered to every part of his Charge, there appeared so much Malice, Folly, and Falshood in the Accusation, that His then Majesty ordered his Discharge without Bail.

L. This was a very malicious Prosecution in hopes to Ruin him; not so much for this, as for what he had done in the Case he was before ingaged in.

T. I believe you are in the right. About this time Mr. *Braddon* was informed, that his Royal Highness (discoursing at a Hunting, concerning the late Earl of *Essex*) had declared he would ruin him, if all the Law or Interest in *England* would Ruin him, for rifling into the Business (or words to that effect); and thereupon Mr. *Braddon* was persuaded to desist; but it was answered, That the Ruin he did expect, he did not fear, neither would by those Threats be deter'd from the Prosecution.

L. Had his Royal Highness been indeed Innocent of this Murder, there had been few things more serviceable to His Highness than a full and clear discovery of the Truth in this matter; for had the Earl been a Self-murderer by a thorough Examination, and strict Scrutiny, the Truth would have plainly appeared, and all Objections would have been answered and vanished, so that there would not have remain'd the least Colour for a Reflection on His Highness; or had the Earl of *Essex* been Murdered by such as did it without His Highness Consent or Privity, upon a diligent and judicious Examination and Prosecution, these vile Varlets that perpetrated this hellish Fact, being detected and punished according to their Demerit (as it had been both His Majesty's and Royal Highness's Interest, as well as Duty they should) His Highness, and all that were Innocoent would hereby have been effectually vindicated from all Colour of Guilt; for the Conviction and Punishment of the Guilty, are Vindications of the Innocent. Whereas the Cause was so managed, as gave all the World just reason to suspect the very truth of the Matter was of so deep a Dye, that it could not endure the Touch-stone of a strict and diligent Inquisition, lest it should then

then appear (as without doubt it would) in its true Sanguine Colours; wherefore this Cause still shun'd the Light, because its Deeds were Evil. *Sed veritas non quærit Angulos*: Truth seeks no Corners.

T. To be short, For it would be very tedious to tell all this Gentleman hath done and suffered upon this Account. In *Hilary* Term, Mr. *Bradden* and *Hugh Speake*, Esq; were try'd upon an Information exhibited against them by the then Attorney General; The chief thing laid to these Gentlemens Charge, was a Conspiracy to procure false Witnesses to prove the late Earl of *Essex* Murdered by Persons unknown, contrary to the Coroners Inquest, &c. Mr. *Speake* was Acquitted of the Conspiracy, and Mr. *Braddon* only found Guilty.

L. Who can *Conspire* alone? A sole Conspirator is a Contradiction.

T. Such a Contradiction the Jury made, and my Lord Chief Justice *Jefferies* approved of the same. When Mr. *Braddon* appeared in Court to be Tried, he that was not the least concern'd in the Prosecution, told him before the Information was read, That he would do his Business for him: Upon which, Mr. *Braddon* desired this Gentleman to have Patience to tarry till the Jury had done it to his hands; to which it was replied, I do not doubt that. The Oppression of the then times, was still sure of both Judg and Jury. This Tryal was carried on with all the Fury and Malice imaginable, and this pretended Crime made worse than a common Theft or Robbery, for that tended to a private Mischief, but this to a general Confusion, &c.

When my Lord Chief Justice *Jefferies* at this Tryal, was thus representing Mr. *Braddon*'s Crime, as one of the highest that could be committed, exposing it as much worse than Burglary, Robbery, or the like, in the midst of his Lordship's Railing, Mr. *Braddon* smil'd; and it was (as I after heard him often declare) upon this Story coming into his mind: A Neighbour of his an illiterate plain Country-Farmer, had a Wife of as violent a Spirit as liv'd, and one day She came into the Room where her Husband was (with several Neighbours); as soon as She came, tho there was not, or it seems had been the least Colour for a Provocation, for he still carried himself well towards her; she flies into the greatest Rage imaginable, calling him all the Names that Malice could invent, or Rage could utter; and had she not been prevented, might have done him some mischief. The Husband in the midst of this great Storm, well knowing all to be false, which the Fury of his Wife charged him with, stood as a Man altogether unconcern'd under this Provocation, but rather appeared very pleasant. One of his Friends asks him, how it was possible for him with that Temper, to receive the scurrilous and unjust Railing of that furious Woman? to which the Husband smiling, calmly replied, That his Wife talked of a Man he did not know, for he was altogether unrelated to, and unacquainted with that Person she so railed against, and therefore what reason had he to be concern'd when he was not the Person she spoke of? Mr. *Braddon* asked his own Conscience (an infallible Evidence according to truth, to condemn or acquit) whether he was this villanous Criminal his Lordship was so furiously Railing against; and he found that Judg (by which at the last day he shall be tryed) did acquit him from that Crime which his Lordship's Corruption (against his belief) unjustly charged him with; and therefore he stood very much unconcern'd at all that his Lordship's corrupt Violence, falsely and maliciously, without the least appearance of a Crime, applied to him; who tho the Person highly accused, was altogether Innocent either of the Offence, or those far-fetched, strained, and groundless Aggravations.

L. If Mr. *Braddon* was well satisfied in his Innocence, he had good reason not to be discouraged: For, *tho the wicked flee when no man pursues, yet the righteous are as bold as a Lyon.*

G. No Terrors ought to affright or discourage the Innocent.

Integer

(73)

Integer vitæ scelerisque purus,
Non eget, &c. Hor. Od. 22. Lib. 1.

L. We have a much better Author, who speaks much to the same effect, and assures us, That to the oppressed, *God is a refuge and strength: a very present help in trouble. Therefore need they not fear, tho the earth be moved, and the mountains be carried into the midst of the sea. Tho the waters thereof roar, and be troubled, tho the mountains shake with the swelling thereof,* &c. Psalm 46. 1, 2, &c.

G. Nothing gives a man that Satisfaction of mind under an unjust Accusation, as his Innocence; and I am verily perswaded that an innocent Man hath greater quiet, even under an unjust Condemnation, than the Guilty can have, tho here acquitted; for tho the Corruption of a Judge or Jury may protect the greatest Criminal from that legal, humane Punishment, which the Law would inflict; yet the Guilt of his own Consciene still haunts him like (or rather much worse than) a Ghost: and therefore is he *like the troubled Sea, when it cannot rest, whose waters cast up mire and dirt; for there is no peace to the wicked, saith my God,* Isa. 57. 20, 21.

T. No Man ought to Condemn or Acquit himself by the Opinion of others; for Men may be led by Misinformation or Prejudice; but his own Conscience, when faithfully observed, will do him the greatest Justice; and when he stands acquitted in his own mind, he ought not much to value the Vogue of the People. For according to the Poet, *Conscia mens recti famæ mendacia ridet.*

G. What this Author saith in the next Verse, may be too truly applied to this corrupt Age, who are so very apt upon the sleightest (and sometimes without any) Grounds, to take up a reproach against their Neighbour.

Sed nos in vitium credula turba sumus.

But to proceed,

T. The Lord Chief Justice, and the Kings Council, often in effect declared (if my Lord was Murdered by others) the King and Duke had an hand in it. Some of these Gentlemen must shortly deny their own Conclusions from the same Premisses, or else maintain (from the Earl's being proved Murdered) that the Duke had a hand in it. The Jury in this Case were twice well treated with a plentiful Entertainment; and that which to some of them was much more grateful, (viz.) three Guineas a Man, so that *Guilty* came to a better Market, than *Not Guilty* would have done by two Guineas a Man.

L. Did the King always pay the Jury, when they found for him?

T. No; but upon such Services they did not go unrewarded.

L. Some of these Mercenary Men, which were corrupted to go contrary to Evidence, will certainly meet with a reward hereafter, which will teach them by woful Experience, what it was thus to put to Sale first their own Consciences; and then in the Corruption of that, to sell the Property, Liberty, and Life of their Fellow Subjects; chiefly to gratify that Blood-thirsty-party, which so eagerly pursued the Destruction of all that stood in their way to those vile Designs then carrying on, for the Ruin of both Church and State. I am apt to believe so Charitably of some of these Jury-men,(tho too Active in such Services) that they did not foresee the Tendency of these things, but were blindly and not maliciously hurried on (the Knaves leading the Fools) to those things which some have long since repented. But pray, what was this Jury?

T. As for the Foreman, Sir *Hugh Middleton,* Baronet, (as I have been credibly informed) he declared himself a Papist soon after King *James* came to the Crown, and then said he had been a *Roman* Catholick in his heart for many years.

L. Mr. *Braddon* had like to have Justice done him by such vile Hypocrites, who continue (in appearance) of a Church, that
L they

(74)

tter opportunity to
e any other of the
tei ?
at any besides this
ift; and I do hope
their Error in this
ithout the least Co-
ll the Witnesses did
m giving, offering,
ng to them, to give
Case. Upon this un-
Braddon was fin'd
000 *l.* and the good
uring Life. Under
e Judgment, Mr.
ince's coming, who
ons, and as the late
o restituit rem. For
restored by his hap-
den as just Success;
s Liberty procured,
eing ever forgiven;
y, That about *Au-*
urton came over to
er to the Discharge
s Prisoners. A List
ses of their Impri-
to Mr. *Braddon*, who
Name cross'd, and
did ask Mr. *Burton*
the only Name so
was answered, That
ed a List of his Pri-
nch under Fines) to
at very List was ac-
rried to His Majesty
his Majesty imme-
s Name, called for a
h his own Hand so

lain, this Gentle-
oxious to His Ma-
n to expect any Fa-

e King's Interest to
Prisoners, and not
rying them alive,
l Reflection on His

L. The Kings prosecuting (with an irreconcilable Hatred) this Gentleman, made
the World justly conclude, that this Gentleman suffered his Imprisonment not for his
own Guilt, but for the Guilt of others,
who would therefore never be reconciled;
for had not others been Guilty of this
Blood, Mr. *B.* would never have been thus
injuriously dealt with, nor his Offence (if
it may be so called) kept in such an hateful
Remembrance.

T. A Gentleman of good Interest in the
late times, told Mr. *Braddon*, he must never
expect to be forgiven, because he had cast
Blood in the King's Face, which none else
had done.

L. His Late Majesties thus marking this
Gentleman out, as an irreconcilable Object
of his Displeasure, was more used as an Argument of His Majesties Guilt in that matter, than any thing I could ever find in
Mr. *Braddon*'s Tryal; for tho what is there
proved, satisfied me, my Lord was Murdered; yet nothing Sworn, appeared directly
against His Highness. But the Government
becoming (as it were) Parties to this Charge,
by their appearing in such an extravagant
Method of (pretended) Justice against the
Prosecutor of this Murder, as tho my Lord
could not be Murdered, but the Government must have an hand in it: This made
Men of Consideration conclude, that had
not Persons of the greatest Character been
chief in this execrable Contrivance, the Government had never thus extravagantly
been hook'd in as *Particeps Criminis*, (in case
my Lord were by others Murdered) to punish him who would have legally Indited
such as the Government ought with an Indignation (due to the most barbarous complicated Murder) to have prosecuted even
unto Death.

T. If a Government shall answer for the
Blood of the Party Slain, when no Inquisition is made by the proper Magistrates in
order to a Detection: How much more
shall that Government appear Criminal,
that instead of making Inquisition for Blood,
became Advocates and Defenders of the
Blood-

Blood-Guilty, and in a violent unprefidented Method of (falfly call'd) Juftice, ruin him, who did humbly offer the Matter to a judicial Confideration?

G. The Government had made Inquiry by the Coroners Inqueft; and therefore, how could the Government be blamed for any neglect?

T. Thofe concerned in this barbarous Fact, intended to ufe (and indeed did) the Coroner's Inqueft (which the Law defigned as the means of difcovery of a violent Death) as the means to prevent the Detection of this Villany; for having prepared a couple of Treacherous and Perjured Varlets (*Bomeny*, and *Ruffel* I mean) to mifinform the Jury, as to the (pretended) manner of Death, inftead of difcovering the Truth, (which would have render'd themfelves obnoxious to Punifhment) they villainoufly contrived a Story, or rather repeated their Inftructions, (for without doubt the Information to be given the Jury, was likewife agreed upon before my Lord's Death; fo that thefe Forfworn Caitifs might not be to feek in their Information when they came to Swear, which would have foon difcovered this bloody Treachery) I fay, repeated their Leffon, and with this Forgery mifled the Jury, who were too eafily impos'd upon. Now, though the Government is not fo much to be blamed in this Coroner's Inqueft, (which Inqueft by the way, in all refpects can never be juftified) yet as to the Governments ftanding by this Inquifition, as what was to remain (like the Laws of the *Medes* and *Perfians*) without alteration: This is what all the World juftly condemns it for. You can't but be fo much a Lawyer and Hiftorian, as to know that the Coroner's Inqueft is not conclufive and final, but may be contradicted, and almoft dayly is; fometimes the Coroner's Inqueft finds Men to have died of a natural Diftemper, which after appear to have been barbaroufly Murdered. To give you one Inftance for many, Sir *Thomas Overbury* (whofe Cafe, in fome refpects, runs parallel with this) was by the Coroner found to have died a natural Death; but as foon as that Faction, which had treacheroufly Murdered him, declined in their Intereft, it appeared this unfortunate Gentleman was treacheroufly Murdered by others. When this Murder of Sir *Thomas Overbery* was firft detected, King *James* the Firft was far from thinking the Profecution of that Murder a Reflection on the Government, though there was the fame reafon in Law for that, as this, feeing in that the Gentleman died in the Cuftody of the Law, and the Coroner found the Perfon to have died of a natural Death, and in this a *Felo de fe*. Now feeing the Contradiction of the Coroner's Inqueft, was the Foundation of Mr. *Braddon*'s Information, there was the very fame ground for the like Profecution of thofe that did detect Sir *Thomas Overbury*'s Murder; but inftead of profecuting the Profecutor, King *James* the Firft, at *Royfton* laid the higheft Injunction imaginable on all the Judges, diligently and impartially to profecute this Murder; for in the midft of his Judges (his Lords and Gentlemen then likewife furrounding him) he ufed thefe words, *My Lords the Judges, It's lately come to my hearing, that you have now in Examination a bufinefs of Poyfoning. Lord! in what a moft miferable condition fhall this Kingdom be (the only Famous Nation for Ho'pitality in the World) if our Tables fhould become a Snare, as none could eat without danger of Life, and that Italian Cuftom fhould be introduced amongft us! Therefore, my Lords, I charge you, as you will anfwer it at that great and dreadful day of Judgment, that you examine it ftrictly, without Favour, Affection or Partiality; and if you fhall fpare any Guilty of this Crime, God's Curfe light on you and your Pofterity; and if I fpare any that are found Guilty, God's Curfe light on me and my Pofterity for ever.* Such was His then Majefties great Zeal for the Detection and Punifhment, and his juft Abhorrence of this treacherous Murder, which he then expreffed upon the firft difcovery of that barbarous perfidioufnefs. But this Cafe is under much higher Aggravations; for

That Gentleman was only charged (and that in truth) with a refusal of the King's Command, in not going on that Honourable Embassy, which would have been both for his Honour and Safety; so that his was a Sin only of Omission. But this Noble Lord was maliciously and falsly accused of the Blackest Treason, *viz. Conspiring the Death of the King*, &c.

That Gentleman's Reputation was not murdered with an Imputation of Self-murder: But

This Honourable Peer was murdered both in Person and Reputation, and by the Perjury of the most perfidious Varlets, corrupting the Law, they villainously transferred the Guilt from those really Criminal, and placed it on him whom they had before (by their privity and consent) treacherously and barbarously Murdered.

That Gentleman's Murder center'd in himself. But the Murder of this Honourable Person was immediately appli'd to the Murdering of another Honourable Lord, whom they were then (by their Instruments not so much corrupted with Malice as blind Obedience) villainously haranguing out of his Life, under form of Law and colour of Justice; and many more since murdered to avoid a Detection of this their first most cruel and barbarous Treachery. Justice zealously espoused the Prosecution of that worthy Gentleman's Murder; but Justice here became Corrupted and Retrograde; for instead of encouraging, and Prosecuting the Murderers, it discouraged, prosecuted and ruined the Prosecutor. That Food which should have sustained the Natural Man, was tainted with a natural, poysonous Composition, and became (or at least was there designed, for he was stifled between the Pillows, and died not of the Poison) the means of that worthy Knight's Destruction: But Justice (which supports the Moral Man) was here twice vitiated; first by Perjury and Treachery in those vile perfidious Caitiffs before the Coroner; and the second time by Perjury (in the same cruel Miscreants in the Kings-Bench Court) at Mr. *Braddon*'s Tryal; and the then bare-faced Wresting of Justice thorough the irreconcileable Malice of the Chief Author of this Murder, and the groundless and illegal Prosecution, Conviction and Punishment of him, who did endeavour by proper legal Methods, to detect this hellish complicated Villany. I shall follow this Comparison no farther, but appeal to all the World, whether the latter of these two Murders, is not aggravated with far higher Circumstances than the former. And as Justice, after some time, overtook those that perpetrated that treacherous Cruelty, so I doubt not but God in Justice will shortly bring to condign Punishment, some, though not all of those concerned in this not to be parallel'd piece of barbarous Cruelty.

L. The hard measure Mr. *Braddon* met with, was more to deterr him and others from this Prosecution, than to punish him for what he had done.

T. That I believe; and my Lord Keeper *North*, who wanted not Words and plausible Insinuations, upon all occasions, represented to Mr. *Braddon*, the great Danger such Practices would bring upon him: To which it was answered by that Gentleman, *That he hoped he had done nothing therein, but what he could answer to God and his own Conscience; and* ● *the Danger, he did not fear, for he did hope that neither Danger nor Death should deter him in the way of his Duty, in which he could as chearfully depart this Life at* Tyburn *in a Halter, as in his Bed of a Fever.*

L. I believe Mr. *Braddon* did not expect to be very kindly received by the then Court.

T. He had no reason to believe he should by them be made very welcome, and he was so told by many of his Friends, which therefore disswaded him from proceeding. But to such he did generally give such answers, *viz. That he could not but expect what they did seem to fear would befall him, nevertheless it should not deter him ; for should none in this case move, the same Bloody Principles that took off that unfortunate Lord, might Poison*

Poison a second, Stab a third, and Strangle a fourth, &c. of those they then had or should take into Custody, pretending (as they falsly did in this Case) that these unfortunate Gentlemen thus barbarously Murdered, had done it to prevent the common Methods of Justice, which their Guilt threatned them with; so that no Man could tell in how many Mens Destruction such their treacherous and bloody Practices would determine; but if once they found that these their dark Designs were suspected, and some of them like to be detected, they might then conclude these clandestine, perfidious, complicated Murders (in Person and Reputation) would do them great prejudice (by raising up in all Mankind a general Averson against those blood-thirsty Men) and therefore they might desist from such barbarous unheard of Measures. And seeing by such Service as this, the Publick would receive far greater Advantage than could be expected by this Gentleman's Liberty; he was resolved to Sacrifice that, or whatever else he had, for the good of his Generation, to whose Interest he thought any Individual was obliged to offer up his private Advantage or Safety. Neither did he believe this to be any other than what he was taught implicitely, by that Doctrine which obliged him to love an individual Neighbour as himself; and therein taught, that much more than Self-love ought that Love to be, which he did owe to so many Millions of such Individuals. I have often heard this Gentleman (when he first engaged) say, That he looked upon the World as an Army, where the bad were still endeavouring the Destruction of their contrary. Now if a General of an Army command a Party of Men to a Post, by the maintaining whereof a certain time, this Party perceive they shall (in all Humane Probability) give Success to their Army; but after their thus maintaining their Post, they shall (in as great probability) fall Sacrifices to the Fury of their Enemies, neither of this Party (though thus assured they shall every Man fall) ought to desert his Post, because every Individual Soldier, or any particular Party, is obliged to prefer and desire the Success of their whole Army, before their private Preservation and Safety. If therefore that Providence, which is the General of all Mankind, should call a Person to that Service wherein he might prove extreamly useful to his Generation, such Service he ought not to desert, though thereby (through the oppression of the Times) he was morally assured he should, in his private Interest and Safety, fall a Sacrifice to the Oppressor; because Self-interest is not to be preferred before the Good of so many Thousands.

L. May all Their Majesties Soldiers be ever influenced by such Considerations, and their Enemies possessed with, and practice the quire contrary Principles.

T. Another Argument of the backwardness (in this case) of the then Government, (and of *Bomeny*'s Guilt in this Murder) is an account which follows, *viz.* About six Weeks after my Lord's Death, there was a Letter (unsealed) left with one Mr. *Cadman*, then living in *Durham-Exchange*; the Letter was directed to the Right Honourable the Countess Dowager of *Essex*; the Substance of this Letter was, That *if her Honour could prevail with the King for the Author's Pardon, he would ingeniously make a full Discovery, how, by whom, and whose order my Lord was Murdered; and this Letter did assure her Honour, that the Duke of* York *and ——— ——— were authorizing this Murder.*
This Letter subscribed   P. B.

L. Who do you believe to be the Author of this Letter?

T. By the Hand that writ it, and the Letters subscribed, it was *Paul Bomeny* before mentioned (who did once Blasphemously say, That *he could as well tell how my Lord came by his Death, as God Almighty himself*) for the Letter was very fairly writ, in a Hand between a *Roman* and an *Italian*, and such an Hand *Bomeny*, when he would write fair, did write; besides, the Letters subscribed, are the Letters of his Name.

G. Can it be supposed that *Bomeny* would write either in his own Hand, or subscribe his own Name, when the Letter, had it been

been brought in Accusation againſt him, would have coſt him his Life, ſeeing herein he confeſſed himſelf Guilty of the Fact.

T. I think *Bomeny* by this Letter, could it have been proved to be his own Writing, was in no danger at all of being puniſhed; for had they hereupon ſeized *Bomeny*, they would have catched a *Tartar*; ſhould they have proceeded againſt him for this Murder, upon this Confeſſion, the World would have believed the whole Contents of this Letter to be true, and conſequently that the Duke of *York* and ——— authorized (or rather) commanded this moſt treacherous Murder. And then pray conſider what that Government would have got by ſuch a Proſecution, Conviction and Puniſhment?

G. What was done with this Letter?

T. This Letter was left with *Cadman* when he was at his Shop within-ſide of the Counter, and very ſleepy; and when he waked, finding this Letter unſealed, he opened it, and perceiving the Contents to be of that Conſequence, he carried the Letter to a Juſtice of Peace, who did promiſe to carry this Letter to the Secretary of State; but this Bookſeller was never ſent for, and examined whom he did ſuppoſe to be the Author of this Letter.

L. By the backwardneſs of the then Government, in not examining into this Matter, it's plain they were too well ſatisfied in the truth of the Contents, which was of ſuch a Nature, as it could not bear an Inquiſition, which would have center'd in his Ruine, who was then by Blood and Cruelty, and other illegal Methods, endeavouring the Subverſion of our Laws, Liberties and Religion: And this by the removal of ſome of the Chief of thoſe Noble Lords and Gentlemen, who had ever oppoſed their Arbitrary and Popiſh Deſigns; amongſt which this Noble Lord, and my Lord *Ruſſel*, they did eſteem two of the Chief.

T. Had they been willing this Murder ſhould have been detected and puniſhed, with what Diligence would they have ſearched out the Author, who deſired no other reward, than the Security of his Life; and in order to his Indemnity (if they could not have otherwiſe found him out) a Pardon would immediately by Proclamation have been iſſued forth, by which the Author would have been aſſured of his Life; and then, without doubt, according to his promiſe, would have laid open this bloody Deed of Darkneſs. Hath this Age ever known, or ſeen Recorded, any Murder (admit this one) committed within this Kingdom, that hath been (in all Circumſtances conſidered) of greater Conſequence than this? We have ſeen a reward of 200 *l.* (as well as a Pardon) by Proclamation offered for the Diſcovery of thoſe bloody Ruffians, who barbarouſly Wounded, but deſigned to have Murdered, that Worthy Gentleman Mr. *Arnold*; and was there not 500 *l.* and a Pardon, by Proclamation, promiſed to him or them that ſhould detect the Murder of Sir *Edmund-bury Godfrey*? Such means as theſe would have been likewiſe in this caſe uſed, if ſuch who then miſled *Charles* the Second, and corrupted the State, had not been the deepeſt in this black Contrivance.

G. This Letter, I perceive, mentions ſome other beſides His Highneſs; Pray, who was elſe named?

T. In this I deſire your Pardon; but of the Name and Perſon you may hereafter hear.

G. Sir, I deſire to know nothing but what you are very free to tell.

T. Some things are not convenient to be ſpoken of, till a more convenient Seaſon.

G. I ſhall preſs to know nothing which may diſſerve this Diſcovery by being divulged. What Religion was this *Bomeny*? I have been informed he was a very good Proteſtant, and one that my Lord had a great kindneſs for. It's much this Fellow (if a Proteſtant) could be prevailed with to connive at ſo Horrid a piece of Cruelty.

T. Bomeny's Religion was (like many other Mens) to be managed and changed in ſhew, according to his Intereſt, but
cordially

cordially I do believe him still a Papist. Whatsoever opinion my Lord might have of this Fellow, as to his Faithfulness, I am very well satisfied this Villain was engaged (before my Lord was brought from his Country-house) in this treacherous Murder; for as my Lord was in the Custody of the Guard, and bringing through *Watford*, when all my Lord's other Servants, and even the whole Town were in Tears for his Lordship's Trouble, this *Judas* rid smiling, and talking of *French* with some of the Guards.

L. In hopes, that within some short time he should receive more for his Perfidiousness, than his Service might expect in many years: But these Gains were his greatest Loss; for what more ready way (could he have taken) to Destruction (here I don't say, against that he was secure enough, but) hereafter? and *what would it profit* this Varlet, *to gain the World, and lose his own Soul?*

T. As for his Religion, you may conclude it belonged to that Church, whose Garments are dipped in the Blood of the Saints; and that this Fellows Religion was really such (tho in appearance he seemed otherwise); may reasonably be concluded from this Story, of which I have been credibly Informed. The Protestant Minister where *Bomeny* lived in *France*, after my Lord's Death, prest *Bomeny* very earnestly to deal ingeniously in this Case; for the Minister declared, he was very well satisfied my Lord of *Essex* was Murdered, and he was well assured that *Bomeny* must know it; therefore the Minister protested he was not free that *Bomeny* should come to Church, much less, be admitted to the Blessed Sacrament, till in this matter he had discharged himself. *Bomeny* finding himself thus pressed by his Minister, thought it best openly to profess what he was, and the very next day declared himself a Papist.

L. That Priest to whom he should confess this Murder, would be so far from enjoyning him a Penance, that he would commend this action, as Meritorious.

T. It was indeed for the Advancement of that Church, (so often drunk with the Blood of the Martyrs, and) the Stones of which Church are Cemented with the Blood of the Saints.

G. Then this traiterous Varlet, who betrayed the best of Masters, was only in shew a Protestant, that thereby he might have the better opportunity of serving a Church, which did ever by bloody means advance its Interest.

L. It's very probable, this vile perfidious Fellow was a constant Spy upon my Lord; but when that Service was to have an end by the Destruction of his Person, then was this barbarous Villain to finish his treachery in being Privy to the most astonishing Piece of complicated Cruelty; and after that, to Crown and Conceal this cursed Butchery, Perjury was to be added, so that this Murder might be laid to my Lord's own Charge, as well to destroy this Honourable Lord's Reputation, as to protect those cruel Miscreants, who had before perfidiously Murdered his Person.

G. Sir, I am very glad you have thus given Mr. *Bomeny*'s Character; for I am very well satisfied that an Eminent Doctor (for whom I am sure you have a very great Reverence) believes quite otherwise of this Fellow; for I have heard the Doctor give this *Bomeny* a very good Character, (which I do suppose he had only by Information); and by what Relation this fellow did give the Doctor, he was strongly perswaded that my Lord did it himself; tho I am sure no Man would be more readily convinced upon good Ground, than this Doctor would; neither would any living be more zealous in a just Prosecution, if once he had good Grounds to proceed upon, which I can now soon furnish him with, and Answer those very Objections which so much influenced the Doctor to a disbelief of my Lord's being treacherously Murdered; and one of his Reasons for the Self-murder, was this, on after my Lord's Death, Mr. *Bomeny* treacherous Villain, of whom I cannot with Patience) gives the Doctor this unt, *That his Lord did use to be taken with a frenzical Passions, and in particular, one that Morning just before his Death: said this vile Judas, As soon as my Lord my Lord Russel go to his Tryal, he struck reast, and said, himself was the cause of my Russel's Misery, seeing he had vouched for Gentleman, whose Treachery would prove my Russel's Ruin, &c. and hereupon fell al-Distracted.* But I perceive this Story is ely forg'd. For the Jury here swear, this very Fellow to them, the next day my Lord's Death, upon Oath declared, *ord was as chearful, (and the Night before, n hearty a Supper) as he did ever see him Life.* And gives them no Account of reacherous Forgery, nor any thing like ut all in Contradiction to it. This ap- by his first Oath.

It's very probable at Mr. *Braddon's* l, he would have forgot this part of esson, had not the Attorney General ther out of any ill Design, or accord- o Mr. *Burton's* false Instruction, I know put him in mind of this particular; when Mr. Attorney said, *Did you observe Lord Melancholly, Mr. Bomeny?*

Without doubt Mr. *Bomeny* under- l what Answer he was to give to this tion.

Yes: And followed not the truth, but art, tho very imperfectly) his Instru- s. For *Bomeny* said, *Yes, he was Melan-* ; but we took no notice of it, for he se to be so, and we had no reason to ect any thing more than ordinary.

Observe now how different, or rather radictory this Answer is to that Rela- this perjured Villain gave this Doctor; both destroyed by that Account, he Oath (the very next day after my l's Death) gave the Jury; for he then re his Lord was very chearful; had the tion given the Doctor been true, how would *Bomeny* to this Question have n it in answer; and what an Harangue thereupon would my Lord Chief Justice at this Tryal have made?

G. I am very well satisfied the Doctor will soon be convinced of the falseshood of that Relation, which *Bomeny* (as before) gave him, when he doth once find that it stands in Opposition to what he hath twice deposed.

L. Whosoever this Doctor be, of whom you give so good a Character, if he shall pretend to believe the Account *Bomeny* gave him, when it thus stands in Contradiction to those Relations *Bomeny* hath twice given upon Oath; he is not deserving of that fair Character, but may justly be suspected as one prejudiced in this Matter against the truth, which maugre all Opponents, will one day (and that speedily) shine through all Clouds of Opposition, which the Malice and Oppression of some, and Impudence of others, have raised against. But blessed be God, as 'tis the Duty, so it hath been the Practice of this Government to incourage this Prosecution.

T. Let the Doctor but reconcile the several Contradictions of *Bomeny's* Informations given the Coroners Jury, and at Mr. *Braddon's* Tryal before at large observed, and I will (then reject all other Evidence, and) believe with the Doctor, That my Lord did indeed cut his own Throat; but till then, I must beg this Doctor's Pardon, if in this matter I will not admit of his belief, as a Rule for mine.

L. I do very much wonder that this Reverend Doctor should in the least be influenced by what this Bloody Rascal told him; for that's allowing a Villains being Evidence in his own Case, which no Law will admit in Opposition to what is Sworn. Now, seeing this false Fellow was to lay the Murder at my Lord's Door, or take it upon himself, either as Privy to it, or Acting in it: I think his ~~~~~~ ought scarce to be received *De bene esse*, as the Lawyers term it, that is, to be believed, or disbelieved, as upon farther Inquiry it shall seem to deserve Credit.

& If

S. If all these Contradictions, before obferv'd, between *Bomeny, Munday* and *Ruſſel*, had appeared to the Coroners Inqueſt, they ought upon theſe only to have quitted my Lord from that perfiduous imputation of Self-murther, and laid it at the door of thoſe Treacherous and Cruel Men, who, by their Perjury (which ſo plainly appeared in theſe groſs Contradictions) villanouſly and falſly charged his Lordſhip with it.

T. In the Hiſtory of *Suſanna* it's related, *That* Daniel *ſtanding in the midſt of the People,* ſaid, *Are ye ſuch fools, ye ſons of* Iſrael*, that without examination or knowledge of the truth, ye have condemned a Daughter of* Iſrael*?* verſe the 48*th.* The People had received the Accuſation of the Elders, whoſe Qualifications gave no ſmall credit to their Evidence; for it's ſaid (verſe the 41*ſt*). *The Aſſembly believed them as thoſe that were the Elders and Judges of the Land.* Nevertheleſs, *Daniel* juſtly condemned the Aſſembly, for pronouncing raſh Judgment without examination, or knowledge of the Truth. In this Caſe an Accuſation was not to be admitted for truth without ſtrict examination of the matter; and ſuch ſcrutiny was proper, as was a-part, ſo that one might not hear the relation of the other, and thereby be enabled to agree in their Evidence, which, without doubt, they would, had they been examined together. If the Teſtimony of theſe two Elders were to be throughly ſifted by a ſtrict, judicious and ſeparate Examination, how much rather the Relation of *Bomeny* and *Ruſſel* in this Caſe? for in that it did not appear (any other ways than by the defence of the Accuſed) that there was the leaſt malice in the Accuſers, or that their Intereſt, much leſs their Lives (before the Charge) depended on the truth of the Fact, for theſe Elders had ſuffered nothing by *Suſanna*'s Innocence provided they had not falſly and maliciouſly teſtified againſt her. But here it was plain to every man's underſtanding, that theſe two Mens (*Bomeny*'s and *Ruſſel*'s) very Lives lay at ſtake; for moſt certain it is, That ſuch as were in the Chamber, and kept the Chamber-door, (the Chamber not being above 14 foot ſquare,

and no other way in or out) muſt be either acting in, or privy to this Barbarity, if ſuch it were; for this very reaſon this Coroner and Jury ſhould have been very inquiſitive and ſcrutinous in their Interrogations, and taken all care poſſible, that the one ſhould not have heard, or been informed of the Examination of the other; by which they would have found theſe two in greater incoherences and contradictions, (if poſſible) than they are now guilty of.

G. Indeed, it's a great wonder they did not agree in every particular, conſidering how fair, or rather favourable, the Coroner and Jury were to them.

T. In the Hiſtory of *Suſanna*, you find in the Charge, not the leaſt incoherence, beſides one Contradiction, and that only as to the place where: but,

In this Caſe, how many, and how notorious Inchoherences and Contradictions have been obſerved in ſeveral reſpects? and therefore how much more rational is it to conclude, as the Aſſembly did in that Caſe (verſe the 61*ſt*) *That theſe Witneſſes are convicted out of their own mouths,* by thoſe many, and thoſe ſo very notorious oppoſitions in their Teſtimonies?

G. In the Contradictions of theſe Sinners there is a clear diſcovery of their Sin, and may they receive the juſt fruits of this their Treachery, which ſo plainly appears by the many oppoſitions in their Relations.

L. I muſt confeſs, I never ſaw ſo ſhort an Account thus cramm'd with Contradictions. I do find the common Obſervation is herein verified, (*viz.*) *The contradiction of Sinners is the diſcovery of Sin:* and, I think, no impartial man, who ſhall hear theſe Contradictions, but muſt be ſatisfied neither of theſe ſpoke true; and he that, through the exceſs of his Charity, (for theſe three Villains, or their Maſter) or his Folly, or rather ſomewhat of a worſe and different nature from either, ſhall in Coffee-Houſes, and other publick Places, make it his buſineſs to weed out theſe Contradictions, to reconcile theſe three Mens Relations in the main, ſo that my Lord may ſtill be

M thought

thought a Self-murderer, and yet at the same time object against my Lord's being Murdered from every Colour of incoherence (in cafe any had happen'd, which I believe there hath not, tho about Sixty in this Cafe have been Sworn) in the Evidence to prove my Lord's Murder. I say, whosoever appears thus Partial, gives great Cause to be thought and censured as very Corrupt, and one whose Zeal is greater for the chief Author of this Murder, and his bloody Party, than for either Truth or Justice. But to return to this Reverend Doctor, of whom you were speaking.

Can the Doctor think that this Fellow, who was immediately attending upon my Lord at the time of his Death, and hath (as before plainly appears by their Contradictions) with two others, forged a Story to transfer their own, and others Guilt upon his Head, whose Throat they barbarously Cut, or permitted to be Cut; I say, How can this Reverend Doctor now give the least dram of Credit to this perfidious Fellow?

G. Sir, I do assure you, I shall (as in Justice bound) do the Memory of this Honourable, but unfortunate Lord, what Justice lies within my Power; and in particular, shall endeavour rightly to inform this Learned Doctor with the whole State of the Case; and if once he be convinced, as he can't but be, if he believe what is herein Sworn, and so strongly confirm'd; his belief will soon draw many Proselytes. But I do admire Mr. *Billingsly*, this unfortunate Lord's Steward, should seem to disbelieve it.

T. This Gentleman of whom you now speak, hath great reason from what himself knows, to believe my Lord was Murdered.

G. What Reason in particular, I pray, Sir?

T. From what *Bomeny* told this Gentleman, he might safely draw that Conclusion; for Mr. B. the *Sunday*, or *Monday* after my Lords Death, asking *Bomeny* how long my Lord lay Dead, before he was known to be Dead; he declared, above two hours; upon which Mr. *Billingsly* (as he justly might) was very angry with *Bomeny* for leaving my Lord so long alone. Now, by comparing this Relation to what was Sworn, he must have found it a point-blank Contradiction; for *Russell* deposed, it was not half an hour from the time of the Razor's being delivered by *Bomeny*, to the time of their finding my Lord Dead in his Closet; so the one Swore it was not half an hour; and the other said, that it was above two hours (and this declared within two days after the Fact, and so may be supposed to be fresh in his Memory); it's plain, that one of these two was false in his Information; and seeing these Mens Ralations were to acquit themselves, as well as charge my Lord; it might be reasonably concluded that both were false, and all forged, as it now plainly appears by comparing these Mens Relations (so full of Contradictions) together.

G. I have Reason to believe, That the Right Honourable the Countess *Dowager* of *Essex* hath been extreamly deceived by what this Mr. *Billingsly* informed her Honour; for I have been told, that this Gentleman pretended to the Countess, that the very Night before my Lord's Death, he being with his Lord, his Lordship seemed extreamly disordered in his Mind; and he took the more notice of it, by his commanding him to sit down and drink a Glass of Wine with him, which made *Billingsly* believe his Lordship was somewhat crazed; and therefore he was inclined to think what he was sorry to say, (*viz.*) *That my Lord committed that Violence on himself*. If this report be false, Mr. *B.* ought to vindicate himself, and therein clear his Lord from this Suspicion of being delirious.

T. Sir, I have little reason to give Credit to what this Steward saith, seeing (as I was informed by one of the Family) he made Oath before my Lord *Sunderland*, *That he did believe my Lord did destroy himself*; whether this be true, I know not; but of this I am very well assured, That this Mr. *Billingsly*

(83)

Billingſly (tho he hath got ſo many thouſands by this Family) would not in the leaſt engage with Mr. *Braddon* in this Proſecution; nay, at laſt, was ſo far from it, that he did refuſe to ſee Mr. *Braddon*, pretending that he did believe Mr. *Braddon* was a Court-Engin, uſed by the Court, for the further Ruin of that Honourable Family (whoſe Misfortunes were before greater than could well be born) ſo that the Court might have a farther opportunity to Proſecute and Ruin the Survivors of his Unfortunate Lord. This was the Subſtance of this Gentleman's Suggeſtion.

L. For this Suggeſtion, Mr. *Billingſly* had not the leaſt Colour; and I do believe this he declared only to avoid being thought backward in that Proſecution, which the higheſt degree of both Juſtice and Gratitude obliged him to engage in. Tho this Mr. *Billingſly*, by this Honourable Family had well feathered his Neſt, his Gratitude was not ſuch, as in Service to (the Memory of his Murdered Lord, and his Honourable Relations then ſurviving) to hazard any part of the Eſtate he had got under them; and that he might not be thought ingrateful, he buried his Ingratitude in the Blood of his Lord, by falſe, diſingenuous, and baſe Inſinuations.

T. If Mr. *Braddon* was the late Courts Inſtrument, I am ſure he was very ingratefully ſerved, to be ſo violently Proſecuted, unjuſtly Convicted, and Sentenced to his perpetual Impriſonment; for ſuch would it have been to him, had it not been for this providential Deliverance.

L. There are a ſort of People (ingrateful as they are!) that will Sacrifice the Honour of their greateſt Benefactors, rather than themſelves ſhould be thought ingrateful. And of this ſort are many, that have been preferred by this Great, but Unfortunate Lord; for I have heard of few that were imployed under him, that would heretofore in the leaſt ſeem to countenance this Proſecution: But I think my ſelf bound (in Juſtice) to vindicate one (in particular) from being thought ingrateful to the Memory of his Murdered Lord. The Gentleman I now ſpeak of, is one Mr. *E.* who in the worſt of times hath gratefully endeavoured to reſcue the Honour of his Lord from falling under this falſe Imputation of Self-murder; and as I have heard Mr. *Braddon* often declare, was very ready to aſſiſt him in any thing, when this Murder was firſt Proſecuted.

T. Your naming this Honeſt Gentleman, puts me in mind of one particular, which I have heard him often aver, the Truth whereof I do not doubt, and this Truth ſeems to deſtroy that great Objection, That my Lord was afraid he ſhould according to his (pretended) Guilt be brought to Condign Puniſhment, for the avoiding whereof he laid violent Hands on himſelf; this was (as before obſerved) often (in effect) ſaid at my Lord *Ruſſell*'s Tryal, and likewiſe at ſeveral other times. The Story is this, When my Lord *Shaftsbury*, my Lord *Howard*, &c. were laſt Committed, this Gentleman, one of General Converſation (having heard the Court deſigned likewiſe to Commit my Lord of *Eſſex* and to take off many in form of *Law* or rather that which they falſely called ſo); went to his Lordſhip, and informed him of what he had been told, and humbly ſubmitted it to his Lordſhip's Judgment, whether it were not proper for ſome time to withdraw, till the Fury of the Court by time was a little appeaſed; this Gentleman told his Lordſhip, *He found by the Papiſts, that they did deſign to deſtroy ſeveral, and his Lordſhip being to their Arbitary and Popiſh Deſigns, as great and profeſt an Enemy, as any, he did fear his Lordſhip might not be ſafe from their pretended Juſtice, when within their Power.* My Lord hereupon ſmiled, and ſaid very ſedately, and yet very reſolutely, *That he would not ſtir, tho he did expect the Court would proceed very far, not only to the Impriſoning, but againſt the Lives of many; and if God in his Providence ſhould think fit to ſuffer him to fall a Sacrifice to the Rage and Maliſe of the Court, he did hope; and did not doubt, but the World ſhould ſee that he could dye with as great Reſolution as ever his Father did; for he was ready at all times, and upon all occaſions, to lay down his Life for his Country.*

M 2   *L.* This

(84)

L. This was his Lordship's true Character, and this the Popish faction was well satisfied in, therefore they dar'd not bring him to his Tryal; for should they either by false Witnesses have proved that which really was Treason against him, or by wresting the Law in Bench, Council and Jury, (which were then more led by the Dictates of *White-Hall*, than the Judgment of *Westminster-Hall*, in the Case of Treason) have adjudged that Treason, which the Law never made or designed to make so, as they did in the Case of the Honourable Lord *Russel*, and some others; I say, should they have thus proceeded, his Lordship's Courage in all probability, would have been such in a bold Defence, that his Enemies would have rather lost, than gained by his Death; besides, had my Lord been really Guilty of Treason, his Lordship had reason to presume upon the King's Mercy, seeing his Father sacrificed his Life in that King's Service; wherefore his then Majesty (as is said) declared, *He wondred the Earl should destroy himself, seeing he owed him a Life.*

T. If that King was (as my Lord Chief Justice *Scroggs* told Mr. *Coleman*) *Merciful, even unto a Fault*, sure he would have extended Mercy to him, whom in ingratitude he was bound to spare; for his Justice in this case would have render'd him as ingrateful as his Mercy (too often shewed to the greatest Criminals) render'd him in some measure culpable, seeing by his sparing so many, who had more than once Forfeited their Lives to Justice, he gave (or at least some, by their repeated Presumptions, did so construe it) a sort of Impunity and Encouragement to Vice; for as *Solomon* observes, *Because* Justice *against an evil work is not executed speedily, therefore the heart of the sons of men is fully set in them to do evil,* Eccl. 8. 11.

G. There is one Objection which I designed to have mentioned before, but forgot; it's probable you can give me truer Information in this particular, than I have met with, for I perceive I have been very much misinformed.

T. In any particular (convenient to be told) I will give you what Information I can.

G. The Story is this: About five Months since, I was very positively told, that the Right Honourable the Countess Dowager of *Essex*, desired several Honourable Lords (some of which were of this Committee) and one worthy Gentleman, to meet at her House, where she spoke to them to this Effect: *My Lords, I have desired this Favour of your Lordships, in order to my own Vindication, which in Self-justice I think my self bound to do, though I am very sorry for the occasion. My Lords, I do understand I am traduc'd (out of Malice in some, and Indiscretion in others) as a Woman that hath sold the Blood of an Husband; and by a Non-prosecution tacitly consent to his Death. My Lords, It's no pleasure, but a great Grief to me, to say any thing which may seem in the least to reflect upon the Memory of my Lord; and I could heartily wish there were not this just occasion offered; Just I say, with respect to my self, and to my Honour, much dearer than my Life; for should I suffer my self to lye under this unjust Scandal, without a just Self-vindication, by such my silence, I should make this dishonourable Calumny become currant and credible. My Lords, My Non-prosecution of my Husband's Death is my Charge; to which I have this to say, That was I well satisfied my Lord's Blood was treacherously spilt, I did deserve this Censure, and there is none could think so bad of me as I should then of my self, for my long silence. (My Lords) The Reasons which makes me disbelieve my Lords being (by others) Murdered, are such as I could never hear answered, though I am sure I should readily be convinced, and rejoyce in my Conviction; but till then I should think my self little less than a Murderer, to prosecute any for the shedding of that Blood, from the Guilt whereof (I am sorry) I must, in my opinion, acquit all Men living. My Lords, The Reasons which have thus influenced my Belief, and tied my Hands, I have at large communicated to my Lord Bishop of S.* ——— *I have desired to make them known to your Lordships, and your Lordships (being satisfied in my Innocence)*

Innocence) will, I am sure, soon rescue me from the vile Slanders of those Tongues, under the lash whereof I have so undeservedly suffered. My Lords, I shall only add this, That if once these Objections are removed, and I become fully satisfied my Lord was perfidiously Murdered, none living upon the face of the Earth, shall more zealously prosecute the Blood of a murdered Husband than I will this, as in Duty and Honour I shall then stand obliged.

L. And I doubt not but her Honour will zealously Prosecute, as soon as she finds what is here deposed, to prove her Lord treacherously Butchered: Such Evidence there is, that nothing can ballance, but the occular Evidence of the Self-murder, and if there be any such, it's strange we should not long since have heard of the Person: But pray proceed.

G. Upon this, that Learned Bishop, as I have been told, gave a large account, what were the several Inducements that moved the Countess to this Belief; but I could never hear what these Reasons were, but without doubt they were such as had some weight with them, or otherwise they would never have satisfied, not only that Reverend Bishop, but most then present, in the belief of the Self-murder; and so throughly convinced Mr. *H.* who (as I have been told) did second the Bishop, and gave some other Arguments for the same purpose, and seemed concerned, that some of those Honourable Lords appeared to disbelieve the Self-murder.

T. I could never yet hear, but a very imperfect Account, of what my Lord Bishop said; for the chief reason, as I have been told, his Lordship then gave, was what my Lord of *Essex* declared just before his Commitment, when his Lordship (appearing under some disorder and trouble of mind) said, that it was not any personal concern that made him thus troubled, but it was the thoughts of his Family; for he was much troubled to think what would become of them after his death; as for himself, it was the least of his care, For therein he was resolved what to do; several times over repeating (in a seeming despondency) that expression, *As for my self I am resolved what to do* —Now admitting this to be true, that the Earl several times repeated that expression, *As for my self, I am resolved what to do*, is there no other Resolutions but Self-murder to be supposed.

G. Being spoken with such Despondency, it argues the Resolution was desperate.

T. It's very natural for love to fear the worst, and to apply such Fears accordingly, now her Honour being startled with these often Repetitions, upon hearing of her Lord's death, might suppose that such had been her Lord's Resolutions, which gave Birth to those repeated Expressions: But whereas it's said my Lord spoke it in a sort of Despondency, it's probable that her Honour might mistake his Lordship's undaunted Courage (which with a higher assistance, kept him above the fear of what the Power and Malice of his greatest Enemies could inflict) for Desparation. This, to me, seems the most likely, considering what his Lordship had before declared, *viz. That he did expect the Court would not only Imprison, but take off several; and if it should be his misfortune to fall a Sacrifice for his Country, to the Court Malice and Rage, the World should see he could dye with as great Resolution as ever his Father did, for he was ready at all times, and upon all occasions, to lay down his Life for his Country.* This Honourable Lord was not ignorant of the Popish and Arbitrary Designs of the Court, and that there were small hopes of any Redress by Parliaments, for such were not suffered to sit when they began to reform our Grievances; and as for the then Judges, they were purely Instruments and Ecchoes to the Corruption of the Court; so that whatsoever *Whitehall* had resolved upon, as fit to be declared Treason in *Westminster-hall*, was declared (not properly adjudged) accordingly; not adjudged, I say, for we found many of them more Knave than Fool, and their Interest corrupted their Consciences, and these their Tongues, to pronounce what their Judgments in the Law could

could not but be satisfied was false, and themselves well knew to be corrupt; wherefore only the last remedy remained, in case the Court proceeded, as there was all reason to believe they would, by such Vile, Illegal, Arbitrary, Popish and Oppressive Methods, to destroy what to every brave true English Spirit is much more valuable than Life (Religion, Liberty and Property I mean.) My Lord of *Essex* had long stood in a true light, wherein he could plainly see the most secret and ultimate end of the Court; and this made him the more resolved to joyn with others, such Patriots as himself, in opposition to those Hellish Plots of St. *James's* (for there indeed lived the true Plotters, which were industriously plotting the total Destruction of our Religion and Liberties, when such true Lovers of their Country, as himself, were designing nothing more than the Preservation of our Laws, which the Corruption of the Bench had in Perjury sold to the Oppression of the Court. But this Bargain was never so plainly proclaimed, as in that Never-too-severely-to-be-punished Judgment, which gave (as far as was within the Power of that perjured Bench) such a Dispencing Power to the Crown, under a necessity (of which necessity the Crown was the sole Judge) as by a natural Consequence dissolved all Law, when a Royal Arbitrary *Ipse Dixit* should so pronounce it: Wherefore (as before observed) we held our Laws, and therein our Religion, Lives and Liberties, as these Forsworn, Mercenary Judges did their Places, *durante bene placito Regis*. Had we in this Lord's days known those Popish and Arbitrary Court-Secrets (which he plainly saw designed our ruine, but no consideration could ever corrupt this Honourable Lord to ingage in those Cursed Cabals) most certainly we should have rescued the Lives of those our best Friends, and not by a corrupt Constructive Treason, have Sacrificed those true Lovers of our Country, for doing of that which we all ought as one Man to have cordially joined in. Had not those brave Patriots, our Church and State Confessors, the most Reverend his Grace, and the Reverend six Bishops, met with an Uncorrupt Jury, which were guided by Conscience, (not imposed upon by the Court, but enlightned with the true State of the Case, as most judiciously, and truly Stated by those their Learned Council in the Law); These Seven Champions for our Laws (and therein for all by them we possess) would most certainly have been offered up by the Bench as Victims of Expiation for that Guilt, which would (in a Court Sense) have robb'd the Crown of its richest Jewel; yea, that Court Philosopher-Stone, (the Dispencing Power) which at pleasure might have turned our Properties, Liberties, yea, Lives, into pure Gold; for the Estates we possess, the Liberty we enjoy, and the Lives we live, we have guarded only (next under God) by our Laws, which this *Leviathan* at once would have swallowed and totally destroyed.

L. When I consider my Lord's declared Resolution of his not stirring, tho then under the like Danger, as in this Case apprehended, and with what Readiness, Courage and Chearfulness, he could lay down his Life for his Country; and likewise, the Knowledg that he may be supposed to have of their Designs (which these Villains, nine days before his Death declared; for it's Sworn they then said, The Earl knew so much of their Designs, and was so very Averse to their Interest, that they could never carry them on, unless his Lordship was taken off, and his Lordship was therefore to be Murdered). I say, when I consider these things, and that the more this Honourable Lord knew of the black Intrigues of the Court, the more so good a Man, and so true a Patriot must be supposed to hate them; I can't but imagine that this brave State-Champion, when he had been once satisfied, that the Court under Colour of Law would have taken him off, had *resolved as to himself*, to lay open those Popish Arbitrary-Court Contrivances, and justified that just Design of standing upon their Guard;

(87)

Guard; there was no other way (under God) to defend what was so grosly invaded. Now, tho his Lordship might suppose by dealing thus plainly, he should the more exasperate the Court, so that their Malice would be more inveterately bent in his Destruction; yet, that he declared, he feared not, but was ready, chearfully, to lay down his life in so just a Cause; and should this daring true lover of his Country have thus expired, by his State-Martyrdom, he would have given such satisfaction in the truth of what he thus couragiously, with his last breath, should have affirmed, as would have raised a general hatred against those Arbitrary and Popish-Court-Resolutions; and this might so suddenly have given another so general a Resurrection to that just Cause, as would have totally routed those our true and only Enemies of both Church and State. Our then Enemies, under colour of Law, were industriously endeavouring the total Subversion of our Laws, and whilst in shew they seemed to maintain the Protestant Church, they were secretly contriving its total Destruction, by wresting those very Laws which were chiefly designed as Destructive to Popery, and making them productive of what they were enacted to destroy; for by a malicious and furious Prosecution of all Protestant Dissenters, they did hope to raise so general Animosities between the Conforming and Non-conforming Protestants, that they might, through such Division, have an opportunity to fulfil that notorious Jesuitical Maxim, *Divide & Impera.*

T. God was pleased not to deliver us, till he had made some sensible of the Danger of that which at a distance they did not so plainly perceive to be hurtful; but Affliction soon made them wise, and convinc'd them of their mistake, and then some of them might truly have said of *Our* Law, what the *Psalmist* did of the *Divine*, *Before* *Psal. 119.* *I was afflicted I went astray, but now have I* *7.* *kept thy word.* The general Danger that threatned all, taught us all, it was our Interest, as well as Duty, to joyn with that (falsly called *unnatural Invasion) which in tender compassion, was undertaken by our present Sovereign, to rescue us from our *true Invaders.

L. Can any imagine, that my Lord's declaring, *As for himself, he was resolved what to do*, could give rise to those many reports in such several and far distant places of the Kingdom?

G. But, which is more plain, I have been informed, his Lordship should, in some cases, justifie Self-murder, and particularly that Action of the Earl of *Northumberland*, who Pistol'd himself in the Tower.

T. As for those Judicious Divines which have been reported to be the men to whom the Earl should justify Self-murther (in some Cases) some of these have declared, *That they never heard any man more strenuously argue against it, (as what was unjustifiable under any consideration) than my Lord hath done.* Nay farther, I have been credibly told, *That when my Lord was Lord Lieutenant of* Ireland, *an Eminent Citizen of* Dublin *cut his own Throat; and his Excellency then declaared, that Citizen ought to be found* Non-Compos mentis; *for it was his Opinion, That no man in his senses did ever cut his own Throat*: But a stronger Argument to me is, what is before at large observed of Major *Hawley*'s suggesting Self-murther (for the avoiding a dishonourable and infamous Death) to be my Lord's fixed Principle; and yet this Gentleman now denies not only this suggestion, but likewise declared, *That he never heard it said to be my Lord's Principle, till their Lordships in this Committee charged him with it.* *Hawley*'s Suggestion to the Jury, I do not doubt, for it's positively sworn against him; but the falsity of the thing suggested is plain from *Hawley*'s now denying it: and that this Story had its rise from the same Malice that contrived his Lordship's Destruction. For had this Principle been true, How readily would *Hawley* have justified it, as of what he had been credibly informed? and how serviceable might he have thought it to prove the Self-murther? But this Gentleman
being

being conscious where this pretended Principle was hatched, and what villanous use he himself (according to Instruction and Order) made of it to the Jury; thought it not safe to justify either his Suggestion, or his having so much as heard it, before my Lord's death, to be his Lordship's Principle: for should he have been forc'd to produce (to him) the Authors of this (pretended) Principle, it would too plainly have appeared, that these his Authors were the Forgers of the Story. But I will for the present admit, what I am well assured you can't credibly prove, That before my Lord's death, his Lordship had declared, *that Self-murther (in some Cases) was lawful*; it doth not from thence inevitably follow, that his Lordship therefore must cut his own Throat; for some have justified the Principle, that never thought fit to put it in practice. I will, for Argument sake, admit yet farther, That *Hawley*'s suggested Principle was true (*viz.*) That the Earl of *Essex* declared he would destroy himself, rather than be brought to a dishonourable and infamous Death; can it be thought, that from this general Resolution (wherein no particular manner of death is declared) all those several previous Reports, before observed, should rise? for (to borrow almost the very words of an Ingenious Author upon this Occasion; *Though they were vented by several persons, yet they not only agreed in the matter of the Earl of* Essex's *Death; but they accorded also in the way, and manner of it, and place where, namely, that he cut his Throat in the* Tower: which plainly shews, that it was not vulgar Tattle, vented at random, but had its foundation in a previous and fixed Resolution, that he should undergo that unhappy Fate, both as to manner and place; nothing but a determinate Cause can produce a steddy and determinate Effect: Had the Report taken its rise in the Jealousies of his Friends, or owed its breath to the fearful Apprehensions of the Common People, they would have rather dreamed of his being poisoned, as being more safe for the Actors to perpetrate, and requiring the accession of fewer hands, than have ever imagined that his Throat should be cut. It's impossible to conceive, that the Reports of so many several Persons should not only agree in the matter of his Death, but all harmonize and center in the very Circumstances and manner of it, and Place where, unless it had originally proceeded from such as had contrived and determined both the Murther it self, and the way wherein it should be committed, and the Place where it should be done. For when Reports have their foundation only in Mens Fancies, they will always vary according to the different Tempers, Passions, and Complexions of the Reporters; how could so many Persons, and at such distances from one another, and betwixt whom there was never any correspondence, agree and combine together to impose upon the World, and to abuse the Faith of Mankind? and as they all seem to be Persons who abhor Tricks, and who would not be guilty of spreading, much less of raising a false Report; so it is beyond the Wit of Man, to declare, how it should come to the Interest of Gentlewomen, Citizens, and Countrey Tradesmen, to be the Authors of such a Story, that my Lord of *Essex* had cut his Throat in the *Tower* before it was done, or before knowledge of his Imprisonment in the *Tower* could arrive at some of these Places, where it was so reported. But that not only the *how*, and *where*, as to my Lord's Death, should be the same in all those Reporters; but the very *wherefore*, two days before his Death, be given, for the having cut his Throat; and *the very same wherefore* that the Papists publickly gave out, and industriously spread just after my Lord's Death: this proves, beyond all doubt, that the Matter was so particularly agreed upon by the Papists, and *this* Reason by them resolved to be given out just after my Lord's Death; it's plain to all, but those that wink hard, that this pretended Reason must be hammered out of the Popish Forge. For this Reason carried in it what none but the most secret in this Hellish. Contrivance could before my Lord's Death give out; for observe, the Reason declares, That the Earl

Earl of *Essex* being Prisoner in the *Tower*, the King and Duke came into the *Tower* to see the *Tower*, of which the Earl having notice, he was immediately afraid the King would have come up into his Chamber, and seen him, *&c.* Now I would willingly know who, besides the most intimately knowing in this matter, could give information two days (*viz.*) the *Wednesday* Morning at *Andover*) before my Lord's death, that the Earl of *Essex* would cut his Throat in the *Tower* when the King and Duke were there, because the King should not see him; the King and Duke's being there was unexpected, and a surprize to all, but to the Men of Secrecy in this Murther, because their being there together was so very rare, that it happened but once in twenty five years. But of this I have already spoken; and also how this so particular a Report, as to the *Manner*, *Place*, and *Reason*, became thus reported in the Countrey so long before my Lord's Death.

L. Was you ever credibly told that his Lordship said he was resolved to destroy himself?

T. No, I never heard that credibly reported.

L. Or, which is more plain and particular, Did his Lordship (before his Imprisonment) say, that he was resolved to cut his Throat in the *Tower*, when the King and Duke should come into the *Tower* to see him, which his guilt and shame could not bear the thoughts of?

G. Certainly my Lord could neither foresee, nor expect that the King and Duke should come into the *Tower*, whilst he was Prisoner there.

L. But you find it depos'd, That before my Lord's Death, (*viz.*) the *Wednesday* at *Andover*: As to his Death, *The manner how, the place where, and the reason wherefore, are assigned*: Now had my Lord so particularly declared his Resolution (in which, by the way, as to the King and Duke's being in the *Tower*, he must have prophesied what could not be expected) then it had been possible, that this, and those several Reports proved by eight Witnesses more (far distant from, and altogether strangers to each other all centering in the *same* manner how, and the place where) might have arisen from this Resolution of his Lordship so particularly declared.

T. It may be, my Lord having heard the Papists had resolved to cut his Throat, was afraid they would (the more to torment him) not do it like themselves, but botchingly (as they cut Mr. *Arnold's*) and therefore that it might be done at a jerk, and all perfectly finish'd at a stroak, he was resolved to do it himself, and did it effectually; for though the Blade of the Razor without the Hand, was not two Inches and a half, he made a Wound about three Inches and half deep (and therein did what by others was Mathematically impossible to be done) and whereas, before that Accident, it was the Opinion of Doctors and Chyrurgeons, that none could cut through both Jugular Arteries to the Neck-bone on both sides the Neck, his Lordship was resolved to give the World demonstration of their mistake; and after all, his Lordship stopt the Orifice from giving issue to such a quantity of Blood and Spirits, as would naturally have instantly killed him; and out of malice to the living, that others might be charged with his Death, threw the Razor out of the Window, and then sent the Maid down for it; which having received from her, he retired to his Closet, lockt himself in, and quietly laid himself down, and the Razor by him, and then gave free passage to that Blood, and those Spirits, which he thus miraculously kept so long in.

G. But to be serious, for this is a Case of grave, yea, very doleful Consideration; did you ever hear all those Reasons the Bishop then gave?

T. No, but I could wish I had; only this further Reason I think was given, (*viz.*) what the Steward said concerning my Lord's desiring him to sit down, and drink a glass of Wine with him the Night before his Death.

L. That

(90)

L. That I do totally disbelieve for the Reasons before mention'd.

T. But whereas you say Mr. *H.* did second my Lord Bishop, I do assure you I did hear that Ingenious Gentleman declare the contrary; and (as a Gentleman told me) desired one to vindicate him from that Report, which he did totally deny.

G. What was then said by the Lords of the Committe after my Lord Bishop had given the Countess's Reasons of her Silence?

T. I have been told (how true it is, I cannot say) that the Right Honourable the Earl of *D.* spake to the Countess to this effect; *Madam, The belief, or disbelief of a fact, neither destroys the Existence, nor alters the Nature of the Fact; and we who are to proceed, not according to* private Opinion, *but* legal Evidence, *have taken the Depositions of many Witnesses in this Case; and unless many of these be villanously perjur'd, (which as yet we have no reason to believe)* my Lord must have been most barberously murthered.

G. Had the Countess, or the Bishop, before this, seen what was sworn?

T. I suppose neither of these had either seen, or been informed what was depos'd to prove this Murther; neither could they then have heard what hath in this Case been depos'd, because many Depositions have been since taken before the Lords, and, since their Lordships Committee was dissolved, before several Justices of the Peace.

G. I cannot but believe, that if the Countess once knew what you have now at large related, her Opinion would soon be changed, and her Zeal in this prosecution would be as great as could be expected from a Lady of her Honour and Quality: and as for my Lord Bishop, I am sure none would be more easily convinced upon such grounds as these, neither would any more zealously ingage in this Prosecution.

T. Of this I doubt not; for no Man can have a greater veneration for this Reverend Father in God, than my self; and I think this happy Revolution is (under God, and His Majesty) not a little indebted to the Inge-nuous and Indefatigable Pen of this Judicious and Learned Bishop.

The next Discouragement I shall mention, was the strict Injunction, with Threats, laid upon many of the Soldiers to be secret in this matter.

J. B. and his Wife, further declare, *That the very next day after my Lord of* Essex's *Death, the aforesaid R. M. told these Informants, how that very morning their Officer called several Soldiers together, and under very severe penalties enjoined them not to speak one word of what they had either seen or heard with relation to the Death of the Earl of* Essex, *and therefore the said M. desired these Informants not to speak one word of what he had informed them (with relation thereunto) the day before, lest it being discovered, he should be severely punished for speaking any thing of this matter.*

L. With what a degree of Impudence was this treacherous Cruelty stifled!

T. R. the Soldier before-mentioned, that very day my Lord was murthered, declared with very great earnestness, *That the Duke of* York *had so barefac'd ordered the matter, that he did believe no man was safe that was not for their Interest, so soon as they began thus (in effect) openly to order cutting of Threats.* This *R.* did further protest, *That his Blood did so boil with indignation against this most Villanous and Barbarous Murther, that could he have got those that would have stood by him, he would have shot the chief Author dead upon the spot.*

L. Altho' this Author did escape the just Indignation of this brave Soldier, yet that Omnipotent Arm (which seldom fails of punishing Blood, even in this World, thus treacherously spilt) in vengeance hath pursu'd him, and (without doubt) the Hell within is ten times worse than the trouble without him; for tho' *the Spirit of a man may bear his Infirmities, a wounded Spirit none can bear:* and certainly a Conscience of flint must be deeply wounded with those self-reflections which so great Guilt must naturally beget.

L. But what is become of these two honest Soldiers.

T. As

T. As for *M.* not long after the Earl's Death, he told *B.* and his Wife, and one *D.* That *he had fallen out with one of the Warders about the said Earl's Death, and the Warder had not courage to fight him; but he did verily believe, and much fear, that he should be basely murthered for what he had spoke concerning the said Earl's Murther, and that very day he did much dread he should be destroy'd*: wherefore he did desire *B.* or *D.* to keep him company that day; but they fearing themselves might be in danger by being in his company, and having work to do, which they were obliged to finish, they both refused it, and the next morning they heard the said *M.* was found dead in the *Tower-Ditch* just over against Major *Webster*'s House.

L. Surely Blood upon Blood must force down Vengeance from Heaven; but what became of *R* ?

T. All the account can be had of him, is this, That not long after the Earl's Death, he was drawn out of the *Tower*, and sent beyond Seas to the *East-Indies*, and there, at some fort, shot to death, but upon what account we cannot learn. I fear several other Soldiers have been murthered, to prevent the discovery of this unheard of piece of Villany; for, as I was not long since discoursing in a Coffee-House, concerning this *M*'s being murthered; A Gentleman told me, That by his Neighbour's Shop-door there stopt three Soldiers a little after *M*'s death; and one looking very melancholly, said, *He did fear he should be murthered (as poor M. was) for speaking somewhat which he knew about the Earl's Death; for he did observe himself dog'd several days by two men (which he did suppose were* Irish-men;) and this Soldier did then desire those his two Fellow-soldiers to take notice of what he had told them; *and if he were missing, and could not be found, they should conclude that he was murthered for this very reason.*

L. Did this Shop-keeper know either of those Soldiers.

T. No; nor did he think it safe to make any inquiry into the matter, left he should fall under such misfortune as had befallen others for medling herein; you can't but find most men are for observing that Maxim *Fœlix quem faciant, &c.* Happy is he whom other mens harms do make to beware.

L. Certainly these things must hasten Vengeance. If that Soldier, who was in this danger, be now living, he may with safety (and I am sure it's his duty) appear, and discover what he knows; or (if with others) he be treacherously murthered, it were well those his two Fellow-soldiers would testify what that poor Soldier had informed them; this in Justice they are bound to do, and there is no danger in doing it; such as now do refuse to testify their knowledge in the Matter, consent to the Blood of the Slain, and one day must expect to answer it.

T. Hawley the Warder intimately acquainted with Major *Hawley*, (at whose House my Lord was murthered) was found dead in the Medways, about *April* next after my Lords death, (having been murthered in a most barbarous manner). This *Hawley* was supposed to be taken off to prevent the discovery of what he knew in this matter; for a little after Mr. *Hawley* was missing, (*viz.*) about a month before he was found dead, a Warder then in the *Tower* (supposed to be a Papist) told Mr. *A. S.* (who had long lain under the pressure of the then misgovernment and then there a Prisoner, without any Evidence to justify the Commitment) *That* Hawley *was run away for prating somewhat about the Earl of* Essex; but how he ran away, a short time discovered.

This *Hawley* was in *Westminster-hall* when Mr. *Bradden* was upon his Tryal; and said, *He much wondered upon what Mr.* Braddon *should stir in this thing, when,* to his Knowledg, *Mr.* Braddon *knew nothing.* A Gentleman, then present, who knew Mr. *Hawley* looked on this Expression, as what argued Mr. *Hawley* not a stranger to the matter; wherefore this Gentleman immediately said, *Mr.* Hawley, *if you know Mr.* Braddon *knows nothing of this matter, what must you then know?* upon which Mr. *Hawley* seemed surprized (having too far expressed himself) and made no Reply.

S. I have been informed by a Warder in the *Tower*, that this Mr. *Hawley*, the Warder, as soon as he heard the News of the Earl's Death, immediately declared *it was a damn'd piece of Roguery throughout.*

T. This Mr. *Hawley* was very rich, and a Warder only to exempt him from Parish Services; but he never waited, unless it were on very solemn Occasions; and that very day my Lord dy'd, he was waiting, and (as declared by several) was one of the Warders that attended on the Person of the Duke of *York*, whilst he was in the *Tower*, that morning the Earl dy'd.

L. If so, he might well observe the Duke's sending the two men to the Earl's Lodgings just before his Death; and their return to his Highness, as Mr. *E.* deposeth; and *M.* and *R.* declared, with several other Passages, which might to him discover that barbarous Murther; and then he had cause enough to say, *it was a damn'd piece of Roguery all over.*

G. Good God, deliver us from such bloody-minded men!

T. Several Reports were as industriously as maliciously spread about Town when Mr. *Hawley* was first miss'd; some to influence people to believe, that this Mr. *Hawly*, through discontent with his Wife, was very melancholly, and had declared, 'twas better to make away with himself, than live such a vexatious life with so turbulent a spirited a Woman; but in this they most grossly abused them both; for no Woman could shew greater respect to a Husband, nor any Husband be more kind to a Wife. Another Report was, That Mr. *Hawley* had often declared, He did really believe, if a man withdrew from his Relations, and Friends, for half a year (and suffered none who knew him to know where he was; but to possess all men by such his concealed absence that he was indeed dead) and then to appear in a surprize amongst his Relations, this great surprize would be as pleasing to the Person that withdrew, as it would be astonishing to his Friends; and therefore it was (pretended to be) believed by some, that Mr. *Hawley* had privately withdrawn under this Consideration; but six Weeks discovered his Person, and time may likewise detect those Bloody and Barbarous Men that murthered him. They were so very cruel in this Murther, that his Face was so changed through violence, that it could not be known to be his; and there was nothing that did more (if any thing did besides) discover the Body to be his, than his having three Stockings upon one Leg, and two Stockings and a Seer-cloath upon the other: as for his Cloathes, they were stript off, and nothing but Stockins and Shooes remaining on when the Body was found.

L. Certainly that God who requires Blood for Blood (and who by this ordered the Discoveries of the Person) will in his great Wisdom and Justice, by some means or other, (of which His Wisdom is never to seek in the choice, or His Power in the use) discover these Instruments of Cruelty, that in this Life they may receive their just Reward, which is for the most part (though sometimes after many years) duly paid towards such vile Offenders.

T. Besides this addition of Blood, other violent Methods were used to prevent a discovery, by punishing such Soldiers as seemed to disbelieve (upon very good grounds) my Lord's Self-murther; this appears by this Information following: *viz.*

Richard Jorden declareth, That (sometime that Summer the Earl of Essex dyed, and not long after the said Earl's Death) *he saw a Soldier ty'd to the Wooden Horse in the* Tower (*by order of Lieutenant-Collonel* Nichols) *and whipt after a very cruel manner.* And this Deponent heard the said Lieutenant-Collonel tell the Soldier *he ought to be hanged.* This Deponent further declareth, *That he was just after informed by the Marshal, that whipt the said Soldier, That by order of Lieutenant-Collonel* Nichols, *he gave the said Soldier* 53 *Stripes (tho' the usual number was but* 12;) *and that the said Soldier had lain a fortnight before in close custody, and been fed only with Bread and Water; and all only for the Offence following (viz.)*
Some

(93)

*Dr. H. of Norfolk, Prebend of Norwich.

Some short time after the Death of the late Earl of Essex, a Divine* coming into the Tower, the said Soldier was sent with him to shew him the Tower; and as the Doctor was almost over against Major Hawley's, the Doctor asked the said Soldier, which was the Chamber wherein the late Earl of Essex did cut his Throat? whereupon the said Soldier (pointing to the Chamber in which the Earl had been Prisoner) declared ; That is the Chamber in which it's said the Earl of Essex cut his Throat ; The Doctor then asked the Soldier, what he did believe? to which the Soldier answered, That he did believe in God ; but being prest by the said Doctor to tell him, whether he did believe my Lord cut his Throat; the said Solder then replied, He would not say he did believe it; for which only saying, the Punishment aforesaid was inflicted.

L. Such Extravagant Punishments upon so slight Grounds, was enough to deter all other Solders from discovering what they knew ; for if this Soldier, for only declaring he would not say he did believe my Lord did cut his Throat, was thus barbarously whipt, what must such Soldiers expect, as should have asserted, my Lord was by others murthered; and gave their Reasons for such belief, by telling what they saw, and heard, with relation to this Perfidious and Cruel Murther; most certain, this would have met with (if possible) worse whipping than Doctor Oates ever suffered, or been punished by some private Stab, or other destruction, to avoid the Matter's being brought upon the publick Stage.

G. I do remember Meake is said to have declared, the day after my Lord's Murther, that many Soldiers were enjoined to secrecy. It were well if these would, according to their duty, appear, and declare what they know, and by whom they were thus basely commanded to be secret ; for this Officer could not but believe, That whoever gave him Orders to lay that Injunction, was privy to the Murther, and therefore this Officer was grosly Criminal in being this Instrument to stifle the detection; and most certainly are those Soldiers Criminal, which

shall not now appear, and judicially declare what they know to be true, so that Justice may have its due course against those most barbarous and vile Offenders. For if the time of this bare-faced Cruelty against such Soldiers that knew any thing of this matter, and revealed it, was *a time of silence* ; most certain, now the Government joins in the Prosecution, *is the time to speak* ; and whosoever refuses now to speak, becomes not a little Criminal in such his silence.

L. I have been informed, the Father of *William Edwards*, was turned out of his Place for what his Son had said.

T. That the Father was turned out about nine days after Mr. *Braddon*'s Tryal, is very true, and this done by special Order, under King *Charles* the Second's own Hand, without any cause shown, or any reason to be guessed at, any other than his Son's Offence.

L. I do remember at Mr. *Braddon*'s Tryal, Mr. *Wallop* (whose Courage and Zeal for the Liberty of the Subject, hath been Notorious in the most dangerous times) did suggest, that the Father thought himself in danger of losing his place, from what his Son had declared. Whereupon my Lord Chief Justice *Jefferies*, very sharply reproved Mr. *Wallop*, for reflecting (in this) upon the Government, as though the Father should be punished for the Son's speaking what he knew. If the suggesting the danger of the Place was a Reflection upon the Government, most certainly the Government did strongly reflect upon its self, in turning Old *Edwards* out, and giving no reason for such Dismission ; which made him conclude, and all the World believe, that the Father was turned out only for his Son's Relation.

T. The old Jewish unjust Proverb was here inverted, for *The Son had eaten sour Grapes, and the Father's Teeth were set on edge*; so that this Transgression (in its punishment) did directly ascend, and the Father answered for the Son's Iniquity or rather for what the then Government falsly called so.

L. I

L. I think every Man's own Transgression is enough for him to bear.

T. I shall conclude all, with what after my Lord's Death passed, as to *Webster* and *Holmes*, which seems to confirm the Truth of their Guilt in this Matter. I shall begin with *Webster*.

The very day of my Lord's Death, *Webster* brought home to his House my Lord's Pocket-handkerchief all Bloody, and shaked it, seeming extreamly overjoyed, saying, *There was the Blood of a Traytor* ; and the very next day, pulls out of his Pocket a Purse of Guineas, and in great Joy shaked it; one of his Neighbours told the Gold, and found there was 49 Guineas, and a French Pistole.

L. I doubt not but he had a much greater reward for so remarkable Service.

T. That without doubt; for this Fellow (which was Under-Baily of the Tower Liberty) immediately puts himself into a Garb much above his Quality, with his Fringe Gloves, either all Gold, or part Gold and part Silk, and all other things answerable thereunto ; and being thus flush with both Gold and Silver, he frequents the Gaming Ordinaries; but his Cloaths, and the quantity of Gold and Silver he then brought, surprized the Company which knew him, and all admired at the sudden Change; for he who before used to play hardly for 10 *s.* at a Sitting, would now throw at ten times so much at a Main ; but his Fortune was so very bad, that it's generally believed he lost at Gaming above 400 *l.* in six Months time next after my Lord's Death: All that knew this Fellow, admired how he came thus supplied with Money, most believed he had used the Pad, for all that were acquainted with him, were satisfied his Principles would act in any thing for his Interest.

' *L.* By what this Fellow gamed away, it's plain the first fifty Guineas was but a small part of his Hire in this Treacherous and Bloody Tragedy ; but it seems his Extravagancy lost what his Villany got by this unheard of piece of Cruelty: So that the old Proverb was herein verified, *Ill got ill spent*.

T. This Fellow, by such his Extravagancy in fine Cloaths, keeping his Gelding, Gaming, Whoring, and almost all that is ill, reduced himself in less than a Twelvemonth, to his former Poverty ; so that one of his Wives Relations was upbraiding her with her Husband's necessity: The Wife replied, *Her Husband not long before was not so poor, for he had 500 Guinea's*: At which the Relation being surprized, told her, *It was impossible for him to have such a Sum by honest means, for his Ale-house, and being under-Baily, could hardly get him Bread.* But his Wife pretended his Trade got it.

G. What Trade, Gaming ?

T. No, she mentioned nothing of Gaming, but his Ale-house-keeping. But that appears to be false, for before my Lord's Death, he could not, out of his Trade, pay his Brewer, but owed him a very considerable Sum, 30 Guinea's whereof he paid just after my Lord's Death ; and the Brewer admired how he came to pay him all in Gold ; but since he hath heard how it's suspected this Money was procured. It seems what Money the Wife received for Beer, this Fellow (without having any regard to the Payment of his Brewer) would take from her, and spend in ill Courses ; and if his Wife refused to give him what she had, he would abuse her, not in words only, but Blows, which made his Wife one time tell him, *That he was a Fool, as well as a Rogue, to use her so ill, when he knew it was within her power to hang him, and one in the Tower* ; once naming (as I have been informed) Major *Hawley* for the Man in the Tower.

L. This Woman was mistaken, for it was not within her Power to touch the Hair of this Fellows Head by her discovery of this Matter, as long as this Villain stood guarded with so great a Protection, as both the Interest and Life of the Chief Contrivers, whose Power then was such, that had this Woman charged her Husband or *Hawley*, with being concerned herein,

her

her Accusation would without doubt redound to her Ruine, and she would have been most barbarously used for declaring this high and dangerous Truth: And of this Safe-guard this Bloody Villain being well assured, he feared not what his Wife or any else could charge him with.

L. If this Woman had a true sense of things, she could not but know it's her duty to discover this Matter, in the Concealment whereof, the Duty to her Husband can never excuse her.

T. But this loose Fellow long since turned away that Wife, pretending she was never married to him, but that she got another Whore to dress her self up in Man's Apparel, and go to *Dukes-place*, there personating him, and so in appearance married.

L. If such a thing was, then this was by contrivance between this Whore and Rogue, so that they might live in shew Man and Wife, which if any should deny, there was a Certificate ready to be produced. But I am inclined to think they were really Married, for it's improbable this Trick should Cheat the Parson.

T. Your saying that the Relation of a Wife, will not justifie the Concealment of a Murder by the Husband, puts me in mind of a very remarkable Story of that kind, and the Relation is this; *A certain Gentleman being Melancholly, Peevish and ill-natur'd, carried himself very ill-humour'd towards his Wife, (a very fine virtuous Lady) many times beating her, though she behaved her self, in all respects, as a Woman of very great Vertue and Observance towards her Husband, and endeavoured what she could to conceal her Husband's Cruelty towards her; but the Matter was so Notorious, that her ill usage could not be kept so secret, but that many of her Neighbours knew it to be too true; amongst the rest, a certain Gentleman extreamly pitied this unfortunate Lady, for whom (though he kept it unknown from the Lady) this Gentleman had a very great kindness, and hoped he might Marry her when her Husband died, of which there had been a long expectancy, the Husband being very Consumptive: But his Disease out-lived this Gentleman's Patience; wherefore he was resolved to Murder the Husband (that he might Marry the Wife) yet this kept so very private from the knowledge of the Wife, that nothing was farther from her thoughts, than such Treachery (for this Gentleman, and her Husband, in shew, were intimate Friends.) This Bloody Man, one day walking with the Husband, nigh a very large deep Pond, endeavoured to throw him in; and as he was about it, the Husband told him, That some of those very Ducks then in the Pond, should detect that perfidious Murder he was about to commit: To which the other replied, He would venture that, and so threw him in, where he was drowned; but being well known to be extreamly Melancholly, it was generally believed, that in some Melancholly Distraction (to which he had been subject) he threw himself into the Pond, and there drowned himself. This was generally believed, and none seemed in the least to doubt the truth of it. Some time after the Husband's Death, thus Murderer Courts the Widow, and Marries her, after which they lived very happy together for some considerable time; at length, one night as some Ducks were roasting at the Fire, the Husband, looking on the Ducks, burst out into a great Laughter; the Wife desired to know at what he laughed; to which he answered, At somewhat of which the sight of the Ducks put him in mind; the Wife desired him to tell what that was; but he pray'd her to excuse him, for he would not tell. The more averse he was to reveal it, the more desirous she seemed of knowing, but the Husband would not then discover it to her: That night as they were together in Bed, the Wife did again renew her former request, in which being very importunate, the Husband (after he had solemnly enjoyned her to Secrecy) gave her a particular account of the Murder of her Husband, which in substance you have before heard. The Wife was hereupon extreamly concerned, though in words seemed then not much to resent it; but the next Morning she repaired to some judicious Friend (and notwithstanding her promise of Secrecy, she could not be quiet in her mind till she had revealed it) and desired advice thereupon; to which she was answered, That if she concealed*

concealed the Murder, she thereby consented to it; and though her first Husband was very cruel, and this as kind, the first Husband's Blood, thus treacherously spilt, cry'd for Vengeance, in which she would most certainly partake, if she did not discover her Husband's Confession, wherein there seemed to be a very remarkable Providence. The Wife objected the nearness of the Relation, and the promise of Secrecy, but to both these she was answered, That there is no Relation so dear as Justice, and no Promise, contrary to the Rules thereof, ought to be made, nor kept if made, for that is not so properly being Faithful, as being a Confederate; for Faithfulness, being considered as a Virtue, it's consequently to be exercised only in things Just and Honest; for in other Matters it is not properly (morally speaking) call'd Fidelity, but a Criminal Concealment. The Wife being thus perswaded, repairs to the Magistrate, who forthwith orders the Husband to be seized, who as soon as apprehended, confessed the whole Matter, and was deservedly executed.

G. I think the Wife, in this case, must be in a very great strait, for the Temptation to Secrecy could not but be very strong; but I find in the Old Law, That if the Wife, or the nearest Relation in Blood, or a Friend which was as his own Soul, did but so much as secretly intice to Idolatry, the Relation or Friendship in this case, was to be no Impediment to the Discovery, Prosecution and Punishment; for the Person thus inticed, was not to pity, spare or conceal his Relation or Friend, but was positively commanded to Kill him; his Hand was first to be upon him, and then the Hand of all the People. Now most certainly such a Villainous and Treacherous Murder, attended with such Aggravations, must be most Odious in the sight of God, whose first express Law did positively Enact, That *whoso sheddeth mans blood, by man shall his blood be shed*; the reason whereof follows, for *in the image of God made he man*.

L. In my opinion this Wife did what she ought to have done; for though it may well be supposed, that there was a strong Conflict between her Affection towards her Husband (especially when the best, in Succession to the worst) and her duty to Justice; yet it's most certain the latter ought to have the ascendant; for whosoever loves Husband or Wife, Father or Mother, Brother or Sister, more than what is Just, Righteous and Good (for that is the meaning of, *more than me*) at the last day most assuredly shall be rejected by *him* who hath positively enjoyned us *to hate all those Relations for his sake and the Gospel*, or (which is the same) for our Duties-sake, considered as Christians. But how much higher Aggravations do attend the unparallel'd Murder of this Honourable, though unfortunate Peer?

T. I shall now say but one thing more, with relation to *Webster*, and that is this; When *Webster* was before the Honourable Committee, Mr. *Braddon* desired their Lordships leave to ask *Webster* one question; which being granted, Mr. *Braddon* demanded of *Webster*, *Whether the next day after my Lord's Death, he did not produce to such a man a Purse of Gold, about* 49 *Guinea's, and a Pistole*. *Webster* denied it; Mr. *Braddon* desired him to recollect himself, and be positive; *Webster* declared, *He was positive he did not, nor to his remembrance in his Life ever shewed that man any Gold, much less so great a Sum*. Mr. *Braddon* perceiving some of their Lordships seemed angry, the question was put so plain, after *Webster* had withdrawn, Mr. *Braddon* informed their Lordships, *That* Webster *(as he had been told) was a sort of a hanger on at Gaming-houses (where he could play but for little, being very poor) and should this fellow understand it was positively sworn against him, that he did produce such Gold, in all probability he would forge somewhat in answer to it and it was not unlikely, but he might pretend that those Guinea's he had won at Gaming, and was overjoy'd at being so rich: with this his Invention (upon deliberation) might furnish him, in which his presence of mind under Guilt, could not be so ready; but if hereafter he should so pretend, it would plainly appear to be false, having so positively denied it to their Lordships; when,*

had

had it been true, it would have immediately occured to his mind, and as readily he would given it in answer.

L. Doth not *Webster* still deny the producing any Gold?

T. No; but pretends the Gold he shewed *Osborne*, was what he had won at Gaming.

G. That Sham can't now take, against his positive denial before their Lordships.

T. I shall lastly speak of *Holmes*, and then conclude. It seems *Holmes* and his Wife often quarrelled, and sometimes *Holmes* would beat her. One day, as he was Abusing her, she was heard to say, *He was a Murderous Rogue*; and she told him, *That he could not but remember that she could hang him when she pleased:* To which *Holmes* answered, *That he little thought she would have spoken of it, who of all the World had the least reason.* For said this scurrilous Follow, *You Bitch, you Whore, don't you remember, that I bought you a good Sattin Gown and Petticoat, and therefore you above all the World ought not to prate:* To which she replied, *He was a Murderous Rogue for all that.*

L. By the falling out of Murderers, Murder is many times detected; a very notorious Instance of which, I have often heard related, which was as followeth: *A Waterman and his Servant in the Night, carrying a Gentleman down the River, whom they perceived to have a great Charge about him, these perfidious Villains by Signs, concluded to throw this Gentleman Over-board, which they did accordingly, and so drowned him, and then shared the Spoil; soon after which, they both lived much beyond their former Circumstances, at which all that knew them, admired; but none but themselves knew the reason, till many years after, when these two being Drunk, and at Play, fell out about their Game, and they were then over-heard to accuse one the other, in this matter, the Master the Man, and the Man the Master, as the most Criminal. Upon which they were both Seized, and they then Confessed the whole Matter, each endeavouring to aggravate the Guilt of the other, in Mitigation of his own. But they were.* both thought deserving of Death for their cruel Treachery, and were Executed accordingly.

G. Had we not already been too troublesome to you in this particular and satisfactory Relation, I should beg one favour further.

T. Your further Satisfaction in this Matter may command from me whatsoever is convenient to be told, and beyond that, I desire you not to move me.

G. More than you have already declared, I don't now desire to know; but I perceive there have been very many Persons in this Case, Sworn to many Particulars, so that the Relation of the whole Matter hath been long, but to me not tedious, because I have received full Satisfaction in that, wherein before I was extreamly Abused by Misinformation. Sir, If it may not be too tiresome to you, I would desire you to Abstract the most material Proofs before mentioned, and give us, as short as you well can, the substance of what is before deposed.

T. In this I shall readily serve you, but I shall not observe the very same Method as before, but shall begin with the *Disproof* of my Lord's Self-murder, by destroying those forged Informations which would prove him so; and Secondly, shall prove him barbarously Murdered.

First, For the disproof of the Self-murder.

The Right Honourable *Arthur* late Earl of *Essex*, was Committed to the *Tower*, *Tuesday* the 10th of *July*, 1683. and there were placed over his Lordship two Warders, (viz.) *Monday* and *Russel*, and one Servant, (viz.) *Paul Bomeny*, permitted to be attending on my Lord; the very next *Friday* morning, about Nine of the Clock, his Lordship was found Dead in his Closet, with his Throat cut through both Jugular Arteries, to the Neck-bone.

Now, seeing our Law presumes every Man destroyed by violent Hands, is Murdered by others, unless such Evidence appears as gives Satisfaction in the contrary,

O and

and proves him a Self-murderer. This Lord had been found barbarously Murdered, had not *Bomeny*, *Monday*, and *Ruſſel*, appeared to prove otherwiſe; and they endeavour to prove it (ſhortly) thus.

My Lord of *Eſſex* (they ſay) called for a Pen-knife to pare his Nails, which Pen-knife not being ready, he required a Razor, which was accordingly delivered him, with which his Lordſhip having pared his Nails, he retired into his Cloſet, and locks himſelf in, and there cut his Throat; the Razor (before delivered to pare his Nails) lying by the Body.

But that this Relation is forged, and that there was, *Firſt*, no Razor delivered to my Lord to pare his Nails, nor had his Lordſhip pared his Nails with any.

Secondly, Neither the Body locked into the Cloſet: Nor,

Thirdly, The Razor lying locked in by the Body, when my Lord was firſt know to be Dead, is evident from what follows, which clearly detects this Forgery. For the firſt of theſe, that there was no Razor delivered to my Lord.

This appears by the Contradictions of *Bomeny*, *Ruſſel* and *Monday*, as to the time of the delivery of this Razor; for *Bomeny* firſt Swears, he delivered this Razor to my Lord to pare his Nails on *Friday* morning at eight of the Clock; and within two hours, poſitively ſwears in the Depoſition himſelf writ, that he delivered it on *Thurſday* morning, at Eight of the Clock (being the day before his Death); and this as to the *Thurſday*, he ſwears Poſitively and Circumſtantially; Poſitively, for he doth expreſsly name *Thurſday*, as the day on which the Razor was delivered; and Circumſtantially, for he doth ſwear the Razor was delivered the very next Morning after my Lord came to Captain *Hawley*'s; and his Lordſhip went to *Hawley*, on *Wedneſday* the 11th of *July*. But

Ruſſel Swears a Point-blank Contradiction to *Bomeny*'s Oath; for *Ruſſel* depoſeth,

and now declares, That on *Friday* Morning, in leſs than half an hour before they found my Lord Dead in his Cloſet, he ſtood as Warder at my Lord's Chamber-door, (*Monday*, that Morning having firſt ſtood as Warder on my Lord, and was then gone down to ſtand below Stairs) and heard my Lord ask *Bomeny* for a Pen-knife to pare his Nails; which being not ready, his Lordſhip required a Razor, which he did immediately ſee *Bomeny* deliver his Lordſhip. But

Monday doth as directly give the lye to *Ruſſel*, as *Ruſſel* did to *Bomeny*; for *Monday* the day may Lord dy'd, declared, he ſaw my Lord have a Razor in his Hand, paring his Nails with it, at Seven a Clock that Morning my Lord died, and this about two hours before *Ruſſel* came up, to ſtand as Warder at my Lord's Chamber-door.

Wherefore, unleſs it can be reconciled how this Razor ſhould be delivered *Thurſday* Morning at Eight of the Clock, according to *Bomeny*'s Oath; and yet not delivered till *Friday* Morning Nine of the Clock, within half an hour of the time his Lordſhip was found Dead, and delivered whilſt *Ruſſel* ſtood Warder at the Chamber-door, as *Ruſſel* depoſeth; and notwithſtanding this, my Lord to have had the Razor, and pared his Nails with it, two hours before *Ruſſel* came up Stairs to ſtand Warder at my Lord's Chamber, as *Monday* declared, the very day my Lord died. I ſay, Unleſs theſe Contradictions can be reconciled, it can't be thought that any Razor at all was delivered: And then, whereas all declared my Lord pared his Nails with the Razor; by ſtrict Obſervation, it appeared his Lordſhip's Nails were not newly, before his Death, either pared or ſcraped.

Secondly, That the Cloſet-door was not locked upon my Lord's Body, appears by the Contradictions of theſe three, as to the opening the Cloſet-door.

Bomeny firſt ſwore, He did open the Door, (when my Lord would not anſwer upon his knocking at the Door) and there ſaw my Lord lying Dead in his Blood, and the Razor by him, and he then called the Warders;

Warders; but immediately swears in Contradiction to his first Oath, that he peeped through a Chink of the Door, and saw Blood and part of the Razor, and then without opening the Door, ran and called *Ruffel*, who thereupon first opened the Door: And at Mr. *Braddon*'s Tryal, Swears he knew not who opened the Door.

Ruffel deposeth he did first open the Door, and makes no difficulty in it; then comes *Monday*, and gives the lye to both: For *Monday* (the very day my Lord died) declared (what he hath since often confirm'd) That neither *Bomeny* or *Ruffel* could stir the Door, my Lord's Body lay so close and hard against the Door; and he being stronger than either, put his Shoulders against the Door, and pressing with all his might, broke it open.

Whosoever there is, that can reconcile these Contradictions (in these three Mens Relations) and make all appear credible,

—— *Erit mihi Magnus Apollo.*

§.3.

A further Argument, That the Closet-door was not locked upon the Body, appears by my Lord's Legs lying upon the Threshold of the Closet-door, when the Body was pretended not to have been stired from its first Posture.

Thirdly, That there was no Razor lying locked in with the Body, when the Body was first found, appears by the bloody Razor's being thrown out of my Lord's Chamber-Window, (which is about seventeen Foot distant from the Closet-door, where the Body lay) and no noise of my Lord's Death, till after the Maid carried up the Razor, which Maid thereupon first discovered my Lord's Death.

And, as yet other Arguments of the Perjury of these perfidious Villains, add the Mathematical Impossibility of the Wound, seeing not above two Inches of the Razor must be without my Lord's Hand, (had he done it Himself) and yet the Wound above three Inches deep. Moreover, by many Eminent Doctors and Chyrurgions, the Wound is thought to be naturally Impossible to have been done by my Lord himself because upon cutting the first Jugular Artery such an Effusion of Blood and Spirit would have immediately thereupon followed, that Nature would not have been strong enough for to cut through the other Jugular Artery, to the Neck-bone on the other side; much less, to make so many, and so large Notches in the Razor against the Neck-bone as an old Foolish or K — Chyrurgion suggested to the Coroners Jury.

Wherefore by what is before observed, as to the many Contradictions, it plainly appears, that these three (as it is said in the History of *Susanna, Verse* 61.) are convicted of false Relations by their own Mouths; and those other Arguments before observed, are further Detections of these three Men's Perjuries. It then remains as at first, (*viz.*) That here is a Body found Dead by violent Hands, and the manner of the Death not discovered, (for it can't be, according to these three Mens Relations, for the Reasons before observed). The Conclusion that the Law makes in such Cases, in this therefore holds good, (*viz.*) That this Honourable Lord was Murdered by the violent and cruel Hands of barbarous and bloody minded Men.

Secondly, For the Proof of the Murder. In this I shall first consider what is most material, which passed before my Lord's Death.

Secondly, The day of his Death. And then *Thirdly* and *Lastly*, After the day of his Death In The

First, Before my Lord's Death. I shall consider,

First, The previous Resolutions by Papists to cut my Lord's Throat. And then,

Secondly, The many previous Reports before my Lord's Death, that his Lordship had cut his Throat in the *Tower*.

For the first of these, *D. S.* declares, *That about nine Days before the Death of the late Earl of* Essex, *she heard several Papists consulting together, concerning the said Earl: And this*

this Informant heard them say, the Earl of Essex was to be taken off, and that they had been with His Highness, and His Highness was first for Poysoning the Earl; but that manner of Death being objected against; it was then said, one did propose to His Highness, Stabbing the Earl; but this way His Highness did not like: at length His Highness concluded, and ordered his Throat to be cut, and His Highness had promised to be there when it was done. Some few days after, some of the aforesaid Persons declared, *It was resolved the Earl's Throat should be cut, but they would give it out, that he had done it himself;. and if any should deny it, they would take them, and punish them for it.*

Secondly, For the previous Reports before my Lord's Death.

It's proved by eight several Witnesses, That before the Earl's Death, (or before it could be known) it was Reported, That the Earl of *Essex* had cut his Throat in the *Tower*; amongst the rest, it was at *Froome*, which is about an hundred Miles from *London*, the *Wednesday* Morning; and at the same time, at *Andover*, about Sixty Miles from *London*, tho at neither of these Places, especially the former, could it then be known, that the Earl was a Prisoner in the *Tower*, his Lordship being not committed to the *Tower*, till the *Tuesday* in the Afternoon. All these Reports agreed in the manner *How*, (viz.) cutting his Throat, and the place *Where*, (viz.) the *Tower*; and (which is further) at *Andover*, the *Wednesday* Morning before my Lord's Death, it was reported, not only in the manner *How*, and place *Where*, but likewise the pretended Reason *Wherefore*, was given; for it was then, and there said, That the Earl of *Essex* being a Prisoner in the *Tower*, and understanding, that the K. and Duke were come into the *Tower*, his Lordship was afraid the K. would have come up into his Chamber, and seen him; of which his Lordship's Guilt and Shame would not bear the thoughts, and therefore he did cut his Throat to avoid it. This being declared two days before my Lord's Death, when it could not have been in the least fore-thought, that the King and Duke would have come together into the *Tower*, where they had not been above twice together since the Restoration. I say, This previous Report, which so particularly cloathed this Action with the *how*, *where*, and *wherefore*, clearly proves, That all things were so resolved upon to be done, or otherwise it is impossible it should have been reported under these three Essential Qualifications, as to *Manner*, *Place*, and *Reason*, before it was indeed done, especially at *Andover*, where it could not then be supposed to be known that my Lord was so much as a Prisoner in the *Tower*; this Reason the Papists themselves gave out just after my Lord's Death.

Secondly, What passed the day my Lord died.

These then attending on my Lord, (viz.) *Russel* and *Monday*, the Warders; *Bomeny* the Servant, and *Lloyd* the Centinel at the Door, did all deny that day my Lord died, that there were any Men let into my Lord's Lodgings that Morning, before my Lord's Death. But it now appears, That there were some Ruffians, a little before my Lords Death, sent into his Lodgings to Murder him, which they did accordingly.

R. M. a Soldier in the *Tower*, that Morning my Lord of *Essex* was Murdered; about one of the Clock, that very day, nigh *Aldgate*, told B. and his Wife, *That the Earl of* Essex *did not cut his own Throat, but was barbarously Murdered by his Royal Highness's Order:* For the said *Meake* declared, *That just before the Earl's Murder, His Highness sent two Men to the Earl's Lodgings to Murder him, which after they had done, they threw the Razor out of the Window.* Likewise, a Soldier that Morning in the *Tower*, about Eleven of the Clock, that very Morning my Lord died, in *Baldwins Gardens*, informed G. and H. *That the Earl of* Essex *did not cut his own Throat, but was barbarously Murdered by his Royal Highness's own Order.* For the said R. then declared, *That a little*

little before the Earls Murder, his Royal Highness parted a little way from His Majesty, and then two Men were sent into the Earls Lodgings, to Murder my Lord; which when they had done, they did again return to his Highness.

Mr. E. declares, That he saw his Royal Highness, just before the Earl's Death, part a little from his Majesty, and then beckoned to two Gentlemen to come to him, who came accordingly; His Highness thereupon sent them towards the Earl of Essex's Lodgings, and about a quarter of an hour after, this Informant saw these very two Men return to His Highness, and as they came, they smiled; and to the best of this Informant's hearing, and remembrance; said, The Business was done; upon which His Highness seemed very well pleased, and then went to His Majesty, to whom the news was immediately brought, That the Earl of Essex had cut his Throat.

Lloyd, the Centinel at my Lord's Door the day my Lord dyed (till the 21st of January last) did deny the letting in of any men, (and Russel and Monday still deny it) but now Lloyd doth confess, That just before my Lord's Death, two or three Men, by Major Hawley's special Order, were let in, and immediately he heard them (as he did suppose they were) go up stairs into my Lord's Room, where there was a very great bustle and stir, so great, that this Centinel declared, he would have forced after them, had not the first Door been made fast; upon the bustle, he heard somewhat thrown down like the fall of a Man, which he did suppose was my Lord's Body; soon after which, it was cryed out, My Lord of Essex hath cut his Throat. Here is not only these mens going in, but a great bustle confessed immediately thereupon to ensue in my Lord's Room, and the Body of a Man in this bustle to be thrown down; this is in a Close Prisoner's Room, where no one is admitted, but his Servant; and those that kept the Door deny'd upon Oath that any were in my Lord's Chamber that Morning my Lord died, before his death. But these Warders being supposed privy to the Fact, would not own the admitting of those Men, which themselves let in with such a murtherous Design;

and it is to be presumed, that this Centinel was not a stranger to the matter, but enjoined to secrecy; for otherwise he would never have declared to a Friend, under a repeated request of secrecy, that this Confession (as before) laid upon his Conscience, and troubled him night and day; for tho' it was indeed very true, that he did let in these Men, it was what he should not have confessed. This Confirmation to his Acquaintance (under a great and repeated injunction of secrecy) argues, *first*, That this Confession was indeed true. And

Secondly, That there is some cursed Confederacy (it's probable by Oath) entred into to stifle this Murther; for what other probable Reason can be assigned for that trouble of Conscience in this Confession, seeing himself at the same declared it was true, tho' he should not have said it? There are some other Arguments that this Sentinel was *particeps Criminis* in the Privity; first, his Retraction in part of what he did confess: for, upon his being first apprehended, he owned the throwing out of the Razor before my Lord's death was known; but he now retracts, and disowns it. Another Instance of his Privity is his now prevaricating, in his now pretending that these men were let in an hour, or more, before my Lord's death; whereas, at first, he declared they were let in immediately before my Lord's death; for, as soon as let in, he heard several go up stairs into my Lord's Room, and heard the bustle, &c. as before. A third Argument of this Centinel's Privity, is his not declaring the whole Truth, which he must know; for one at a greater distance, that saw these Ruffians as they were bustling with my Lord, and heard the bustle, did likewise hear one of these in the bustle (as it seemed to be) and therefore presumed to be my Lord, cry out very loud, and very dolefully, *Murther, murther, murther*. The Centinel who could hear the trampling, or indeed the very walking in my Lord's Chamber, could not but hear this *Murther*, so loud and often repeated. It appears by five

(102)

Cuts in my Lord's Right Hand (viz.) two upon his Fore-finger, one upon upon the Fourth Finger, another on the Little Finge, and the fifth about two Inches long in the Palm of his Right Hand; that his Lordship in this bustle made great resistance, for these Cuts can be supposed to be done no otherwise, than by endeavouring to put off the Cruel Instrument of his Death.

The next thing that I should observe, which happened the day my Lord dy'd, and gives us reason to belive the Murther, is the Irregularities committed upon the Body, before the Jury saw the Body; the Body was stript and washed, and the Room and Closet washed, and my Lord's Cloathes carried away (tho' all men know the Body should have remained in its first posture till the Coroner's Jury had seen the Body.) Sir T. R. (as himself saith) declared to the Lords, *That the Body was not stirred from its first posture till the next morning about Ten of the Clock*; to this Sir *Thomas* hath not sworn (for he was not sworn before the Lords) and its well he hath not, for herein he is so much mistaken, that the contrary can be proved by almost twenty Witnesses. Had the Body remained in its first posture, by my Lord's Cravat's being cut in three parts, the Jury would have plainly seen, that his Lordship could not so do it with the Razor; and then secondly, they would have perceived the print of a bloody Foot upon my Lord, as he lay in the Closet, by which it appeared some one had been with the Body in the Closet; and several other Material Circumstances might have been discovered, which by the total (illegal) alteration of the Circumstances of the Body, &c. were destroyed.

About Three of the Clock in the Afternoon, that day my Lord died, some of those bloody Men (who had been at the Consult) met at *Homer's* House, and one of them leaped about the Room, as overjoyed; and as the Master of the House came into the Room, he strikes him upon the Back, and cry'd, *the Feat was done, or, we have done the Feat*; upon which the Master said, *is the Earls Throat cut?* to which the other replied, *Yes*; and farther said, *he could not but laugh to think how like a Fool the Earl of* Essex *looked when they came to cut his Throat.*

To destroy the Testimony of this *D. S.* *Homes* hath produced Two Witnesses, who (by many Witnesses) appear to be forsworn in every part of their Depositions. His Defence being false, his Charge therefore may be concluded true.

Thirdly, and *Lastly,* What past after the day of my Lord's Death.

That very Morning several Soldiers (which were presumed able to discover what was material, with relation to my Lord's Death) were called together (as *M.* then said) and enjoined to secrecy under very severe Penalties.

About Ten of the Clock in the Morning, the next day after my Lord's Death, the Jury met, and were surprized to see all the Circumstances of my Lord's Body changed from what was first discovered.

After the Jury had seen the Naked Body at *Hawleys*, the Coroner adjourned them to a Victualling-House in the *Tower*, one of the Jury demanded a sight of the Cloathes; but the Coroner was immediately called into the next Room, from which returning to the Jury in some heat, he told them, *It was the Body, and not the Cloathes, they were to sit upon; the Body was there, and that was sufficient.*

One of the Jury then said, *My Lord of* Essex *was esteemed a very Sober, Sedate and Good Man* (which *Bomeny* then confirmed, saying, *His Lord was a very Pious Man*) *and therefore it was improbable so Good a Man should be Guilty of the worst of Actions.* Upon which M. *Hawley* told the Jury, *They were misinformed in my Lord's Character, for every Man that was well acquainted with my Lord, well knew, that it had ever been a fixed Principle in my Lord, that any Man might cut his Throat, or any otherwise dispose of his Life, to avoid a dishonourable and infamous Death; wherefore this Action which they thought unlike his Lordship, was according to my Lord's avowed*

avowed and fixed *Principles*. This made the Jury the more easie believe, that my Lord had indeed done it.

Some of the Jury were for Adjourning their Inquisition to some further day, and in the mean time to send notice to the Earl's Relations, so that if any thing appeared on my Lord's behalf, it might be produced. *Hawley*, hereupon, assured the Jury, *That they could not adjourn their Inquiry, for His Majesty had sent one for their Inquisition, and would not rise from Council till it was brought him.* This the Jury believing, immediately made all haste possible, whereas otherwise they might have been more strict and particular in their Examinations.

☞ *Hawley*, in answer to this, totally denies all, and protests that he was not nigh the Jury in the Victualling-house all the time the Jury sate, though most of the Jury can say the contrary; and as for the suggesting Self-murder to be my Lord's Principle, he did protest he did never hear it said to be my Lord's Principle, till their Lordships in this Committee told him it had been so ☞ declared. This clearly proves, that the pretended Principle of Self-murder, was a Forgery of that Bloody Party which murdered my Lord, and *Hawley* pitched upon as the most proper Person to corrupt the Jury with the belief of it.

The backwardness of the then Government from examining into this Matter, and their unjust Proceedings against the Prosecution, (for they Discouraged, Prosecuted, and Ruined him who did humbly offer the Matter to a Judicial Consideration, though no Crime or Colour of Offence was proved against him) is farther Evidence of this Murther.

The Government turned the Old *Edwards* out of his place, for what his Son said in this Matter, and hereby inverted the old Proverb, *For here the Son's eating Sower Grapes, had set the Father's Teeth on edge.*

A poor Soldier was barbarously Whipt (after he had been cruelly managed in Prison) for only saying, That *he would not say, he did believe the Earl of* Essex *cut his own Throat*: But a more barbarous Cruelty is justly suspected t[o] in the *After-murth[er]* *Meake* and *Hawley*, tection of this.

Though the Gov[ernment] received private In[telligence] publick Applicatio[n] thereupon a Promi[se] and in both these t[imes] cularly charged, a[s] this Horrid Cruelty ment would never tion to be made, b[ut] dispersed those pu[blications] His Highness been would have been n[ ] Proclamation of P[ ] *fires a Tryal, and it'[s] Justice.* Another A[ ] and likewise of Maj[ ] in, is *Webster*'s produ[ ] handkerchief all B[ ] Neighbours, rejoy[ ] Traytor; and the [ ] of the same Person the Price of Blood wherein there was 4[ ] which he shewed in all this was but a lainous Reward; fo[r] Lord's Death, when with her Husband [ ] *Her Husband long sin[ce] had* 500 *Guinea's*; a[nd] startled, answered, *come by them Houes[tly]* said, *That he got the[m]* that it was replied *hardly get Bread*: T[ ] some other way.

L. The Wife mi[ght] Trade, *viz. Murthe[r]* posed he hath bee[n] cerned, might get Wife might mean, understood her.

7. That his Wife his Guilt, appears by (upon her hard usag[e]

e, to use her so very ill, with-
he well knew it was, to Hang
ther in the Tower. Another
kind there happened, when
Wife (some time after my
quarrelled; *Homes* abusing
n, *He was a murderous Rogue,*
ll know that she could at any
r it. To which *Homes* an-
his usual Scurrilous Lan-
h, *you Whore, you of all the*
reason to speak, for do not you
ht you a good Sattin Gown and
ereupon the Wife replied,
ing Rogue for all that. .
hieves fall out, Honest Men
ecome of their Goods.
t this Woman of a loose
bigotted to that Bloody Re-
n such Cases esteem Murder
his Gown would have been
into of that Blood, for the
hereof, this Garment (in

:, as briefly as I well could,
our request, and I hope you
:ed of your former Mistake.
: you I am, and I give you
this great Satisfaction, and
r, what in me lies, to rescue

the Memory of this Right Honourable Lord,
from that dishonourable, undeserved Imputation of Self-murder, by laying the Guilt
at that door which seems most deserving;
and though herein I may displease some of
my most intimate Acquaintance, yet I
think in Justice I stand bound to unde-
ceive many of their mistake in this Self-murder: Especially when these, through what
I have declared, have been deceived in this
Matter; and whatsoever my former opinion may have been, through Misinformation, it is now such, that none living
shall more cordially Pray, *That the God of*
Justice, who hath so many times remarkably
appeared in the Detection and Punishment of
Blood, may eminently manifest himself in the
full Discovery and just Punishment of all Con-
trivers, Actors; Aiders and Abettors herein;
and likewise that all Concealers of what they
know in this matter, and all such as endeavour
to stifle or frustrate this Just Prosecution, may
be made exemplary in this World; in order to
which, may that only Just and Wise God (whose
are every good and perfect Gift) pour down
upon our Senators, such a Spirit of Wisdom, as
may conspicuously detect every Arcana of this
Blood-thirsty and most barbarous Murder, with
all its vile and astonishing Dependences.
L. Amen.

www.ingramcontent.com/pod-product-compliance
Lightning Source LLC
Chambersburg PA
CBHW020142170426
43199CB00010B/845